Case Law in Roman, Anglosaxon and Continental Law

Case Law in Roman, Anglosaxon and Continental Law

by

María José Falcón y Tella

Professor of Philosophy of Law
Complutense University of Madrid

Translation into English, from

La Jurisprudencia en los Derechos Romano, Anglosajón y Continental
Madrid-Buenos Aires, Marcial Pons, 2010

by

Stephen Churnin

MARTINUS
NIJHOFF
PUBLISHERS

LEIDEN • BOSTON
2011

This book is printed on acid-free paper.

Library of Congress Cataloging-in Publication data

Falcón y Tella, María José
[Jurisprudencia en los derechos romano, anglosajon y continenta. English]
Case law in Roman, Anglosaxon and continental law / by María José Falcón y Tella ; [translated] by Stephen Churnin.
p. cm.
Translation into English, from La Jurisprudencia en los derechos romano, anglosajon y continental by Stephen Churnin. Madrid-Buenos Aires : Marcial Pons, 2010.
Includes bibliographical references and index.
ISBN 978-90-04-20416-4 (hardback : alk. paper) 1. Judge-made law. 2. Law--Cases. 3. Comparative law. I. Churnin, Stephen. II. Title.
K574.F34813 2011
340.5--dc23

2011029982

ISBN 978 9004 20416 4

To Pablo, Marta and Carlos

Table of Contents

Preface xv

Chapter 1 Introduction 1

Chapter 2 Roman *Iurisprudentia* as *Prudentia Iuris* 7

1. Introduction to Roman Law, Especially Classical Law 7
2. Roman *Iurisprudentia* as Science of Law, as Distinct from its Modern Conception as *Jurisprudenz* in German and *Jurisprudence* in Anglosaxon Authors 9
3. Priority of *Iurisprudentia* over Law in Roman Law 10
4. Etymology of the Term *Iurisprudentia* as *prudentia* Applied to Law in a Practical Manner; Cognitive and Scientific Differences Regarding *Scientia* and *Sapientia* 10
5. Decisive Creative Role in Roman *Iurisprudentia* – Neither via Legislator Nor Judge – of Two Bodies: Jurisconsults and *Praetor* 11
6. Origin of Roman *Iurisprudentia* in the College of Pontiffs, as a "Secret" Concept, and Subsequent Conversion into "Lay" and "Public" Jurisprudence 12
7. Value of *Iurisprudentia* and *Ius Publicae Respondendi*: Original Scope and Reduction by Augustus 12
8. Grandeur of Roman *Iurisprudentia*, Owing to Casuistics, Inductiveness and Intuitiveness; Value of Science of Law Today as a Theoretical-Doctrinal Concept 14
9. Value of *Iurisprudentia* in Roman Law: The Source of Law? 15
10. Why *Iurisprudentia* and not *Iuriscientia?* 16
11. Roman *Prudentia* 18

Chapter 3 The Anglosaxon Precedent 19

1. The Anglosaxon System of Sources 19
    - 1.1. The Term "Anglosaxon" compared with "English" or "British" 19
    - 1.2. The English System of Sources 22
        - 1.2.1. List and Hierarchy of English Sources of Law 24
            - A. Judge-made Law 24
            - B. Statute Law 27
        - 1.2.2. The *Stare Decisis* 31
        - 1.2.3. Distinctions 33
        - 1.2.4. The *Ratio Decidendi* 34

1.2.5. Declarative and Constitutive Theories of the Nature of Common Law 36
1.2.6. Types of Precedent 37
1.2.7. Hierarchy of Courts 38
1.2.8. Publication of Precedents; The Law Reporting System 39
1.3. The North American System of Sources 40
1.4. The Scottish System of Sources 43
2. Distinction between "Jurisprudence" – Science of Law – and "Case Law" – a Judicial Phenomenon 44
3. Differences between Common Law and Continental Legal Systems 45
3.1. The Distinct Influence of Roman Law 47
3.2. The Influence of Legal Codes on the Continent compared with Case Law Character of the Anglosaxon System 48
3.3. The Rationalist, Rule-based and Formalistic Conception of the Continental Systems Compared with Anglosaxon Realism and Empiricism 49
3.4. The Evolution of and Respect for Tradition in the Anglosaxon System Compared with the Continental Revolutions 50
3.5. A "Procedural" Law compared with a Law of "Rules" 50
3.6. A Social Organisation Model Based on Individual Initiative and Free Enterprise Compared with the Interventionist and State-centred Continental Model 50
3.7. An Open and Incomplete Law Compared with the Plenitude, Completeness and Closed Nature of the Continental Systems 51
3.8. A Casuistic System Compared with the Pre-established and Preconceived *a Priori* Ideas of the Continental Systems; An Inorganic Doctrine without Codes; The Case Method 51
3.9. Disregard of the Separation between Public and Private Law – a Key Issue in Continental Law 52
4. Main Differences between Anglosaxon Precedent and Continental Case Law 52
4.1. Provenance of Precedent from any Jurisdictional Body regardless of Hierarchical Rank 52
4.2. One Single Ruling sufficient for Judicial Precedent 53
4.3. Precedent as the Main Source of Anglosaxon Law 53
4.4. The System of Dispersed Jurisdiction Compared with Concentrated Jurisdiction 53
5. Current Harmonisation of Statute Law and Case Law Systems 54

Chapter 4 Continental Case Law **57**
1. Concept and Main Requirements of Case Law in the Spanish Legal System 57
1.1. The Provenance of Case Law 57

1.1.1. The Supreme Court; Appeal to the Highest Instance (Appeal for Cassation) 60
A. History of the Supreme Court and Appeal to the Highest Instance (Appeal for Cassation) 60
B. Main Purpose of Cassation 61
C. The Various Chambers of the Supreme Court 61
D. Evolution of Concept of "Legal Doctrine" as a Basis for Cassation; Effect of the Reform of the Rules of Civil Procedure of 2000 61
1.1.2. The Constitutional Court – Main Functions 64
A. Introduction: the North American Model of Dispersed Jurisdiction Compared with the Austrian Model of Concentrated Jurisdiction 64
B. Nature of the Spanish Constitutional Court 67
a. Jurisdictional Nature 67
b. Political Nature 68
c. "Mixed", Special, *Sui Generis* and Complex Nature 68
C. Relations between the Constitutional Court and the Supreme Court and other Judicial Authorities: A Question of Hierarchy or Jurisdiction? 69
D. Place Occupied by Case Law Established by Constitutional Court Rulings and Orders 70
1.1.3. The Higher Courts of Justice of the Autonomous Communities; Territorial Jurisdiction 74
1.1.4. The European Courts 77
A. The European Court of Human Rights of Strasbourg 77
B. The European Court of Justice of Luxembourg 78
C. The International Criminal Court 79
1.1.5. Value of Rulings by the General Department of Registers and Notaries Public 81
1.2. Reiteration of Rulings 82
1.3. *Ratio Decidendi* Compared with *Obiter Dicta*; The *Ratio* and Similar Concepts in Law 82
1.3.1. The *De Facto* Assumption, Legal Consequence and *Ratio* as Elements of the Law; Historical Development of the Concept of *Ratio* 83
A. The Greek *Logos* 85
B. Appearance of the Term *Ratio* in Roman Law with a Different Meaning: The Arithmetical and Geometrical *Ratio* of Mathematical Content – Proportionality 85
C. The Middle Ages 85

a. The Glossators and Devotion to the Letter and Literal Interpretation 86
b. The Post-glossators or Commentators and Use of Logical Interpretation in Search of the *Ratio* 86
1.3.2. The *Causa Legis* in Transactions compared with the *Ratio Legis* in Law 87
1.3.3. The *Ocassio Legis* Compared with the *Ratio Legis* 87
1.3.4. The *Anima Legis* Compared with the *Animus* 87
1.3.5. The *Ratio Legis* Compared with the *Ratio Legislatoris* 88
1.3.6. The "Historical *Ratio*" Compared with the "Presumed or Hypothetical *Ratio*" 90
1.3.7. The *Corpus* Compared with the *Ratio* and the "Criteria for Interpretation" 91
1.3.8. The *Opinio Iuris* in Custom 91
1.3.9. The *Ratio* in Legal Argumentation; Types 97
A. The *Eadem Ratio* in Analogy 98
B. The Major Ratio in the *A Fortiori* Argument 98
C. The Minor or Contrary *Ratio* in the *A Contrario* Argument 99
1.3.10. The *Ratio Decidendi* of the Judgement Compared with the *Obiter Dicta*; Fundamental Points of Law 99
2. The Functions of Case Law 100
2.1. The Interpretation of Law 100
2.2. The Application of Law 101
2.3. The Integration of Law 102
2.4. The "Limited" and "Derived" Creative Function of Case Law 103
2.5. Other Functions 104
2.5.1. The Function of Decantation and Application of the General Principles of Law 104
2.5.2. The Updating Function of Law 105
2.5.3. The Function of Forming and Creating Legal Concepts 105
3. Is Case Law, Especially that of the Supreme Court, a Source of Law in the Spanish Legal System? 105
3.1. Arguments in Favour of it Being a Source 107
3.1.1. The Evolution of the Principle of Separation of Powers 107
3.1.2. Kelsen's "Stufenbau" Theory and Hart's "Open Texture" Theory; Problems Resolving the Improvement of Strict Legal Positivism and the Conception of Law as a Legal System 107
3.1.3. The Infringement of Case Law as Grounds for Appeal to the Highest Instance (Appeal for Cassation) 108
3.1.4. Association of Case Law with Other Sources of Law 108
A. Association with Custom, *i.e.* Judicial Practice – *Usus Fori* 109

B. Association with the General Principles of Law, as a Source of Said Principles 110
C. Association with Legislation 110
a. Case Law as "Special", "Individual" or "Specific" Law 111
b. The Legislator's Tacit Approval via a *posteriori* "Reception" or Prior "Delegation" of the Case Law Rule 112
c. The Legislator's Express Approval in the Additional Provisions of the Civil Code, by reference to the *Comisión de Codificación* (Council of Law Reporting) 112
3.1.5. The New Value of Case Law due to Progressive Importance of "Agreements Adopted by the Non-jurisdictional Meetings of the Supreme Court" 113
3.2. Arguments against it Being a Source 115
3.2.1. A Strict Interpretation of the Principle of the Separation of Powers and the Judge's Position 115
3.2.2. The General and Abstract Nature of Statute Law and the Specific Area of Case Law Maxims for Isolated Cases 117
3.2.3. The Imperative Nature of Statute Law as a Source of Law compared with the Merely Persuasive, Non-binding and Merely Authoritative Value of Case Law 118
3.2.4. Inclination of Legislation in Principle towards Permanence, Stability and Coherence compared with Freedom to Vary Doctrine and Contradiction in Case Law 118
3.2.5. The Presumption of *Res Judicata* Compared with the Merely Exemplary Value of Case Law for all Cases Comparable with the One at Issue 119
3.2.6. The Creation of Objective Law by Legislation Compared with the Award of Subjective Rights by Case Law 120
3.2.7. The Requirements of Legal Certainty 120
3.2.8. The Originating Value of Legislation Compared with the Borrowing Nature of Case Law 121
3.2.9. The Creative Nature of Legislation Compared with the Function of Mere Interpretation, Application and Integration of Case Law 121
3.3. Case Law and Equity 122
3.4. Analogy and Resultant Maxims of Decision 131
3.5. The Consideration of Case Law as an Improper, Material Source or Source of Knowledge of Law: "Legislation Reigns and Case Law Governs" 134

3.6. The "Sources-Argument" Theory 136
3.6.1. The *Ab Exemplo* Argument 137
3.6.2. The Authority Argument 137
3.6.3. The Principle of Formal Justice in Coordination with the Principle of Inertia 140
3.6.4. Respect for Tradition 141
3.6.5. The Pragmatic Argument 141
3.7. The Models of Judge: Hercules, Jupiter and Hermes 141
3.8. Formalism and the Anti-formalist Revolt, with Particular Reference to Case Law 143
3.8.1. French Legal Anti-Formalism 145
A. The French Scientific School of François Gèny 145
B. The French Sociological School of Leon Duguit 146
3.8.2. German Conceptual Anti-Formalism 147
A. The Jurisprudence of Interests of Ihering and Philipp Heck 147
B. The Free School of Law of Hermann Kantorowicz and Eugen Ehrlich 150
3.8.3. Jurisprudential Anti-formalism: The North American Sociological Jurisprudence of Oliver Wendell Holmes, Roscoe Pound and Benjamin Cardozo; North American Realism 151
3.8.4. Other Anti-formalist Trends 153
4. Changes in Case Law, Especially by the Supreme Court 157
4.1. Can Case Law Be Changed? 157
4.2. Is it Advisable to Change Case Law? 157
4.3. If there Is a Change of Case Law, Which Prevails? 158
4.3.1. The Oldest Case Law 158
4.3.2. The Most Recent Case Law 159
4.3.3. A Third, Distinct Line of Case Law 159
5. Main Rules on the Sources of Law and Case Law in the Spanish Legal System 160
5.1. The Pre-1978 Situation 160
5.1.1. The Civil Code 160
A. Pre-reform of the Preliminary Title of 31 May 1974, article 6 160
B. Post-reform of the Preliminary Title of 31 May 1974, article 1.6 161
a. The Systematic Argument or *Sedes Materiae* 163
b. The Literal Argument and the Exhaustive List of article 1.1 of the Civil Code 163

c. Case Law "Complements" but does not "Complete" the Legal System 163
d. The Expression "Certain Legal Transcendence" in Reference to Case Law in the Preamble of the 1974 Reform of the Preliminary Title of the Civil Code 164
e. The Express Recognition of "Analogy" Post-reform of the Preliminary Title of the Civil Code 165
5.1.2. The Rules of Civil Procedure; the Reform of 2000 165
5.2. The Post-1978 Situation 166
5.2.1. Spanish Constitution of 1978 and its Main New Contributions on the Matter 167
5.2.2. The Organic Law regarding the Judiciary 169
6. Case Law in Other Continental Legal Systems 170
6.1. German Law 170
6.2. The Swiss Civil Code and the Legislator Judge 172

Bibliography **173**

Index **211**

Preface

If, from the viewpoint of continental legal systems, one can define case law as a common interpretation of legal regulations, with those regulations leading to a convergent series of judicial decisions, then to a large extent the phenomenon of case law may be seen as a paradox.

On the one hand, case law can effectively seem to be entirely integrated into the legal regulations whose meanings it interprets. From this point of view, case law apparently fulfills a purely declarative role, thereby running the risk of being viewed as merely an accessory to the legal regulations it describes.

Nonetheless, one cannot ignore the fact that identifying and properly understanding legal norms requires a careful study of case law. In this respect, and from a more realistic standpoint, it can be accepted that case law – partially, at least – helps to establish the scope of the norms that may be in play.

Bearing in mind the uncertainties outlined above, it is understandable that the role and rules of case law itself have taken their place among the problems which the science of law seeks to research and analyse, whether in relation to the inherent principles of a specific legal system or to the properties of law in general. The questions of whether case law has a creative or merely declarative function, in addition to whether – and under what conditions – case law can be considered to be a source of law, represent key problems upon which to reflect.

These issues have indeed been the object of debate since at least the nineteenth century, as much in terms of General Theory of Law as in the doctrinal study of the various national legal systems. In this sense, the understanding of the role performed by the judge, insofar as it derived from certain interpretations of the principle of separation of powers and taking into account the prestige that the judiciary enjoyed in the majority of European legal systems, has driven numerous jurists to consider in depth the question of the proper role and scope of case law.

In any case, it is worth highlighting that, at the present time, the outlined issue has an even greater importance. In effect, certain aspects of the contemporary evolution of European legal systems are contributing towards making questions concerning role and scope of case law ever more difficult to resolve. These aspects include the increase in written law, in addition to the strengthening of the judicial role in general – a strengthening shown clearly, among other things, by the extension of jurisdictional control of constitutionality of laws in various States, or the growing influence of supranational jurisdictions in areas such as European Union law, or applicable rules in the field of human rights. These are among the factors which have taken the case law phenomenon to a new level of significance. In this regard, and beyond their traditional theoretical and legal dimensions, problems relating to the role and rules of case law demand an in-depth reflection, taking into account the context of the modern day.

The preceding observations alone would justify our interest in this new work by María José Falcón y Tella dedicated to case law. This study, in fact, offers readers an outstanding study of the case law phenomenon.

The reflections offered by the author are concerned with the specific scope of case law in Continental legal systems. This definition derives from a methodological comparison concerning both the meaning of the term *iurisprudentia* in Roman law, and the practice of case law that characterises common law systems (English law particularly being considered with regard to the latter).

Following this first stage, María José Falcón y Tella analyzes, in the light of the Spanish model, the role performed by the various jurisprudential institutions in the formation of case law, and similarly the conditions on which its existence depends. Later, having identified the various functions of case law, the author reviews in detail the arguments advanced in favour of and against the role of case law as a source of law. This is specifically considered with relation to the case law emanating from the Spanish Supreme Court (*Tribunal Supremo*).

The immense interest that the author's work holds is particularly evident in its digressions on Theory of Law, which supplement the arguments made in the work and allow the reader to recognize their scope. These analyses deal not only with the notion of a source of law, but also with the varying understandings of the role played by the judge which have been outlined by the contemporary mainstream of Theory of Law.

The reader will be able to benefit from clarifying analyses provided by the author regarding changes in case law, in addition to considerations of the role it performs in different national legal systems.

The historical focus of the issues, the use of methodology from the perspective of comparative law and of doctrinal studies of positive law, as with the use of resources offered by general Theory of Law, together constitute some of the elements which enrich this work by María José Falcón y Tella and confer real scientific value on the work. Hence, as with previous works of real value written by the author in the field of Theory of Law,[1] this essential study of case law carried out by María José Falcón y Tella will occupy, without a shadow of a doubt, a key position among the more significant reference works dedicated to this form of manifestation of law.

Philippe Gérard
Professor of Philosophy of Law
and political Philosophy
Facultés Universitaires Saint-Louis
(Brussels)

1 See, among others, M.J. FALCÓN Y TELLA, *El argumento analógico en el Derecho*, Preface by J. ITURMENDI MORALES, Madrid, Civitas, 1991. *Id, Concepto y fundamento de la validez del Derecho*, Preface by F. OST, Madrid, Civitas, 1994. *Id, La desobediencia civil*, Preface by F. GARRIDO FALLA, Madrid, Marcial Pons, 2000. *Id, Equidad, Derecho y Justicia*, Preface by J. IGARTUA SALAVERRÍA, Madrid, Editorial Universitaria Ramón Areces, 2005. Id – F. FALCÓN Y TELLA, *Fundamento y finalidad de la sanción: ¿un derecho a castigar?*, Preface by A. GARCÍA PABLOS, Madrid, Marcial Pons, 2005.

Chapter 1

Introduction

Case law is a widely studied field.[2] It creates various questions, the first of which being how it should be defined, as case law cannot be given a single meaning. There is no universal sense of the term "case law", but rather a plurality of meanings depending on the historical era (temporal variant), and the place or legal system in question (geographical variant). In this sense, the old Roman law concept of *iurisprudentia,* referring to a concept comparable to Science of law, does not carry the same meaning as the current idea of case law.[3] While in Anglosaxon legal systems the idea of case law is one in which judicial precedents form the principal source of law, jurists in Continental systems continue to debate whether case law may be considered at most a source of definition of subjective rights, or also a source for creation of objective law.[4]

2 F. M. CALVO VIDAL, *La jurisprudencia ¿Fuente del Derecho?,* Valladolid, Lex Nova, 1992, pp. 23-26. F. C. DE DIEGO, *La jurisprudencia como fuente del Derecho,* Madrid, 1925, pp. 105-106.

3 J. H. VON KIRCHMANN, *La jurisprudencia no es ciencia,* translation into Spanish and Introduction by A. TRUYOL SERRA, Madrid, 1949.

4 See, on jurisprudence, H. J. ABRAHAM, *The Judicial Process,* New York-Oxford, Oxford University Press, 1986. J. ADAME GODDARD, "Jurisprudencia", in *Diccionario Jurídico Mexicano,* V, México, Instituto de Investigaciones Jurídicas, UNAM, 1984, p. 289. M. ALBALADEJO GARCÍA, "La jurisprudencia", in *Revista de Derecho Privado,* 54, 1970. *Id, Curso de Derecho Civil español, I, Introducción y Parte General,* 3rd. ed., Barcelona, Bosch, 1983. *Id, Derecho civil, I, Introducción y Parte General, vol. I, Introducción y Derecho de la Persona,* 12nd. ed., Zaragoza, 1991. N. ALCALÁ ZAMORA Y CASTILLO, *Jueces. Jurisdicción, Jurisprudencia. (Estudios de Derecho procesal),* Madrid, 1934, pp. 303-326. N. ALCALÁ ZAMORA Y TORRES, *La jurisprudencia y la vida del Derecho.* Discurso leído en el acto de recepción. Contestación de Rafael de Ureña y Smenjaud el día 22 de febrero de 1920, Madrid, Real Academia de Ciencias Morales y Políticas, 1920. L. ALEXANDER, "Precedent", in D. PATTERSON, *A Companion to Philosophy of Law and Legal Theory,* Oxford, Blackwell, 1996. A. ANZON, *Il valore del precedente nel giudizio sulle leggi,* Milano, Giuffrè, 1995. ARCHIVES DE PHI-

LOSOPHIE DU DROIT, *La jurisprudence,* XXX, Paris, Sirey, 1985. M. AZUELA GUITRÓN, "Importancia, límites y riesgos de la jurisprudencia", in *La Interpretación Constitucional de la Suprema Corte de Justicia de la Nación en Materia de Impuestos 1917-1985,* México, Instituto de Investigaciones Jurídicas, UNAM, Tribunal Fiscal de la Federación, 1986. D. BARBERO, *Sistema del Derecho Privado, I -Introducción, Parte preliminar, Parte general-,* translation into Spanish by S. SENTÍS MELENDO, Buenos Aires, Ediciones Jurídicas Europa-América, 1967. G. BELLONI PERESSUTTI, "Metodo e strategie nell'utilizzazione di precedenti giudiziali: riflessioni di un avvocato civilista", in U. VINCENTI (a cura di), in cooperation with G. SANTUCCI, *Il valore dei precedenti giudiziali nella tradizione europea,* Padova, CEDAM, 1998, pp. 147-163. M. BIBENT, *L'informatique appliquée à la jurisprudence. Une méthode de traitment de la documentation juridique,* preface by P. CATALA, Paris, Librairies Techniques, 1976. J. BONNECASE, *Elementos de Derecho Civil, I (Nociones preliminares, persona, familia y bienes),* translation into Spanish by CAJICA, México, 1945. G. A. BORDA, "Reglas prácticas para la interpretación de la ley civil", in *Revista General de Legislación y Jurisprudencia,* 190, 1951, pp. 507 ff. P. CALAMANDREI, "La funzione della giurisprudenza nel tempo presente", in *Rivista Trimestralle di Diritto e Procedura Civile,* 1955, pp. 252-272. J. CASTÁN TOBEÑAS, *La formulación judicial del Derecho (jurisprudencia y arbitrio de equidad),* 2nd. ed., Madrid, Reus, 1934. *Id, Teoría de la aplicación e investigación del Derecho (Metodología y técnica operativa en el Derecho privado positivo,* Madrid, Reus, 1947. *Id, Derecho civil, común y foral,* I, 1, 12nd. ed. revised by DE LOS MOZOS, Madrid, Reus, 1982. C. CHECCHINI, "Storia della giurisprudenza e interpretazione della legge", in *Archivio Giuridico Filippo Serafín,* XC, 1923, pp. 167 ff. A. L. COBDEN, "El juez y la regla de Derecho", in *Revista de Derecho Privado,* December, 1989. M. COIPEL, "Les reactions de la doctrine à la cuestion de droit par les juges en droit civil", in *Travaux de l'Association Henri Capitant, Les reactions de la doctrine à la creation du droit par les juges (Journeès italiennes, XXXI),* Paris, 1980. V. COLESANTI, "Giurisprudenza", in *Novissimo Digesto Italiano,* VII, Torino, 1961, pp. 1101-1106. A. COLIN – N. CAPITANT, *Curso elemental de Derecho Civil, I (Introducción, estado civil, domicilio y ausencia),* notes by D. DE BUEN, Madrid, Reus, 1922. A. D'AMATO, *Jurisprudence. A Descriptive and Normative Analysis of Law,* Netherlands, Martinus Nijhoff Publishers, 1984. R. DE ASIS ROIG, *Jueces y normas. La decisión judicial desde el ordenamiento,* Madrid, 1995. C. DE LA VEGA BENAYAS, *Introducción al Derecho judicial,* Madrid, Montecorvo, 1970. Lord DENNING, *From Precedent to Precedent,* Oxford, Clarendon Press, 1959. Lord DEVLIN, "Judges and Lawmakers", in *Modern Law Review,* 39,1, 1976, pp. 1-16. C. DE SILVA Y NAVA, "La jurisprudencia", in *Curso de Actualización del Amparo,* México, División de Estudios Superiores de la Facultad de Derecho, UNAM, 1973. R. W. D. DIAS,

Jurisprudence, London, Butterworths, 5th. ed., 1985. L. DIEZ PICAZO – A. GULLÓN BALLESTEROS, *Sistema de Derecho civil, vol. I, Introducción. Derecho de la persona. Autonomía privada. Persona jurídica,* Madrid, Tecnos, 1990. G. DOLEZALEK, "I precedente giudiziali nello ius commune", in U. VINCENTI, (a cura di), in cooperation with G. SANTUCCI, *Il valore dei precedenti giudiziali nella tradizione europea,* Padova, CEDAM, 1998, pp. 55-81. O. DUPEYROUX, "La jurisprudence, source abusive de droit", in *Mélanges offerts à Jacques Maury,* II, Paris, 1960, pp. 349-377. M. DUVERGER, *Instituciones políticas y Derecho constitucional,* 6th. ed. española, Barcelona, Ariel, Caracas, México, 1980. R. DWORKIN, *Los derechos en serio,* translation into Spanish by M. GUASTAVINO, preface by A. CALSAMIGLIA, Barcelona, Ariel, 1984. *Id, A Matter of Principle,* Cambridge -Massachusetts-, Harvard University Press, 1985. *Id, Law's Empire,* Cambridge -Massachusetts-, Harvard University Press, 1986. E. EHRLICH, *Escritos sobre sociología y jurisprudencia,* translation into Spanish by J. A. GÓMEZ GARCÍA, G. ROBLES MORCHÓN and J. L. MUÑOZ DE BAENA, Madrid, Marcial Pons, Ediciones Jurídicas y Sociales, S.A., 2005. J. ESCRICHE, "Jurisprudencia", in *Diccionario Razonado de Legislación y Jurisprudencia,* III, México, Manuel Porrúa, S.A., 1979. J. ESSER, *Principio y norma en la elaboración jurisprudencial del Derecho Privado,* translation into Spanish by E. VALENTÍ FIOL, Barcelona, Bosch, 1961. L. FERRAJOLI, (1940-), *Derecho y razón. Teoría del garantismo penal,* 3rd. ed., Madrid, 1998. F. FERRARA, "Potere del legislatore o funzione del giudice", in *Rivista di Diritto Civile,* II, 1911. H. FIX ZAMUDIO, "Breves reflexiones acerca del origen y de la evolución de la jurisprudencia obligatoria de los Tribunales Federales", in *Lecturas Jurídicas,* 41, Chihuahua, México, Universidad Autónoma de Chihuahua, December, 1969, pp. 87-105. M. L. FRIEDLAND, "Prospective and Retrospective Judicial Lawmaking", in *University of Toronto Law Review,* 24, 1974, pp. 170-190. H. T. FROEHLICH, *Observations on the History of Judicial Precedent, Especially During the Middle Ages,* 1931. F. FUEYO LANERI, *Interpretación y juez,* Santiago de Chile, Universidad de Chile and Centro de Estudios "Ratio Iuris", 1976. R. GARCÍA ORMAECHEA, "Notaciones sobre jurisprudencia", in *Revista General de Legislación y Jurisprudencia,* CLXIII, II, Madrid, 1933, pp. 306-329. J. J. GIL CREMADES, "Jurisprudencia", in *Gran Enciclopedia Rialp,* XIII, Madrid, Ediciones RIALP, S.A., 1973. J. GILISSEN, *Introduction historique au droit. Esquisse d'une histoire universelle du droit. Les sources du droit depuis le XIIIe siècle. Eléments d'histoire du droit privé,* Bruxelles, Bruylant, 1979. P. GÓMEZ DE LA SERNA-MONTALBÁN, *Tratado académico forense de procedimientos judiciales,* II, Madrid, Calleja, 1848. J. GONZÁLEZ, "Jurisprudencia constructiva", in *Revista Crítica de Derecho Inmobiliario,* Madrid, 1935, pp. 342 ff. G. GORLA, "Giurisprudenza", in *Enciclopedia del Diritto,* XIX, Milano, Giuffrè, 1970. *Id,* under "Precedente Giudiziario", in

Enciclopedia Giuridica Treccani, Vol. XXIII, Roma, 1990. J. CH. GRAY, *The Nature and Sources of Law*, New York, The Macmillan Company, 1927. J. C. GUERRA AGUILERA, "Apuntes sobre la jurisprudencia méxicana", in *Revista Michoacana de Derecho Penal*, 19, México, Michoacán, Facultad de Derecho y Ciencias Sociales de la Universidad Michoacana de San Nicolás de Hidalgo, 1986. E. GUERRERO LARA, "Jurisprudencia judicial", in *Diccionario Jurídico Mexicano*, V, México, Instituto de Investigaciones Jurídicas, UNAM, 1984. KOTTENHAGEN, *Van precedent tot precedent*, Arnhem, Gouda Quint, 1986. A. LEÓN HURTADO, "Valor de la jurisprudencia", in *Revista de Derecho y Jurisprudencia*, 56, First Part, Santiago de Chile. E. T. LIEBMAN, "Giurisprudenza", in *Nuovo Digesto Italiano*, VI, Torino, 1938, pp. 411-414. L. LOMBARDI VALLAURI, *Saggio sul diritto giurisprudenziale*, Milano, Giuffrè, 1967. *Id*, under "Giurisprudenza", in *Enciclopedia Giuridica Trecanni*, XV, Roma, 1989. J. I. MANJARREZ ALONSO, *Concepto y función de la jurisprudencia*, México, 1950. J. MAURY, "Observations sur la jurisprudence en tant que source de Droit", in *Etudes ofertes à Georges Rippert, (« Le droit privé français au milieu du XX siécle »)*, I, Paris, 1950, pp. 28 ff. M. NOVALVOS PÉREZ, "Arbitrio y actividad judicial", in *Revista de Derecho Privado*, June 1978. E. PATTERSON, *Jurisprudence. Men and Ideas of the Law*, Brooklyn, The Foundation Press Inc., 1953. V. PETEV, "Structures rationnelles et implications sociologiques de la jurisprudence", in *Archives de Philosophie du Droit*, 30, *La jurisprudence*, Paris, Sirey, 1985, pp. 181-190. E. PIOLA CASELLI, "Giurisprudenza", in *Il Digesto Italiano*, XII, Torino, 1927, pp. 831-853. F. POLLOCK, *Jurisprudence*, London, MacMillan and Co., 1918. R. A. POSTNER, *The Problems of Jurisprudence*, Cambridge (Massachusetts) Harvard University Press, 1990. L. PRIETO CASTRO FÉRRANDIZ, *Meditaciones sobre la jurisprudencia*, Madrid, 1966. H. REICHEL, *La ley y la sentencia (Orientación acerca de la doctrina actual sobre fuentes del Derecho y aplicación del último)*, translation into Spanish by E. MIÑANA VILLAGRASA, Madrid, Reus, 1921. Lord REID, "The Judge as a Law Maker", in *Society of Public Teachers of Law*, 12, 1, 1972, pp. 22-29. J. L. REQUEJO PAGES, "Juridicidad, precedente y jurisprudencia", in *Revista Española de Derecho Constitucional*, 29, 1990, pp. 223-240. M. E. ROBLES DE SOTOMAYOR, "Los sistemas de interpretación de la ley", in *Revista de la Facultad de Derecho de México*, XXVIII, 110, México, UNAM, Dirección General de Publicaciones, May-August, 1978. L. ROCA-SASTRE MUNCUNILL, *La jurisprudencia*, Barcelona, Colección "Ciclo de conferencias sobre el nuevo Título Preliminar del Código Civil", organized by the "Ilustres Colegios de Abogados y Notarial de Barcelona y la Academia de Jurisprudencia y Legislación de Cataluña", 1975. A. N. CH. ROSS, *Towards a Realistic Jurisprudence*, Copenhagen, 1946. J. B. ROSSLER, "Prospective Application of Judicial Decisions", in *Alabama Law Review*, 33, 2, 1982, pp. 463-492. S. SENTIS MELENDO, *El juez y el Derecho*, Buenos Aires, EJEA,

If we limit the concept of case law in the context of geography and time to these various meanings – basically, a trichotomy of characterizations – it is therefore essential to find an answer to our second question: is case law a source of law? Whether the answer is positive or negative will depend on our understanding of a "source of law" – sources of production or of knowledge, formal or substantive sources, direct or indirect sources – and on the legal system we are considering.

To ensure the greatest expositive clarity, and with the aim of dealing with the question of whether case law can be considered a source of law in an organized and coherent fashion, our investigation will be divided into

1957. F. SENN, *Les origines de la notion de jurisprudence*, Paris, Recueil Sirey, 1926. R. SILTALA, *A Theory of Precedent: From Analytical Positivism to a Postanalytical Philosophy of Law*, Hart Publishing, 2000. A. SMITH, (1723-1790), *Lecciones de jurisprudencia*, translation by A. RUIZ MIGUEL, Boletín Oficial del Estado, 1996. M. TARUFFO, "Precedente ed exempio nella decisione giudiziaria", in *Rivista Trimestrale di Diritto e Procedura Civile*, XLVIII, 1994, pp. 19-36. *Id*, "Dimensione del precedente giudiziario", in *Rivista Trimestrale di Diritto e Procedura Civile*, XLVIII, 1994, pp. 411-430. *Id*, "Per un'analisi comparata del precedente giudiziario", in *Ragion Pratica*, 6, 1996, pp. 55-64. A. TUNC, "Jurisprudence", in *Enciclopedia Universalis*, 9, 1968. J. L. VILLAR PALASÍ, *La interpretación y los apotegmas jurídico-lógicos*, Madrid, Tecnos, 1973. A. WALD, *Rapport brésilieu al T. XXXI, 1980 de les Travaux de l'Association H. Capitant (Les reationes de la doctrine à la création du droit par les juges), Journées italiennes de Florence*, Paris, Ed. Economica, 1982. M. WALINE, "Le pouvoir normatif de la jurisprudence. La tecnique et les principes du droit public", in *Melanges Scelle*, II, Paris, 1950, pp. 613 ff. E. WANBAUGH, *The Study of Cases*, 2nd. ed, Boston, 1894. *Id*, "How to Use Decisions and Statutes", in A. VANDERBILT (ed.), *Studying Law*, New York, Washington Square Publishing Comp., 1945, pp. 537-598. R. WASSERSTROM, *The Judicial Decision towards a Theory of Legal Justification*, Stanford, Stanford University Press, 1961. O. WEINBERGER, "Basic Puzzles of Discourse Philosophy", in *Ratio Juris*, 9, 1996, pp. 172-181. A. WINCKLER, "Précédent: l'avenir du droit", in *Archives de Philosophie du Droit*, 30, *La jurisprudence*, Paris, Sirey, 1985, pp. 131-140. J. WRÓBLEWSKI, "Legal Syllogism and Rationality of Judicial Decisions", in *Rechtstheorie*, 3, 1974, pp. 33-46. *Id*, "La jurisprudence et la doctrine juridique en tant que source de droit", in *Rapports Polonais*, Varsovie, Ossolineum, 1974. *Id*, *"Sentido" y "hecho" en el Derecho*, translation into Spanish by F. J. EZQUIAGA GANUZAS, San Sebastián, Universidad del Pais Vasco, 1989. *Id*, "The Judicial Application of Law", in Z. BANKOWSKI and N. MACCORMICK (eds.), Dordrecht, Kluwer, 1992. M. ZANDER, *The Law-Making Process*, London, Weidenfeld and Nicolson, 3rd. ed., 1989.

three main sections:[5] *iurisprudentia* as a Science in Roman law; judicial precedent in Anglosaxon systems (distinguishing here, in turn, between the English and North American systems); and case law in Continental law, this final section focusing particularly on the Spanish legal system.[6]

5 See, CH. GREGORZYK, "Jurisprudence: phènomene judiciaire, science ou méthode", in *Archives de Philosophie du Droit*, XXX, *La jurisprudence*, Paris, Sirey, 1985, pp. 35-52; there is a translation into Spanish by M. CASADO, in *Revista General de Legislación y Jurisprudencia*, XCIII, 3, September 1986.

6 L. M. DOMÍNGUEZ RODRIGO, *Significado normativo de la jurisprudencia: ¿Ciencia del Derecho o decisión judicial?*, I and II, Madrid, Centro de Publicaciones General Técnico, Ministerio de Justicia, 1984. A. CADOPPI, *Il valore del precedente nel Diritto penale: uno studio sulla dimensione in action della legalità*, Torino, G. Giappichelli, 1999. *Id*, "Introduzione allo studio del valore del precedente giudiziale nel diritto penale italiano", in U. VINCENTI, (a cura di), in cooperation with G. SANTUCCI, *Il valore dei precedenti giudiziali nella tradizione europea*, Padova, CEDAM, 1998, pp. 106-147. G. COMOTTI, "Il valore del precedente giudiziale nella tradizione canonica", in U. VINCENTI, (a cura di), in cooperation with G. SANTUCCI, *Il valore dei precedente giudiziali nella tradizione europea, op. cit.*, pp. 81-106. F. GALGANO, "Giurisdizione e giurisprudenza in materia civile", in *Contratto e impresa*, 1, 1985, pp. 29-48. L. JAUCH, "Il precedente giudiziale nel diritto del lavoro", in U. VINCENTI (a cura di), in cooperation with G. SANTUCCI, *Il valore dei precedenti giudiziali nella tradizione europea, op. cit.*, pp. 163-167. M. PUECH, "La jurisprudence pénale", in *Archives de Philosophie du Droit*, 30, *La jurisprudence*, Paris, Sirey, 1985, pp. 141-156. E. SERVERIN, *De la jurisprudence en droit privé (Théorie d'une pratique)*, Lyon, Presses Universitaires de Lyon, 1985.

Chapter 2

Roman *Iurisprudentia* as *Prudentia Iuris*

1. Introduction to Roman Law, Especially Classical Law

Roman law, along with Christianity and Greek Philosophy, occupies a central position in the legal history of the West. From Roman law we take our distinctions between possession and property and facts and law, in addition to notions of obligation, contract and wills. The virtue of Roman law, and the reason its contribution to the social order of the West not only survives but continues to provide a source of inspiration in the resolution of legal problems – having constituted a form of *ius commune* in Europe, a common and shared legal culture – stems precisely from Roman law having been a jurisprudential form of law, something scientific, as opposed to an order imposed by a legislator.[7]

Of all the ages of Roman law – ancient, classical, postclassical, common, Justinian and common Roman – the second of these, Roman classical law (130 B.C. to 220 A.D.), enjoys the greatest significance for our purposes, given that the splendor of Roman *iurisprudentia* originated in that era. Therefore, following Professor Juan Antonio Martínez Muñoz, this section undertakes an introductory study of the features characteristic of Roman classical law.[8]

7 G. NOCERA, *Iurisprudentia. Per una storia del pensiero giuridico romano*, Roma, Bulzoni, 1973. J. A. MARTÍNEZ MUÑOZ, *El conocimiento jurídico*, Madrid, Servicio de Publicaciones, Facultad de Derecho, Universidad Complutense de Madrid, 1rst. ed. 2005, pp. 283 ff. There is a second edition, 2006. U. ÁLVAREZ SUÁREZ, *La jurisprudencia romana en la hora presente*, discurso leído el día 2 de mayo de 1966, en su recepción pública, y constestación de Leonardo Prieto-Castro y Ferrandiz, Madrid, Real Academia de Jurisprudencia y Legislación, 1966. S. RICCOBONO, "Jurisprudentia", in *Nuovo Digesto Italiano*, VII, Torino, 1938, pp. 477-502.

8 See, P. BONFANTE, *Historia del Derecho romano*, I, translation by SANTACRUZ TEJEIRO, Madrid, Editorial Revista de Derecho Privado, 1944. W. W. BUCKLAND – A. D. MACHAIR, *Derecho romano y common law: una*

- Firstly, it is important to highlight that the origin of Roman classical law was not the result of a State initiative, but rather the work of *iurisprudentia* and the jurists who advised thereon. We are talking here of the principle of spontaneity, of the isolating of private law from political power and of aversion to the extension of bureaucracy – even if it is true that, later, in the Imperial era, we can see disagreeable indications of bureaucratic tyranny (of a *princeps legibus solutus*, above the law: *quod principi placuit legis habet vigorem*).
- Roman classical law is based on "procedural actions", on judicial remedies investing it with value – *actio, exceptio, interdictum, in integrum restitutio.* It is neither a law of norms nor of faculties – subjective rights – given the absence of the notion of a "person" or even an "individual" as understood by the Enlightenment as an emancipated human being, with complete autonomy (maximum freedom).
- It is a "case-specific" law, formed by case law, the product of disagreements and controversies.
- It comprises succinct and concise, liturgical, brief and immediate formulae, and as clearly seen in aphorisms today considered classical – *pacta sunt servanda, audiatur altera pars,* and so on – the formulae are abstract, precise and clear. Grandiloquent declarations of rights, similar to those in modern International and Constitutional Declarations, are absent in Rome.
- It is an "individualistic" law, in spite of the lack of a notion of a sovereign individual, and in contrast to Germanic law, in which rights are acquired as and when they belong to the community. This also implies that the State would not have been the "guardian" of the citizen as in the Welfare State, lacking as it did paternalism and associations to protect citizens as seen in Welfare States.[9] This does not indicate a lack of solidarity in Rome, but instead implies that this solidarity was more readily considered the role of the family than the State.
- The Romans were very "religious", though their religion was essentially animistic and superstition was prevalent. Both the lawful – *fas* – and the unlawful – *nefas* – depended on the will of the Gods. The virtues of the citizen, of *paterfamilias,* and of the jurist – *fides,*

comparación en esbozo, translation by I. CREMADES UGARTE, Madrid, Editorial Centro de Estudios Ramón Areces, S. A., 1994.

9 J. A. MARTÍNEZ MUÑOZ, *El conocimiento jurídico, op. cit.*, pp. 285-293, p. 288.

pietas, humanitas, prudentia – determined by the law itself, were religious in character.

- Roman classical law was to a limited extent influenced by philosophy, economics and politics. Roman jurists sought to define what was and what not law, possessing immunity from the influence of manipulation by political powers.
- There is a rigid separation between "public" and "private" law, although neither correspond to our modern-day understanding of the terms. Public law is linked to the city, while private law focuses on the family setting. The fundamental legacy of Roman law to posterity bears greater relation to private than to public law. It revolves around property (without a social function), wills, and such matters.[10]
- The principle of autonomy of the *paterfamilias* plays a fundamental role in Roman classical law. Only the *paterfamilias* possesses full legal and patrimonial capacity, and women and children are subordinated to his legal guardianship.
- Finally, Roman classical law can be characterized as demonstrating an elevated level of "technical perfection". This makes it an ideal model for study, as previously perceived by medieval jurists.

2. Roman *Iurisprudentia* as Science of Law, as Distinct from its Modern Conception as *Jurisprudenz* in German and *Jurisprudence* in Anglosaxon Authors

The word "jurisprudence" can be attributed a number of meanings – it is not an unambiguous term. Firstly, we can understand it as referring to science of law. This is the understanding of the term that existed in Roman law, referring to the writings of *iuris prudentes* and legal experts. In this regard, Ulpiano in the Digest (D. 1.1.10.2) offers a classic definition of *iurisprudentia* as "*divinarum atque humanarum rerum notitia, iusti atque iniusti scientia*". *Iurisprudentia* here refers to knowledge of divine and human things, and the science of the just and unjust.

In the Anglosaxon and Germanic world, the word "jurisprudence" carries this meaning of science of law. However, the *iurisprudentia* of ancient Roman law is not equivalent to the modern concept of science

10 See, R. SOHM, *Instituciones de Derecho privado romano. Historia y sistema*, 17th ed., corrected by MITTEIS and WENGER, translation into Spanish by W. ROCES, Madrid, Ed. Revista de Derecho Privado, 1928.

of law, but rather to the meaning this phrase had for Roman law itself, unlike German writers – developers of *Jurisprudenz* – and Anglosaxons – with their conception of *Jurisprudence.*

3. Priority of *Iurisprudentia* over Law in Roman Law

In modern, post-codification times, Continental law of Roman origin recognizes legislation as pre-eminent. However, in ancient Roman law, the "jurisconsult" rather than the legislator played the fundamental role in the process of formation and creation of law. The jurisconsult, via *iurisprudentia,* adapted the scope of the existing law to new needs and requirements created by the expansion of the Roman Empire. Law was basically shaped by the judgements of the jurisconsults, those judgements constituting the principal and almost the only source of law. In this environment, legislation was seen as an element that may disturb the spontaneous creation of law via *iurisprudentia.*

4. Etymology of the Term *Iurisprudentia* as *prudentia* Applied to Law in a Practical Manner; Cognitive and Scientific Differences Regarding *Scientia* and *Sapientia*

The origin of the Latin term *iurisprudentia* can be found in the Latin expression *prudentia,* which in turn constitutes a translation of the Greek term *frónesis,* meaning evaluation and knowledge of justice and injustice, with the aim of practising the former and avoiding the latter. The Latin term *iurisprudentia* has spawned numerous similar terms in modern European languages: *jurisprudencia* in Spanish, *jurisprudence* in French, *Jurisprudenz* in German, and *jurisprudentia* in Italian, for example.

However, and although we can state that Roman *iurisprudentia* equated to science of law, we are not referring here to what is today understood as "science". The Romans did not have an adequate term for our science, given that *scientia* implied simple understanding, while *ars* referred to technology or systems.[11]

For the Romans, *prudentia* is not *sapientia,* knowledge in itself, but rather an art aimed at achieving some things and avoiding others.[12] In Ro-

11 See, A. AGÚNDEZ FERNÁNDEZ, "La jurisprudencia: ciencia, técnica y arte del Derecho", in *El Poder Judicial,* I, Madrid, 1983, pp. 353-379.

12 S. PUGLIATTI, "La giurisprudenza comme scienza pratica", in *Rivista Italiana per le Scienze Giuridiche,* 87, 1950, pp. 49-86.

man law, *iurisprudentia* is in fact "*prudentia* in the field of law" – the art of seeking the just and omitting the unjust. It therefore does not consist of the discernment that we all tend to employ in our daily lives in order to achieve the greatest result, but rather of discernment when applied to the field of law – to *ius*. From here, we find the word: *iuris-prudentia*.[13] The jurist who practiced this art of the good and just – *ars boni et aequi* – was therefore precisely called *iurisprudens, prudens* or *prudentior.*

We can therefore affirm that Roman *iurisprudentia* did not seek to investigate a true "science", via logical constructs, but instead sought a "practical" result, in terms of the administering of justice in social relationships. Science was not conceived of as separate to life, but as operating in its service. The *iurisprudens* was not an expert or specialist in any particular scientific area. He was a person acting prudently in the field of law. Perhaps for this reason, the first jurisconsults were the Pontiffs, given that originally, when Law and Religion were being founded, priests were the persons considered most just and prudent of all. To achieve its aim, Roman *iurisprudentia* valued all types of knowledge: Religion, Morality, Philosophy, History, Philology and Rhetoric, among others. The jurist made use of all of these. From this, we see the definition of *iurisprudentia* in Rome as "*divinarum atque humanarum rerum notitia*". The idea would later limit its scope to the legal arena, separating itself from Religion and Morality.

5. Decisive Creative Role in Roman *Iurisprudentia* – Neither via Legislator Nor Judge – of Two Bodies: Jurisconsults and *Praetor*

Roman *iurisprudentia* had a particularly important impact on the development of civil law. This law was constituted, together with legislation,

13 See, J. CONSTANTINOFF, "Two Creations of Praetorium Jurisprudence Under French Law", in *Tulane Law Review*, XXIV. A. D'ORS, "De la prudentia iuris a la jurisprudencia del Tribunal Supremo", in *Información Jurídica*, 55, 1947, pp. 63-82. G. PIERI, "Ius et prudentia", in *Archives de Philosophie du Droit*, XXX, *La jurisprudence*, Paris, Sirey, 1985, pp. 53-60. L. VACCA, "Sulla relevanza dei 'precedenti' nel diritto giurisprudenziale romano", in U. VINCENTI, (a cura di), in cooperation with G. SANTUCCI, *Il valore dei precedente giudiziali nella tradizione europea*, Padova, CEDAM, 1998, pp. 29-55. U. VINCENTI, "I precedente giudiziali: prospettive romanistiche", in U. VINCENTI, (a cura di), in cooperation with G. SANTUCCI, *Il valore dei precedenti giudiziali nella tradizione europea, op. cit.*, pp. 1-29.

by the interpretation of those with wisdom. *Iurisprudentia* in Roman law is, then, a source of law which is dependent neither upon legislation nor judges, but upon experts. Answers to emerging problems did not come from the legislator or from judges, but from the slow workings of two bodies: jurisconsults and Praetors, who eventually came to form Roman classical law, and moderated and modulated, by way of fusion with this new law, the institutions of the archaic *ius civile*. The jurisconsults and Praetor together dealt with problems as they arose, resolving issues on a case-by-case basis. They preferred their solutions to the rigid written formulations of legislation. As a result, a duality of legal systems came about: on one hand, the *ius civile* with its archaic and traditional institutions, while on the other, *iurisprudentia* sat alongside Praetorian law, a new creation, a flexible law which could be adapted to changing circumstances.

6. Origin of Roman *Iurisprudentia* in the College of Pontiffs, as a "Secret" Concept, and Subsequent Conversion into "Lay" and "Public" Jurisprudence

The origin of Roman *iurisprudentia* is found, according to Roman law specialists, in the "secret" College of Pontiffs. It later became "lay" and "public", and, by the end of the Republic, had acquired a "universal" function. In 254 BC, *iurisprudentia* ceased to be the preserve of the few – Pontiffs and patricians – and became common. Then, *iurisprudentia* opened its doors to all, freeing itself from the Pontiffs' custody and becoming part of national culture.[14] Jurisconsults replaced the Pontiffs. Their activities were aimed at: *respondere* – giving opinions regarding specific issues; *cavere* – preparing schemes of contracts to facilitate the achievement of the various practical results desired; and *agere* – helping interested parties to choose the best procedural model to defend their interests.

7. Value of *Iurisprudentia* and *Ius Publicae Respondendi*: Original Scope and Reduction by Augustus

In the era of the Republic, the views of the jurisconsults were not binding on judges, their force deriving instead from the prestige or authority of the author. Over time, the emperors, looking to take advantage of the undeniable value of the institution of *iurisprudentia*, created the *ius publi-*

14 F. M. CALVO VIDAL, *La jurisprudencia ¿Fuente del Derecho?, op. cit.*, pp. 64-74, p. 68.

cae respondendi, or *ius respondendi ex auctoritate principis*: at first, every author who was capable of doing so was entitled to deliver their opinions "in the name of the emperor" – *ex auctoritate principis*. Later, Augustus, with the aim of giving the institution more distinction and dignity, limited the "right to reply" to a reduced circle of illustrious jurists. It would then have been the jurisconsults who "requested" of the prince the awarding, as a privilege, of *ius respondendi*. The practical judgements of these jurists, privileged by the emperor, would acquire over time the force of law, binding on judges. During the Monarchy, the value of the jurists' "*responsa*" did not derive from "personal *auctoritas*" – as happened in the age of the Republic – but from the "*auctoritas* of Augustus". This caused a certain reduction in the freedom that the jurists had enjoyed during the Republican period, and also a greater link to Imperial opinion. The character of these *responsa* in Rome was that of an authentic source of law – to such an extent, in fact, that judges rarely dissented from the opinion of a jurist with "*ius respondendi*". The force of the *responsa* was even greater when various jurists agreed on the same solution in relation to a particular issue. On the other hand, when opinions diverged, the judge could follow whichever he considered most pertinent to the case. While the old Republican jurists stuck rigorously to tradition and rarely strayed from the letter of the law, the jurists of the classical period were more relaxed and free in their work. They were guided more by the spirit of a norm, placing themselves to an extent above the law, or at least above a grammatical or literal interpretation – as opposed to the judges of today, at least in Continental systems. Perhaps never in the history of law have jurists enjoyed such influence, in being more than mere interpreters of the law. This zenith of jurisprudence occurred especially during the Principality, when it was clearly shown that the archaic law of the XII Tablas legislation was unable to address the problems caused by the expansion of the Roman Empire. Developing alongside sources such as legislation or Imperial Constitutions, the work of jurisprudence proved greater even than that of legislation in the formation of private law. The creative function of Roman jurisprudence "decays", however, as we move from classical pluralism to the Imperial monism reminiscent of contemporaneous statehood.

8. Grandeur of Roman *Iurisprudentia*, Owing to Casuistics, Inductiveness and Intuitiveness; Value of Science of Law Today as a Theoretical-Doctrinal Concept

The grandeur of Roman *iurisprudentia* lies specifically in its great control of "casuistics", in which it was not affected by dogmatic, historical or philosophical interests (as in modern legal science), and was not detained by conceptual or abstracts discussions, but developed "inductively". It went directly to the subject, seeking the practicality, justice and equity necessary for straightforward coexistence within society.[15] The Roman jurists possessed an accurate "intuition" concerning concepts, far from the theoretical speculation characteristic of the constructive approach which defines and distinguishes modern jurisprudence. Roman jurisprudence aimed to be practical rather than speculative – to suggest, in the field of law, what would comprise reasonable behaviour. The goal was not to write erudite and wise treatises or to construct systems and doctrines, so much as to be in contact with life, and satisfy the requirements that arose in the world of law in order to fulfill this aim. Today, we expect everything from legislation; the Romans, in contrast, expected everything from the wisdom of the *iuris prudens*. The key to the success of this system was to meet the practical requirements of daily life, rather than to formulate complex systems of abstract concepts.

This does not mean that Roman jurisprudence was not rational. Its authority derived more from reason than experience, unlike customary law. For this reason, it was possible to base the Justinian Codes on Roman jurisprudence. Furthermore, and for the same reason, Roman law was picked up and adopted as the basic torso of "common law" by medieval jurists in Universities – law which survived in Western European culture up to the era of codification.

The scientific doctrine comprises the opinions and perspectives held by essayists and writers – the authors – of works in the various branches and fields of law. This is simply the "doctrine of the authors" – the "prudent", the "doctors". Following this initial conceptual approximation, we will now analyse their legal value.

Historically, the scientific doctrine enjoyed great prestige and even binding force. This is the case of the "prudent" in Roman law, who gave jurisprudence the identity of an authentic science, as with the glossators

15 See, M. J. GARCÍA GARRIDO, *Casuismo y jurisprudencia romana: responsa*, 2nd. ed., Ediciones Académicas, S.A., 2006.

and post-glossators of the Middle Ages. The glossators studied Roman law (basically, the *Corpus Iuris Civilis* of Justinian) as an object for analysis, and therefore completed an essentially grammatical interpretation in relation to their method. This represents a key difference from the later doctrinal trend of post-glossators, or commentators, who worked on the annotations of those who came before (hence "post-glossator"), and used more interpretative than literal criteria. The annotation, then, was a clarification of the words – *littera* – of the norms, while the commentary sought to investigate their spirit – *sensus*.

The historical proliferation of this scientific doctrine was such that it had to be limited to the opinions of a few, via use of "cited laws". On other occasions, a certain doctrinal consensus was required – *communis opinio doctorum* – for a view to have legal significance. The codification movement – specifically the Prussian and French Codes – deprived the doctrine of its value. The only significant law could be that posited in the Codes themselves. In contrast, the Historical School of Law – including Puchta, Savigny and Windscheid – spoke of a "jurist's law". However, this idea did not achieve general acceptance.

Currently in Spain, *de lege data* the scientific doctrine does not constitute a source of law, but simply a means of "knowing" law. It is, then, a source merely of knowledge, and not of creation. The reason for this state of affairs is that the doctrine does not emanate from Imperial guardianship or sovereign power, but from the science, or personal judgement, of the jurists. For this reason, it has no more value than the "authority" of its author and the vigour of its arguments. This is the distinction between guardianship and authority. The first implies a superiority imposed from outside, via force; the second, acceptance in accordance with a recognition of merits and intrinsic value.

Hence, not even the *communis opinio doctorum* binds the courts, although the courts will turn to it for illustrations and confirmations. On the other hand, jurisprudence, since before the Civil Code, has denied the character of legality to the doctrine of authors.

9. Value of *Iurisprudentia* in Roman Law: The Source of Law?

In particular historical contexts, such as ancient Roman law, judicial decisions constituted in some shape or form sources of law – a law which to a great extent was judicially created, via the Praetor's edicts, which contained rules in accordance with which the edicts must be developed at a later stage. These edicts involved, in turn, the humanization of the *ius civile* by way of *ius praetorium* or *ius honorarium*, with the employment of the *aequitas*. Something similar occurred in the Middle Ages, during which time judicial decisions – *fazañas* ("deeds") and *albedrios* ("wills") – also gave rise to a form of judicially created law. But, without doubt, the prototype modern legal system in considering case law to be a source of law is Anglosaxon law, or more accurately Anglosaxon legal systems, to the study of which we will dedicate later sections.

10. Why *Iurisprudentia* and not *Iuriscientia?*

Professor Martínez Muñoz offers an answer to this question. For him, the choice of the term *iurisprudentia* and not *iurisciencia* appears not to be coincidental or a result of improvisation, but something which is justified for various reasons.

First, we must take into account that the Romans did not possess an idea of science comparable to our modern understanding of the term. Even in Rome, separation of science and practice of law was almost entirely absent. We should bear in mind that the Roman world was not a technical one; there was very little scientific innovation or theoretical development. So, when Ulpiano in the Digest defined *iurisprudentia* as "*iusti atque iniusti scientia*", he would have been using the term "science" in a generic and imprecise sense, equivalent to "knowledge", very probably with the aim of avoiding repetition of the defined word in the definition itself.

However, it is obvious that *iurisprudentia* designated the results of the activity of a special group of men, qualified due to their roles in public life, those roles demanding specific qualities and in particular *prudentia* – which conferred on them moral *auctoritas* by virtue of their personalities, as *auctor*, as eminent men. The jurist was a man of *officium*, a virtuous man. The position required knowledge similar to that necessary in the art of war – *prudens rei militaris*; or knowledge of land – *prudens locorum*; or business – *prudens rerum*. Therefore, etymologically, the word *iurisprudentia* is simply a name composed of *iuris* and *prudentia*, where *prudentia* supplants *scientia*.

To understand the meaning given to the term *prudentia* in Rome, by a population lacking any in-depth education in philosophy, we need to trace the term back to Greek philosophy, and particularly Aristotle and Stoicism. Aristotle addressed the issue of prudence in Book VI of his *Nichomachean Ethics*.[16] For the philosopher, jurisprudence or *prudentia*

16 See, P. AUBENQUE, *La prudence chez Aristote*, Paris, 1963.

iuris was the application of the virtue of prudence to a specific object: the law. The Aristotelian doctrine is "teleological" given that it does not consider actions in themselves but rather the extent to which those actions drive towards the good of mankind, which is the real objective. The virtue of prudence would be relative to the action – *praxis* –, an approach which provides a radical distinction from a scientific activity. It concerns the will more than intelligence. This means that it is not possible to practice prudence with the same precision as, for example, solving a mathematical problem. We are in the arena of contingency rather than necessity. Prudence, here, is an instrumental rather than a rational virtue, the aim of which is to draw inferences in relation to the good of oneself and that of the *polis*, taking into consideration to that end both general and specific questions. It is not a science, and not objective, but "subjective". It cannot be taught or transmitted, but must be acquired through one's own experience of specific situations, this being in synchronicity with the absence of theoretical teaching of law in Rome – at least until Cicero. Prudence is considered an aristocratic quality, expected of men fulfilling public roles – whether judges, legislators or jurisconsults – and must be possessed in order to obtain justice. It does not aim for originality or cleverness – instead, greatness is found in maintaining a valuable tradition via model men stocked with virtues such as strength, temperance, generosity, charity, and decorum. Both general legal knowledge and experience of specific analogous cases are required. The key is finding the ideal applicable solution to the specific problem, as with a genuine "art" or pragmatic science. Effectively, the Romans – such as Celso – considered law to be an art. But in Rome, the word *ars* was not intended to mean art in its modern sense. It would be better put as "skill and competence", analogous to understanding how to be in harmony with nature. The aim was not so much to deduce, to theorize, or to abstract. It was to seek to apply the law, even in cases where the law itself remained silent or obscure, via a "prudent" solution, comparing apparent analogies with loyalty to the *officium* yet without having to be coerced – as in the Napoleonic Code – by the duty always to provide an answer, or otherwise run the risk of losing a post and even a judicial career. In this way, there is a distancing from the positivist model of science, just as there is from the Latin and Medieval roots of the study of law.[17]

17 J. A. MARTÍNEZ MUÑOZ, *El conocimiento jurídico, op. cit.*, pp. 298-308.

11. Roman *Prudentia*

In the Middle Ages, as in Rome, the intellectual activity of the jurist depended on a specific "model" of man, characterized not so much by social or political status as by elevated moral qualities, understood to be a strenuous striving for excellence. In contrast, in the Modern Age, the study of law is not considered a professional or personal activity but a scientific one, independent of any "model" of man. The scientist is no more than an operative of the system. In Rome, jurists performed an active rather than merely passive role. Jurists were not limited to receiving information which was already sufficiently configured, but carried out a creative – and to a point, artistic – role. The artist – a painter, for example – is not a mere "professional" of painting. On every canvas, the painter creates beauty and art. No work is repeatable. For this purposes, a particular quality is needed – a quality to which the Greco-Romans and Medieval authors attributed a fundamental role in general life and in the legal profession specifically – that of prudence: *frónesis, prudentia, Klugheit, prudence.* For the jurist, prudence – which gives rise to jurisprudence – is an effort to acquire specific knowledge and moral qualities to prevent reckless behaviour. With prudential knowledge, one appeals to a specific model of the professional, of the intellectual, which the law develops and in which the jurist is personally involved. This professional and intellectual model is characterized by "excellence", which cannot be achieved without prudence, in the same sense that playing the piano requires a certain virtuosity and skill, acquired through study and technicality, but also an artistic sensibility which allows a score to be "felt and transmitted". In both cases – for the jurist and the artist – the aim is not money or fame (though often, indirectly, these are also obtained), but, above all, doing the job well. From this, we understand that prudence cannot be uncoupled from personal, professional and intellectual improvement, these qualities influencing each other in the forging of the personality.[18]

18 *Ibid.*, pp. 351-363.

Chapter 3

The Anglosaxon Precedent

1. The Anglosaxon System of Sources

1.1. The Term "Anglosaxon" compared with "English" or "British"

Before pressing ahead, it is convenient to indicate how the use of the generalized expression "legal system" – whether civil or common law – can lead to errors, and therefore, for our purposes, it would be more appropriate to use instead the phrase "legal tradition", or "legal family".[19] This is due to the fact that the phrase "legal system" implies a collection of "legal institutions, procedures and rules". In this sense, nations such as Spain, France and Germany do have their own legal systems, with differentiated legal rules, institutions and so on. However, in the same sense, there is no such thing as "the" system of common law or "the" civil law system.[20] More precisely, there are many different legal systems within both of these groups, or legal families.[21] Furthermore, the phrase "legal

19 On Continental civil law, see, J. H. MERRYMAN, *The Civil Law Tradition*, Standford -California- Stanford University Press, 1985. J. L. DE LOS MOZOS, "El sistema del 'common law' desde la perspectiva jurídica española", in *Revista de Derecho Privado*, LXVII, April 1983.

20 On these, see, H. W. EHRMANN, "Civil Law Systems", in R. J. JANOSIK (ed.), *Encyclopedia of American Judicial Systems*, III, New York, Charles Scribner's Sons, 1987, pp. 490-499.

21 See, on the subject matter, R. DAVID, *Les grands systèmes du droit contemporains*, 4th ed, Paris, Dalloz, 1971. 7th ed. 1978. D. LYONS, "Formal Justice, Moral Commitment and Judicial Precedent", in *The Journal of Philosophy*, 10, 1984, pp. 380-387. *Id*, "Formal Justice and Precedent", in *Vanderbilt Law Review*, 38, 1985, pp. 495-512. K. N. LLEWELLYN, *The Common Law Tradition*, Boston – Toronto, Little, Brown and Company, 1960. *Id*, *The Case Law System in America*, edited and with an introduction by P. GEWIRTZ, translation by M. ANSALDI, Chicago (etc.), University of Chicago Press, 1989. A. L. MAGALONI KERPEL, *El precedente constitucional en el sistema judicial norteamericano*, McGraw-Hill / Interamericana de España,

tradition" relates a legal system with "culture" – of which the legal system is a partial expression.[22]

It is clear that, as opposed to those we define as Continental, the Anglosaxon systems do share a minimum common denominator, a hard and identical nucleus. However, despite the existence of this nucleus, an in-depth analysis of reality leads us to recognize clear differences between the various countries which make up the Anglosaxon legal bloc. It is not possible to refer to a uniform Anglosaxon culture, given that there are very distinct common law systems if we look beyond English law. There is Scottish law, Irish law, a law for every one of the States of America.[23] There is the law of Canada, of Australia, and of New Zealand.[24]

S. A., 2001. F. W. MAITLAND, *Las formas de acción en el common law*, translation by CREMADES UGARTE, Madrid, Marcial Pons, Ediciones Jurídicas y Sociales, S. A., 2005. D. LLOYD OF HAMSTEAD, *Introduction to Jurisprudence*, London, Stevens & Sons, 4th ed. 1979. On the Australian legal system, see, A. I. MACADAM – J. PYKE, *Judicial Reasoning and the Doctrine of Precedent in Australia*, Sydney, Butterworths, 1998.

22 V. ITURRALDE SESMA, *El precedente en el* common law, Madrid, Civitas, 1995, pp. 13-14. See, also, on the subject P. S. ATIYAH, – R. S. SUMMERS, *Form and Substance in Anglo-American Law*, Oxford, Clarendon Press, 1987. J. H. BAKER, (ed.), *Judicial Records, Law Reports, and the Growth of Case Law*, Berlin, Duncker & Humblot, 1989. *Id*, "Records and the Origins of Case – Law in England", in J. H. BAKER (ed.), *Judicial Records, Law Reports and the Growth of Case Law, op. cit.*, pp. 15-46.

23 See, O. RABASA, *El Derecho angloamericano*, México, Porrúa, 2nd. ed., 1982. RADCLIFFE-CROSS, *The English Legal System*, London, Butterworths, 6th ed., 1977. A. P. SERENI, "L'equity negli Stati Uniti", in *Rivista Trimestrale di Diritto e Procedura Civile*, 2-3, 1952, pp. 311 ff. Also in *Studi di Diritto Comparato*, I, Milano, 1956, pp. 68-147. S. DE FIGUEREIDO TEIXEIRA, "Consideraciones y reflexiones sobre el Derecho norteamericano", in *Revista de la Facultad de Derecho de México*, XXIX, 13, México, UNAM, Dirección General de Publicaciones, May-August 1978. G. F. J. PUERTAS GÓMEZ, *El precedente judicial y la jurisprudencia en los sistemas norteamericano y mexicano*, thesis, México, Universidad de Monterrey, March 1981.

24 A. GARAPON, "Peine fixe v. individualisation: analyse d'un clivage culturel", in *Justices. Revue Générale de Droit Processuel. Justice et Équité*, 9, January-March 1998, p. 148; C. AE. UNIKEN VENEMA, *Law en equity in het Anglo-Amerikaanse privaatrecht: rechtsvergelijkende beschouwingen bettreffende de belangrijkste structuren en begrippen in het Anglo-Amerikaanse privaatrecht*, Rjeenk Willink, Zwolle, 1990. London, Butterworth, 1924; A. TUNC, "L'équité en droit anglais et en droit américain", in Vari-

It could be said that, except for certain exceptions, almost all the Anglophone countries belong to the common law family of systems. However, due to their importance it is worth highlighting two members of this family in particular: English law, which has historically occupied the most exalted position,[25] and American law, breaking away from the maternal influence of old England and of great significance in the modern day, with its own characteristics and peculiarities.

In the context of English law there is a need to make a series of clarifications regarding its scope. The sphere of application of English law does not extend beyond England and Wales. English law does not predominate in Scotland (where a hybrid system, in part similar to Continental law, exists), or in Northern Ireland, the Channel Islands, or the Isle of Man.[26]

We need, then, to clarify terms and employ them with precision. We need to consider when we use the term "Anglo-American law" (a mix of English and American such as exists in the USA), when we use Anglo-saxon (referring to the Anglophone countries in general), when we refer to the United Kingdom (which includes Northern Ireland and Great Britain),[27] when to be more specific and refer only to Great Britain (England, Wales and Scotland),[28] and when we make exclusive reference to

ous Authors, *Justice et équité. Justices. Revue Générale de Droit Processuel*, January-March 1998, Dalloz, pp. 123-131.

25 See, on the subject, W. B. ODGERS, *The Common Law of England*, I, London, Sweet & Maxwell, 1911.

26 See, M. L. MARÍN CASTÁN, *Significado y alcance de la equity inglesa*. Thesis, directed by J. ITURMENDI MORALES, Madrid, Editorial de la Universidad Complutense de Madrid, 1985, pp. 10 and 38-39. *Id*, "Razón y Ciencia en la Equity Inglesa del Siglo XVI. Algunas Consideraciones sobre la Obra de C. Saint Germain 'Doctor and Student'", in *Reason in Law*, vol. II, Milano, 1988, pp. 63-74.

27 J. HEATH, "'Aequitas' and 'Lex' in the United Kingdom: Motive and Material for Research", in *La Formazione Storica del Diritto Moderno in Europa*, III, Firenze, 1977, pp. 127-166.

28 On equity in Scots law, see: D. M. WALKER, "Equity in Scots Law", in R. A. NEWMAN (ed.), *Equity in the World's Legal Systems. A Comparative Study*. Papers to the Congress held by the Hastings College of Law, of the University of California in Bellagio, in August 1972. Dedicated to René Cassin, Brussels, Établissements Émile Bruylant, 1973, pp. 187-205; E. ÖRÜCÜ, "Equity in the Scottish Legal System", in A. MORDECHAI RABELLO (ed.), *Aequitas and Equity: Equity in Civil Law and Mixed Jurisdictions*, Jerusalem, The Harry and Michael Sacher Institute for Legislative Research and

English law (England and, by extension, Wales). These terms – Anglosaxon, British and English – are not synonymous and should not be used as such.[29]

With relation to geography, with respect to the United Kingdom, common law reigns in England, Wales and Ireland. We can state that there are three British laws: English law (England and Wales), Irish law, and Scottish law. While the first two belong firmly to the common law tradition, Scottish law is of Roman origin and should be considered a mixed system. The United States belong, similarly, to the legal tradition of common law – except for the State of Louisiana, whose allegiance lies with civil law. Additionally, there are other States – such as Florida, Texas, New Mexico, Arizona, and California – in which the civil law tradition enjoys great influence. Countries like Canada (except Québec), Australia, New Zealand, India and South Africa all form part of the common law tradition.[30]

Later, we will carefully consider the differences related to case law in the main types of Anglosaxon legal systems (basically, English, American and Scottish). But prior to analyzing the Anglosaxon system from the inside, it would be useful to study it from the external perspective, counterpointing it against the Continental systems of Romano-Germanic origin. Here we can highlight the curiosity of the fact that despite the Anglosaxon system not generally being based on Roman law – in fact, quite the opposite – there nonetheless exists a great analogy between Anglosaxon, particularly English, law, and Roman law – between English "Jurisprudence" and Roman *iurisprudentia*.

1.2. The English System of Sources

English law is essentially based on case law, as opposed to Continental law – "civil law" – which is of Roman origin and expressed via legisla-

Comparative Law, The Hebrew University or Jerusalem, 1997. Second International Conference on Aequitas and Equity, 1993. (1rst. 1990: Equity and Contemporary Legal Developments, 1992), pp. 383-395.

29 See G. RADBRUCH, "El espíritu del Derecho inglés", translation into Spanish by F. VELA, *Revista de Occidente*, 1958.

30 V. ITURRALDE SESMA, *El precedente en el* common law, Madrid, Civitas, 1995, p. 17.

tion.[31] One can also point here to the lack of a formal, written constitution in England. It would be better to talk of a so-called "flexible" constitution, one which has not been created once and for all by way of a single act, but is the fruit of fourteen centuries of continuity, as opposed to the Continental systems' constitutions. This remains the case even though, after the United Kingdom having joined the European Community, legislation has been passed in many sectors. In terms of fundamental institutions, of great judicial and political importance, we find Parliament and the Crown, in addition to co-operative organisations of jurists – the "Inns of Court" – with clear medieval heritage. The current Parliament is comprised of two Houses – the Lords, its role being more judicial than legislative, and including some who are members by birthright – and the Commons. It should be noted that the division of powers does not formally exist in the English system, although the political power is well distributed and well balanced. This leads to a situation where the courts are involved in controlling legislation – they judge as much regarding legislative excess as they do regarding excesses of the executive or individuals. In this sense, the English administration lacks prerogative and is strongly decentralised, being subject to the same laws as individuals – as opposed to centralised Continental bureaucracy. [32]

31 See, E. W. IVES, *The Common Lawyers of the Pre-Reformation,* England, Cambridge, Cambridge University Press, 1983. R. M. JACKSON, *The Machinery of Justice in England,* Cambridge, Cambridge University Press, 7th ed., 1977. J-A. JOLOWICZ, "La jurisprudence en droit anglais, aperçu sur la regle du précédent", in *Archives de Philosophie du Droit,* 30, *La jurisprudence,* Paris, Sirey, 1985, pp. 105-116.

32 J. A. MARTÍNEZ MUÑOZ, *El conocimiento jurídico, op. cit.,* pp. 266-269. See, on Anglosaxon precedent, W. BLACKSTONE, *Commentaries of the Laws of England (A Facsimile of the First Edition of 1765-1769, I, 1765),* Chicago-London, University of Chicago Press, 1979. B. N. CARDOZO, *La naturaleza de la función judicial,* Buenos Aires, Ed. Arayú, 1955. Translation into English, *The Nature of the Judicial Process,* New Haven and London, Yale University Press, 1949. J. EVANS, "Change in the Doctrine of Precedent during the Nineteenth Century", in L. GOLDSTEIN (ed.), *Precedent in Law,* Oxford, Clarendon Press, 1987, pp. 35-72. R. W. FONSECA *(et al.),* "The Legitimacy of Civil Law Reasoning in the Common Law: Justice Harlan's Contribution", in *The Yale Law Jornal,* 82, 2, 1972, pp. 258-285. F. FRANKFURTER, "Some Reflections and the Reading of Statutes", in *Columbia Law Review,* 47, 4, 1947, pp. 527-546. A. K. R. KIRALFY, *The English Legal System,* London, Sweet & Maxwell Ltd., 2nd ed., 1956. 7th ed., 1984. D. LEE, *The Power of Parliamentary Houses to Send for Persons, Papers & Records:*

1.2.1. List and Hierarchy of English Sources of Law

A. *Judge-made Law*

Perhaps, however, the separation between the two systems is best exem-

A Sourcebook on the Law and Precedent of Parliamentary Subpoena Powers for Canadian and Other Houses, University of Toronto Press, 1999. H. K. LÜCKE, "The Common Law: Judge Impartiality and Judge Made Law", in *The Law Quarterly Review,* 98, 1982, pp. 92-93. C. MANCHESTER – D. SALTER, *Exploring the Law: The Dynamics of Precedent and Statutory Interpretation,* Sweet & Maxwell, 2006. J. L. MONTROSE, *Precedent in English Law and Other Essays,* H. G. HANBURY (ed.), Shannon-Ireland, Irish University Press, 1968. R. J. C. MUNDAY, "New Dimensions of Precedent", in *Society of Public Teachers of Law,* 14, 3, 1978, pp. 201-217. A. G. L. NICOL, "Prospective Overruling: A New Device for English Courts?", in *The Modern Law Review,* 39, 1976, pp. 542-560. J. PANIAGUA, "La regla de oro de la jurisprudencia inglesa", in *Revista de los Tribunales,* Madrid, 1933, pp. 380 ff. E. A. PETERS, "Common Law Judging in a Statutory World: an Address", in *University of Pittsburg Law Review,* 43, 4, 1982, pp. 995-1011. F. POLLOCK – F. W. MAITLAND, *History of English Law,* 2 vols. 1923. D. F. PUGSLEY, "L'origine della regola stare decisis nella House of Lords e il Caso London Tramways (1898)", in U. VINCENTI, (a cura di), in cooperation with G. SANTUCCI, *Il valore dei precedente giudiziali nella tradizione europea,* Padova, CEDAM, 1998, pp. 235-252. J. W. SALMOND, "The Theory of Judicial Precedents", in *The Law Quarterly Review,* 16, 1900, pp. 376-391. *Id, Jurisprudence,* London, Sweet & Maxwell, 9th. ed., 1937. J. J. SANTA PINTER, *Sistema de Derecho anglosajón,* Buenos Aires, Depalma, 1956. R. SATTER, "Changing Roles of Courts and Legislature", in *Connecticut Law Review,* 11, 2, 1979, pp. 230-246. F. SCHAUER, "Precedent", in *Standford Law Review,* 39, 1987, pp. 571-605. R. A. SPRECHER, "The Development of the Doctrine of Stare Decisis and the Extent to Which it Should Be Applied", in *American Bar Association Journal,* 31, 1945, pp. 501-509. J. P. STEVENS, "The Life Span of a Judge-Made Rule", in *New York University Law Review,* 58, 1, 1983, pp. 1-21. J. STONE, "The Ratio of the Ratio Decidendi", in *The Modern Law Review,* 22, 6, 1959, pp. 597-620. *Id,* "1966 and All That! Loasing the Chains of Precedents", in *Columbia Law Review,* 69, 7, 1969, pp. 1162-1202. Id, *Precedent and Law. Dynamics of Common Law Growth,* Sydney, Butterworths, 1985. R. STONE, "The Precedence of Precedents", in *The Cambridge Law Review,* 26, 1, 1968, pp. 35-38. P. L. SZANTON, "Stare Decisis; A Dissenting View", in *The Hastings Law Journal,* 10, 4, 1959, pp. 394-403. C. WOODARD, "Common Law and Common Law Legal Systems", in R. J. JANOSIK (ed.), *Encyclopedia of American Judicial Systems,* II, New York, Charles Scribner's Sons, 1987, pp. 500-516. Lord WRIGHT, "Precedents", in *The Cambridge Law Journal,* 8, 2, 1943, pp. 118-145.

plified by their system of sources. English law is a case law system, case law here being used in a broad sense, an eminently judge-made law. It functions in the following way:[33]

a.– Judge-made law, assuming the three following forms:[34]

- A consensual law, "customary law", which comprises traditional uses declared by the popular courts.
- "Case law", in the strict sense, consisting of legal decisions made by judges.[35]
- "Equity", not understood in the Roman-Germanic way as outlined above, as moderating justice in the specific case, but viewed in the Anglosaxon fashion, as a jurisdictional system in itself, derived from the discretion of arbitrators and judges when applying general considerations of justice to legal disputes.[36]

33 See, on the subject, Sir C. K. ALLEN (1887-1966), *Law in the Making*, 2nd. ed. revised, Oxford, Clarendon Press, 1930. *Id*, "Case Law: an Unwarrantable Intervention", in *The Law Quarterly Review*, 51, 1935, pp. 333-346. *Id*, *Las fuentes del Derecho inglés*, Introduction by A. ORTIZ GARCÍA, Madrid, Instituto de Estudios Políticos, 1969. N. H. ANDREWS, "Reporting Case Law: Unreported Cases, the Definition of a Ratio and the Criteria for Reporting Decisions", in *Legal Studies*, 5, 1, 1985, pp. 205-235. L. ANTONIOLLI DEFLORIAN, "Il ruolo del precedente giudiziale nel common law inglese", in U. VINCENTI, (a cura di), in cooperation with G. SANTUCCI, *Il valore dei precedenti giudiziali nella tradizione europea, op. cit.*, pp. 167-235.

34 See on the subject, SIR R. CROSS, "Stare Decisis in Contemporary England", in *The Law Quarterly Review*, 82, 1966, pp. 203-214. *Id*, "The Ratio Decidendi and a Plurality of Speeches in the House of Lords", in *The Law Quarterly Review*, 93, 1977, pp. 378-385. *Id*, "The House of Lords and the Rules of Precedent", in P. M. S. HACKER – J. RAZ (eds.), *Law, Morality and Society*, Oxford, Clarendon Press, 1988, pp. 145-160. *Id*, *Precedent in English Law*, Oxford, Clarendon Press, 1961; J.W. HARRIS (editor), Oxford, Clarendon Press, 4th. ed., 1991. T. S. CURRIER, "Time and Change in Judge-Made Law: Prospective Overruling", in *Virginia Law Review*, 51, 2, 1965, pp. 201-272.

35 See, W. HOLDSWORTH, "Case Law", en *The Law Quarterly Review*, 40, 1934, pp. 180-195. *Id*, *Some Makers of English Law*, Cambridge, Cambridge University Press, 1938. *Id*, *A History of English Law*, 17 vols., London, Methuen & Co., 7th. ed. 1956. T. INGMAN, *The English Legal Process*, London, Blackstone Press, 2nd ed. 1987.

36 See: G. F. BELL, *What do we Mean by Equity?* 1993; H, RAJAK, "Equity v. Statute", in S. GOLDSTEIN (ed.): *Equity and Contemporary Legal Develop-*

As regards equity, the current Anglosaxon concept has nothing in common with the Continental notion apart from its name – which naturally leads to error – and its initial, historical origin. Its origin goes back to the *aequitas canonica* which was the basis of not only Continental equity but also of English equity in its beginnings, when, in the Middle Ages, the Chancellors of England were ecclesiastics.[37] Today, however, the idea equivalent to the notion of "Continental equity" is not "English equity" but rather what is called natural justice.

The institution referred to in this section is not natural justice, but what is known as English equity. It is a branch of case law, and constitutes a category different from both statute law and common law. Its existence was indissolubly linked to that of a specific historic institution, the Chancery Court, for 500 years of its history, from the 14th to the end of the 19th century.

English equity is characterised principally as secret, inquisitorial and written, with professional judges and no jury. This is in contrast to common law, which is predominantly oral, can be contradictory, and relied upon the jury system and publicity. The principles applicable are also different. Roman canonical principles predominate in equity, while the traditional national law takes precedence in common law.[38]

Still, what are common law and equity as counterposed systems and jurisdictions?[39] English common law is the systematic conjunction of principles taken from the legal precedents emanating from the Royal Courts at Westminster Hall. These courts are in fact called the "Courts of Common Law". Here, cases of interest to the Crown are heard, creating a public law which is common to all England as opposed to law based on local custom. These principles cease to be of exceptional jurisdiction and become of "common" jurisdiction, perfectly applicable to any case whatever.

ments. Papers presented to the First International Conference on Equity. The Faculty of Law. The Hebrew University of Jerusalem. June 1990, The Harry and Michael Sacher Institute for Legislative Research and Comparative Law, The Hebrew University of Jerusalem, 1992, pp. 100-115.

37 See DE LUCA, "Aequitas canonica ed equity inglese alla luce del pensiero di C. Saint-Germain", in *Eph.* i.c., 1947.

38 J. A. MARTÍNEZ MUÑOZ, *El conocimiento jurídico, op. cit.*, p. 275.

39 *Cf.* W. W. BILLSON: *Equity in its Relations to Common Law,* Boston, Boston Book Co., 1917.

For its part, and as distinct from common law, equity is the conjunction of principles taken from the precedents of the old Chancery Court, whose origins date back to two centuries after the Courts of Common Law. These precedents were then applied by English Courts, though, prior to the enactment of the *Judicature Acts* (1873-1875), they would be exclusively applied by those legal institutions called "Courts of Equity".

Today, following the *Judicature Acts* of 1873-1875, common law and equity may be applied by the same Courts. However, their principles are so different that, even in very recent times, they constitute separate branches of judge-made law. These differences in their rules and principles are a consequence of their distinct historical origins.[40]

B. Statute Law

As is widely known, judicial precedent is not the only source of English law. It is in fact one of three, the other two being legislation and custom. Various writers also include – in a subsidiary sense – equity and books of authority. [41]

English "statute law" can be found in a series of texts from various periods, such as the Magna Carta, signed by King John on 15 June 1215, which forms the cornerstone of English political freedoms and contains such fundamental legal principles as "no taxation without approbation", the right to freedom and personal security, and recognises the right to "due process of law". This latter recognition caused protest from the privileged classes. Other texts include the Petition of Rights (7 June 1628), the Habeas Corpus Amendment Act (26 May 1679), and the Bill of Rights (12 February 1689).[42]

40 We have followed here the work by M. L. MARÍN CASTÁN, *Significado y alcance de la equity inglesa,* thesis, directed by JOSÉ ITURMENDI MORALES, Madrid, Facultad de Derecho, Universidad Complutense de Madrid, 1985, pp. 19-89. And also N. ANDRADA HERRERO, *La equidad como elemento catalizador entre la norma jurídica y la justicia,* thesis, directed by J. ITURMENDI MORALES, Madrid, Editorial de la Universidad Complutense de Madrid, 1988, pp. 221, 240 and 247.

41 See, on the subject, J. F. BURROWS, "The Interrelation Between Common Law and Statute Law", in *Otago Law Review,* 3, 4, 1976, pp. 583-600. F. A. R. BENION, *Statute Law,* London, Oyez Pub., 1980. G. CALABRESI, *A Common Law for the Age of Statutes,* Cambridge – Massachusetts / London – England, Harvard University Press, 1982.

42 See, J. A. MARTÍNEZ MUÑOZ, *El conocimiento jurídico, op. cit.*, pp. 269-271.

Statute law has for centuries been considered an exception to case law in England.[43] English legislation was concerned with small details of law. This has changed dramatically from the second half of the 19th Century. Today, the preponderance of case law has been seriously affected by the progressive increase in statute law, with many general rules being incorporated into legislation, particularly in the so-called "Consolidation Acts".

Legislation tends to be classified as:

1. Primary legislation, consisting of laws approved by Parliament – "Acts of Parliament". This legislation may take two forms – public or private – depending on whether the legislation in question is aimed at all citizens or merely a specific group.
2. Delegated legislation – also known as secondary, subsidiary or subordinate legislation. This legislation is enacted by other institutions which form part of the executive part of the government: the Crown, the Ministeries, Departments of State, Public and Local Authorities. This legislation may take various names in England: rules, regulations, orders, by-laws, schemes, measures, and so on. Delegated legislation also falls within the scope of "Administrative law".
3. Community legislation. Community law comprises:
    a. Primary legislation, meaning the founding Treaties of the European Community – those of Paris in 1951 and Rome in 1957, including its various amendments, the last of which – the Treaty on European Union, of Maastricht – came into force on 1 November 1993.
    b. Secondary or derived legislation, meaning regulations, directives, decisions, recommendations and opinions.

The relationships between the various types of legislation can be summarised as follows:

1. Firstly, Community legislation takes precedence over the laws of Member States, in this case those of the United Kingdom – even in the event that the domestic legislation is posterior to the Community legislation. In general terms, all primary legislation can be said to be directly applicable. In relation to secondary legislation, regulations are directly applicable. Directives are binding in terms of their intended effect, but the national government – via Parlia-

43 J. DAVIES, "A Response to Statutory Obsolescence: the Nonprimacy of Statutes Act", in *Vermont Law Review*, 4, 2, 1979, pp. 203-231.

ment or the administration – retains the competence to determine the form and means of developing those directives. Decisions can be directly applicable depending, above all, on the addressee. The remainder – recommendations and opinions – do not have binding effect, for which reason they cannot in the strict sense be considered sources of law.

2. Secondly, legislation of the English Parliament is superior to the delegated legislation emanating from subordinate legislative authorities.
3. Enactments are either expressly or implicitly repealed by later and contradictory enactments.

Although at first glance one might consider, given the importance of precedent in English law, that law of legislative origin is in itself quantitatively less than in civil law countries, this is far from being the case: there is in fact a great deal of legislative law. The dominant way of creating law today in England is that of legislation. There is a great amount of delegated legislation – on average, the annual amount of such legislation easily exceeds that of Parliamentary legislation. Despite the importance of precedent in English law, there is no doubt that case law is a source of law subordinate to legislation – this is the principle of legality. Legislation is superior to judicial precedent and, in the event of conflict, will prevail. Judges and courts cannot refuse to apply a Parliamentary law, and no common law development can reject a Parliamentary law, this state of affairs having been recognised since the beginning of the 19th Century. The superiority of statute law means that a precedent may be amended by legislation, while legislation can never be altered by a precedent. It should also be noted that the courts do not have the freedom to create new law in the same manner as Parliament. Parliament is free to create law concerning whatever matter it wishes, whereas the courts are constrained by the facts of the case before them. Once a rule established by common law has been repealed by legislation, that rule cannot be cited in a later court hearing.[44]

"Legislation" or "statute law" refers to written law. This includes not only the law properly speaking – formal laws or Acts of Parliament – but also administrative rules of a rank inferior to the law itself.

44 V. ITURRALDE SESMA, *El precedente en el* common law, Madrid, Civitas, 1995, pp. 116-128.

The great collection of legislation is called public law. In the field of private law, the Courts remain pre-eminent. Within that sphere, rules enacted by the legislator are only fully assimilated into the English legal system once they have been interpreted and reiterated by the Courts of Justice. Should a conflict arise between such legal rules and the legal principles of common law, then the following maxim is applied: "*laws which go against the common law must be interpreted restrictively*".

Furthermore, the idea of a legal rule in the English system does not have the same general character as it does in the Continental jurisdictions. It cannot be separated from the factual considerations of the specific cases to which it is applied. This is in keeping with the clearly procedural character of English law. This further explains the special shaping of the legal rule, and the importance of the factual element. The English legal rule may be considered a legal norm aimed directly at resolving the case at hand, and consequently its scope is determined by each and every one of the elements of the case for which it has been specifically formulated. Therefore, translating the Continental notion of a legal rule into the English language would result not in a "legal rule" or "legal provision", but in something more similar to an "abstract precept", a "legal principle" or a "general directive".

As opposed to the legal rule, we find the rule of precedent.[45]

A judicial "precedent" [46] is a judgement or decision of a Court of Justice, which can be cited as an authority to determine a similar case in the same manner, or at least in accordance with the same principle or via analogy. In a jurisprudential system such as the Romano-Germanic one, the conception of the law or the system has a "closed" character, within which any subject can and should – at least theoretically – be resolved by way of "interpretation" of a legal rule which has generally been previously formulated by the legislator in relatively wide terms. On the other hand, Anglosaxon systems are "open" and inconclusive orders, where the existence of numerous gaps is taken as read – and in these gaps, the objective of the jurist is fundamentally based on discovering and establishing specific rules, aimed at resolving specific cases and applicable to the

45 See, on the topic, L. MORAL SORIANO, *El precedente judicial*, Preface by Z. BANKOWSKI and N. MACKORMICK, Madrid, Marcial Pons, 2002.

46 M. L. MARÍN CASTÁN, "Consideraciones sobre el Derecho inglés como prototipo de sistema de Common Law y sus diferencias respecto a los sistemas romano-germánicos", in *Revista General de Legislación y Jurisprudencia*, February 1984, pp. 173-174.

particular situation at hand. Not without reason has it been said that the Continental jurist "defines", whereas the English jurist "enumerates".

1.2.2. The *Stare Decisis*

The English precedent is binding, of coercive effect as opposed to the merely "persuasive" effect of case law in the Continental system. In this area, the governing principle is that of *"stare decisis"* or *"stare decisis quieta non movere"* – "abide by what has already been decided and do not modify what exists", persisting in the judgement. However, this rule does allow for exceptions where the prior judgement is clearly contrary to reason, and even more so where it is contrary to divine law. The doctrine of the law is the following: precedents and rules must be followed unless they would lead to absurd or unjust results.[47] The principle of *"stare decisis"* was not formally adopted in judicial practice until the latter part of the 19th Century.[48]

Before *"stare decisis"* can be established, two conditions must be fulfilled: 1) there must be an established hierarchy of courts, since otherwise it would not be possible to know whose decisions were binding and who they would bind. 2) Reliable compilations of cases must exist. These conditions were only met around the middle of the 19th Century, and at that point the modern *"stare decisis"* doctrine rose to prominence.

In England, the flexibility of *"stare decisis"* comes about via the following means:

47 See, M. L. MARÍN CASTÁN, "Consideraciones sobre el Derecho inglés como prototipo...", *cit.*, p. 171.

48 See, on the subject, D. C. BRATZ, "Stare decisis in Lower Courts: Predicting the Demise of the Supreme Court Precedent", in *Washington Law Review*, 60, 1, 1984, pp. 87-100. S. BRENNER – H. J. SPAETH, *Stare Indecisis: the Alteration of Precedent on the Supreme Court, 1946-1992*, New York, University of Cambridge, Cambridge University Press, 1995. J. DRION, *Stare Decisis. Het gezag van precedenten*, Den Haag, Martinus Nijhoff Publishers, 1950. G. DWORKIN, "Stare Decisis in the House of Lords", in *The Modern Law Review*, 255, 1962, pp. 163-178. A. KOCOUREK – H. KOVEN, "Renovation of the Common Law Through Stare Decisis", in *Illionois Law Review*, 29, 8, 1935, pp. 971-999. F. W. CATLETT, "The Development of the Doctrine of Stare Decisis and the Extent to Which it Should Be Applied", in *Washington Law Review*, 21, 1946, pp. 159-170. E. B. WHITNEY, "The Doctrine of Stare Decisis", in *Michigan Law Review*, 3, 2, 1904, pp. 89-107. E. M. WISE, "The Doctrine of Stare Decisis", in *Wayne Law Review*, 21, 4, 1975, pp. 1043-1060.

1) When the circumstances of a case change, making it advisable to move away from precedent.
2) Via consideration of common law as a living organism which expands, grows and develops in step with the requirements of the nation.
3) When a precedent contradicts the "rules and general principles" which underpin and inspire judgements and constitute the core of the law.
4) By virtue of the maxim *"cesante ratione cesa ipsa lex"* – when the grounds for a rule cease to exist, the rule itself ceases to exist.
5) Through the technique of distinguishing, which allows for differentiation between very similar cases.
6) Occasionally by disregarding a precedent, simply asserting that it "is or is not relevant", without further justification to explain this standpoint.
7) Discrediting the level of authority of the person who has compiled the collection of case law within which the precedent in question has been found.

Obviously, the behaviour of judges varies from one to another. Some are rigorous defenders of the stability of the law, while others prefer to emphasise its dynamic nature, changing as society does.[49]

It can be said that, on the "vertical" plane, only hierarchically superior courts can revoke decisions of inferior courts – though it must be recognised that, on occasions, the latter pass judgements that go against the judgements of superior courts. "Horizontally", the various courts are authorized to move away from their own previous judgements.

Derogation from precedent can be express or implicit, the first of which does not present real problems. Express derogation occurs when a court with the necessary power says that the previous precedent no longer holds authority. The key in respect of derogation is that a precedent, once overridden, can no longer be cited with authority in relation to the principle of law that constituted its *ratio decidendi*.

When this process occurs, the derogation can have a retrospective or prospective effect. In England, derogations have retrospective effect. Retrospective derogation is a legacy of the declarative theory of the common law, according to which judges do not create or change law – they

49 See, D. F. KEEFE – A. H. MERRILL, "The Attitude of Lower Courts to Changing Precedents", in *The Yale Law Journal*, 50, 8, 1941, pp. 1448-1459.

simply declare it. In this sense, derogation did not indicate a change in the law, but rather a correction of an erroneous assertion. In the words of Blackstone, "if it be found that the former decision is manifestly unjust or absurd, it is declared, not that such a sentence was bad law, but that it was not law".

There exist arguments in favour of retrospective derogation and hence against prospective derogation:

1) It allows courts to create new law without applying it to the case before the court.
2) A judge using prospective derogation would be too similar to a legislator.
3) If derogation were prospective, it would go against legal certainty.
4) Prospective derogation promotes normative reform on the part of the judiciary, whereas it would in fact be correct only for Parliament to undertake such reform.[50]

1.2.3. Distinctions

A judicial precedent must be followed, except where it can be distinguished – in other words, where it can be shown that there is an important distinction between the facts of the precedent and those of the instant case. The question posed in these cases is always the same: is there any substantial difference between the facts of the two cases which justifies the creation of a different rule?

Distinguishing precedents is often a gradual process, as opposed to the process of derogation, but its effects are the same.[51]

In this section, we consider what has been described as the fundamental technique of English law – that of distinguishing. This technique is used with the aim of achieving a "mitigation" of the inflexibility the rule of precedent contains – or, better said, would contain. In this manner, the danger of stiffness or stagnation of law is avoided. By virtue of distinguishing, the courts can focus on the specific case, allowing the judge to evaluate specific elements that may not have previously occurred in the same form or may have been ignored in previous analogous situations.

50 V. ITURRALDE SESMA, *El precedente en el* common law, Madrid, Civitas, 1995, pp. 25 and 69-77.

51 *Ibid.*, pp. 77ff.

The judge can introduce new solutions and elude rigidity, immobility and lack of expansion of the law.[52]

Distinctions essentially work in the following manner: the legal principle laid out in the precedent is only binding insofar as it is necessary for the resolution of the specific case before the judge – *ratio decidendi*, the grounds on which a case is determined and the foundation of the normative decision for future cases. In contrast, if the principle is not fundamental but constitutes an incidental element in the decision of the judge – known as *obiter dicta*, the antecedents of fact and law, marginal opinions which do not affect the essential content of the decision – it lacks normative value.

1.2.4. The *Ratio Decidendi*

In reality, courts are only obliged to follow the *ratio decidendi* of previous judgements. The concept of *ratio decidendi* is therefore a central notion in the doctrine of precedent.

Questions of fact and considerations regarding questions of law which appear in the judgement but are not considered necessary for the final decision are excluded from the *ratio decidendi* of a case.

The "Wambaugh test" is used as one method to determine *ratio decidendi*. According to this test, *ratio decidendi* constitutes the main premise of a syllogism whose minor premise is the factual context of the case. The "Goodhart test" is another method, distinguishing between fundamental and non-fundamental facts. The "Oliphant thesis", meanwhile, represents an extreme trend of North American legal realism related to finding "stimulus-response", or the "fact-decision" technique, meaning the response of the court to the stimulus of the facts of the case. While not explicitly so, the Oliphant thesis deduces that "the opinion of the court is a rationalization undertaken after the decision, which gives 'good' but not 'real' grounds".

There are a series of problems in establishing *ratio decidendi*.[53]

52 See, L. GOLDSTEIN (ed.), *Precedent in Law*, Oxford, Clarendon Paperbacks, 1987. A. L. GOODHART, *Precedent in English and Continental Law; an Inaugural Lecture Delivered Before the University of Oxford*, London, Stevens and Sons, 1934. Also in *The Law Quarterly Review*, 50, 1934, pp. 40-65. *Id*, *Essays in Jurisprudence and the Common Law*, Cambridge, Cambridge University Press, 1937. *Id*, "The Ratio Decidendi of a Case", in *The Modern Law Review*, 22, 2, 1959, pp. 117-124.

53 V. ITURRALDE SESMA, *El precedente en el* common law, *op. cit.*, pp. 81 ff.

1. An initial inconvenience is the interpretation of precedents and the plurality of *ratio decidendi*. The basic question in applying precedents is not only the analogy between the previous and current case, but whether, according to the court, the presence in the case of any fact (existing in a previous decision) is more relevant for the case in question than the absence of others (which may not appear in the same decision).

   There can be as many *rationes decidendi* as there are potential combinations of elements. Therefore, a correct *ratio* does not exist, but rather a multiplicity of possible *ratios*, between which the courts have to choose. This means we can say that there are not rules to determine the *ratio decidendi* of a case, although we can find various guidelines.
2. A second issue derives from the audience of appeal courts. While questions are normally determined by one judge at first instance, appeals are generally examined by a panel of judges. Furthermore, it is normal for the judges comprising the court to have individual votes.
3. A further possible source of difficulty is "lack of reasons". In principle in English law, there is no rule establishing an obligation to give reasons for judgements, although this obligation does exist in relation to numerous administrative courts. In any case, in practice the higher courts tend to explain the reasons for their decisions in great detail. In this respect, more than a failure to provide reasons for judgements, there can often be an excess of reason-giving. In the common law system, furthermore, the giving of reasons is particularly important, given that the *ratio decidendi* is binding, rather than the decisions in themselves. *Ratio decidendi* can only be obtained by analysis of the reasoning of the court, and it is therefore essential to provide this reasoning for a judgement to have any binding force. Despite this, there remain cases in which insufficient reasoning is given for the judgement made.
4. Another difficulty in determining the *ratio decidendi* of a judgement comes from the fact that it is not easy to trace the dividing line between *ratio decidendi* and *obiter dicta*. It is usually understood that *ratio decidendi* is a rule necessary for a judgement, meaning that, *a sensu contrario*, considerations in the sentence which are not necessary for the judgement are merely *obiter dicta*, as explained previously. Besides this, the problem of *obiter dicta* has become extremely confused, and as the authorities hence continue to multiply, it be-

comes more difficult to determine what is essential and what merely incidental in a judgement.[54]

1.2.5. Declarative and Constitutive Theories of the Nature of Common Law

It is essential at this point to turn to the question of the nature of common law. The following issues need to be considered: is common law created by the judges or does it simply consist of the declaration of something that already exists? Is common law the result of judicial decisions, or are those decisions no more than the manifestation of the common law, which constitutes a *prius* in relation to those decisions?

According to the "declarative theory", decisions of the courts do no more than provide evidence, or manifestation, of the law. Blackstone advances this theory in his *Commentaries* (it has also been supported by other writers). Summarising, we can say that for Blackstone, common law is constituted of the immemorial customs of the Kingdom, just as judges have declared them in precedent decisions. These precedent decisions are the proof of existence of those customs. This theory has been accepted in many judicial pronouncements, for example *Ray v. Western Pennsylvania Gas Co.* (1981). This exact doctrine was taken up and developed in the United States by writers such as Carter.

The second theory – which can be entitled "constituent theory" – came about as a consequence of criticisms by many writers, including Gray, Holmes, Cardozo, Pound, and Salmon, of the declarative theory. These writers pointed out that it was a base fiction to conceive of the law as having an existence independent of and previous to judicial decisions. In contrast, common law was not constituted by immemorial custom, but by norms created by judges when considering the specific cases before them. The courts would be continuously creating *ex post facto* law.

The theory that court decisions do not form law but merely provide evidence of the same makes it probable that the perspectives of federal and state courts regarding the law will diverge. As these concurrent jurisdictional systems do not have a "superior" in common, the different courts may establish different rules. This gives rise to independent court systems applying conflicting rules in the same jurisdiction, meaning that the rights of a person will depend on the court hearing their case.

Another example of the paradoxes resulting from the declarative theory is the following: when a later decision does not follow an earlier

54 *Ibid.*, pp. 89-106.

precedent, a third case may bring about the question of what the law was after the original decision but prior to the dissenting later judgement. Applying the declarative theory, the original decision must be considered never to have been law, and is not followed for that reason. But if the judgements of courts make the law, the original decision does not necessarily have to have retroactive effect beyond what affects that judgement itself, because the judgement simply changes the law from the time it is made, leaving the law previous to that judgement unaltered. In one case, the effects are in the past – *ex tunc* – and, in the other, the effects only look to the future – *ex nunc*.

In this sense, *stare decisis* means the obligation of the courts to follow precedents, except where it is possible to establish a relevant distinction between the facts of the previous and the instant judgement.[55]

1.2.6. Types of Precedent

According to Llewellyn, the concept of precedent is "two headed" – it is not a single doctrine or line of doctrine, but two, which when applied to the same precedent are contradictory. There is a doctrine to avoid having to follow precedents considered inconvenient, and at the same time there is another doctrine to make use of those precedents which appear useful.

The Anglosaxon doctrine tends to distinguish between various types of precedent:[56]

1) "Declarative" and "creative" precedents. A declarative precedent involves a mere application of a pre-existing legal rule, while a creative precedent creates and applies a new rule. In the first case, the rule is applied because it is already law, while in the second, the rule becomes law in the future, by dint of its application. In any developed legal system, declarative precedents will be more numerous than creative ones. Creative precedents, although they may be less common, are of great importance. A declarative precedent, just as a declarative law, is a source of law, though not a source of new law.
2) "Obligatory" and "persuasive" precedents. These are distinguished in terms of the type of influence they exert on the future course of the administration of justice. An obligatory precedent is one that judges must follow, whether or not they approve of it. A persuasive precedent, meanwhile, is one that the judges must take into account

55 Ibid., pp. 25-32.

56 C. CRISCUOLI, "La sentenze della giustizia inglese: i precedenti 'vincolanti' e i precedenti 'persuasive'", in *Economia e Credito*, 3, 1976, pp. 1-32.

– they are not obliged to follow it. A judge choosing to follow a persuasive precedent must be convinced of its correctness, in contrast with declarative precedents, which are followed regardless of whether they convince the judge.[57]

3) "Absolutely obligatory" and "conditionally obligatory" precedents. Those precedents in the first category are entirely binding, and must be followed even if considered erroneous or irrational. On the contrary, conditionally obligatory precedents can be disregarded if they are seen to be so clearly incorrect that a fair administration of justice would require their disapplication. For a court to ignore a conditionally obligatory precedent, the judgement creating the precedent must have been incorrect. A judgement is incorrect in two circumstances: where it is contrary to law, or where it is contrary to reason.[58]

1.2.7. Hierarchy of Courts

The judicial system of England and Wales is the following:

1) The Supreme Court, which on 1 October 2009 replaced the House of Lords as the final court of appeal for England, Wales and Northern Ireland in civil and criminal matters, and for Scotland in civil matters. The judgements of the Supreme Court are binding on all other courts. The House of Lords was bound by its own previous judgements, until Lord Gardiner – the Lord Chancellor at the time – issued a Practice Statement in 1966. According to this document, the House of Lords could in future freely depart from its own judgements, via the technique of distinguishing. A decision must be distinguished where it creates uncertainty, is considered unjust, where the distinction would lead to a clear improvement in the law, or where a change in circumstances dictates that the decision should be distinguished. A judgement regarding criminal law should only be departed from in exceptional circumstances. Furthermore, in accordance with the *per incuriam* principle, any judgement arrived at "completely by lack of care" – for example, "due to ignorance or forgetting some legal resolution or authority which is binding on the court" – should not have the force of precedent.

57 R. BRONAUGH, "Persuasive Precedent", in L. GOLDSTEIN (ed.), *Precedent in Law*, Oxford, Clarendon Press, 1987, pp. 217-247. V. ITURRALDE SESMA, *El precedente en el* common law, *op. cit.*, pp. 33-35.

58 V. ITURRALDE SESMA, *El precedente en el* common law, *op. cit.*, pp. 33 ff.

2) Court of Appeal. Initially, this court only had jurisdiction over civil matters, but following the Criminal Appeal Act 1966, it also has power to consider criminal matters. As the name suggests, it is an appeal court.[59]
3) High Court of Justice. This court is divided into three divisions: the Queen's Bench Division, the Chancery Division, and the Family Division.
4) Crown Court. This court has first instance jurisdiction in relation to all serious and very serious crimes. It is also a court of appeal.
5) County Courts. These are local courts, resolving civil disputes of low value, such as contractual claims, civil offences, mortgages, adoption, guardianship, etc.
6) Magistrates' Courts.
7) Courts with special jurisdiction. These include the following: the European Court of Justice (which with effect from the United Kingdom joining the EU on 1 January 1973 took its place above the House of Lords as the court of last resort, albeit only in relation to cases the ECJ was competent to hear), the Judicial Committee of the Privy Council, the Employment Appeal Tribunal, the Restrictive Practice Court, the Administrative Tribunals, and the Domestic Tribunals.[60]

1.2.8. Publication of Precedents; The Law Reporting System

Given the essential nature of precedent within common law systems, it is necessary to ensure precedents are accessible in some way – although, in theory, an unreported case has the same authority as one which has been reported. Law reporting – the compilation of judgements – is the way in which common law is made accessible, as much for legal professionals as for the general public. Although law reporting has a long history, even today there is no totally official method or systematic organization.

Historically, there have been three periods in the history of law reporting. The first, from 1282 to 1537, is the time of the annual Year Books. The second phase, dating from 1573 to 1863, saw the end of the Year Books

59 CH. E. CARPENTER, "Court Decisions and the Common Law", in *Columbia Law Review*, 17, 7, 1917, pp. 593-607. H. CARTY, "Precedent and the Court of Appeal: Lord Denning's Views Explored", in *Legal Studies*, 1, 1, 1981, pp. 68-76. CH. E. F. RICKETT, "Precedent in the Court of Appeals", in *The Modern Law Review*, 43, 1980, pp. 136-158. G. ZELLICK, "Precedent in the Court of Appeal", in *The Criminal Law Review*, 1974, pp. 222-238.

60 V. ITURRALDE SESMA, *El precedente en el* common law, *op. cit.*, pp. 39-68.

and the beginning of private collected reports, which began to incorporate summaries of the claims of the parties and the declarations of the judges. The third period began in 1865, when the English Bar established a committee whose recommendations led to the preparation and publication, at a reasonable price, of compilations of the judgements of the high courts and appeal courts of England, known as The Law Reports. In addition to these, there is a large variety of series of compilations and collections. However, not all cases are collected – and whether they are will depend on the opinion of the editor of the publication, not the opinion of the judge (though the judge can indicate that a case is badly reported). Approximately eighty per cent of judgements emanating from the House of Lords are compiled. Even so, the tendency in relation to the admissibility of citing a non-compiled case in court is restrictive.

While the modern compilations are far superior in quality to their predecessors, they have nonetheless been subject to criticisms. Some of these objections are related to the basis for the compilations, while others highlight the difficulties for the compiler deriving from the quantity of precedents to be compiled. It is also argued that, as the establishment of law will on occasion depend on fortunate accidents of litigation, key legal issues can be marginalized simply because no one has yet brought a relevant claim. In addition, an erroneous judgement can acquire undeserved authority simply because the losing party decides not to appeal. A further problem is the existence of unrecorded precedents. Finally, the same cases may be published in different compilations, this carrying with it the danger of textual variations and imprecision.[61]

1.3. The North American System of Sources

Two fundamental differences distinguish North American law from English law:[62]

61 *Ibid.*, pp. 106-116.

62 A. DE COSSÍO Y CORRAL, "La concepción anglosajona del Derecho", in *Revista de Derecho Privado*, 361, April 1947, p. 249. F. M. CALVO VIDAL, *La jurisprudencia ¿Fuente del Derecho?, op. cit.*, p. 90. A. KOCOUREK, "Sources of Law in the United States of North America and their Relation to Each Other", in *American Bar Association Journal*, 18, 10, 1932, pp. 676-682. E. BODENHEIMER – J. B. OAKLEY – J. C. LOVE, *An Introduction to the Anglo-American Legal System*, St. Paul – Minnesota, West Publ. Co., 1988.

1. The considerable extension of the tendency to legislate and pass statutory law, which in America has a more decisive value – even if this legislation is not genuinely considered to be "living" law until applied by the Courts of Justice.
2. The federal character of the USA, which recognises individual States as having full legislative and jurisdictional powers, this being reflected by different lines of case law in every instance.[63]

Given the English colonization of what would become the United States of America, it is only logical that the system adopted in case law – as in many other matters – should correspond to the English case law model, though, of course, it would have certain peculiarities corresponding to the particular idiosyncracies of the new country.[64] One exception to this general rule came about in the State of Louisiana, colonized by the French. Its legal system corresponded rather to the Continental systems, with substantive, French civil law predominating. The consolidation of English law came about with colonial emancipation in the middle of the 18th Century. Despite settling on the dual English system–making a divide between common law and equity– in the United States there are as many stable common law systems as the Union has States.

The power of the courts has a different origin in each order. This is because, while what corresponded to common law appeared by the mere fact of the Courts being instituted, without any express jurisdiction

63 M. N. KNIFFIN, "Overruling Supreme Court Precedents: Anticipatory Action by United States Courts of Appeals", in *Fordham Law Review*, 51, 1, 1982, pp. 53-89. G. RUIZ, *Federalismo judicial (El modelo americano)*, Madrid, Civitas, 1994.

64 See, on the subject, BRENDAN F. BROWN, "Equity in the Law of the United States of America", in R. NEWMAN (ed.), *Equity in the World's Legal Systems. A Comparative Study, op. cit.*, pp. 205-223. J. I. BROWNSON, *Equity in Pennsylvania from the Historical Point of View*, Washington, Washington Bar Association, 1914. W. W. COOK, "The Place of Equity in our Legal System", in *American Bar Association Report*, XXXVII, 1912, pp. 997-1009. K. S. COOK – D. M. MESSICK, "The Powers of Courts of Equity", New York, *Columbia Law Review*, XV, 1915. "Equitable Defences", in *Yale Law Journal*, XXXII. *Cases and Materials on Equity*, 3rd. ed., Ed. W. A. SEAVEY (American Casebook Series), St. Paul, Minnesota West Publishing, 1940. T. A. COWAN, "Legislative Equity in Pennsylvania", in *University of Pittsburgh Law Review*, 4, 1, 1937; J. P. PUTNAM: *Digest of the Decisions in the Courts of Equity in the United States*, Boston, Little, 1851.

needing to be granted, something very different happened in relation to equity. Equity, being a special form of jurisdiction, required express recognition in order to be exercised, this even causing a certain reluctance to make use of it – although this situation changed gradually to the point that equity found a place in a national jurisdiction of the different States, with a reach similar to that of common law.[65]

While the status of case law differs greatly from State to State, certain general comments may be made. First, it may be said that the authority of precedent is much weaker in the United States than in England. The American judge's freedom to make judgements as he sees fit in the context of the specific case before him is greater than that of his English counterpart. In England, it is easy to find a judge who laments the decision he is obliged to take. It would, in contrast, be unthinkable for an American judge to issue the same lament. Moreover, judges are elected in the United States, a fact which eliminates the capacity to be self-critical.

On the other hand, the American Constitution contains an Amendment, the fourteenth, prohibiting a citizen being deprived of his "life, liberty or property *without due process of law*" – equivalent to requiring "a trial where all possible guarantees are provided".

Another small anecdote is relevant here. Earl Warren – who presided over the United States Supreme Court from 1953 to 1969– would listen to what lawyers had to say during the half hour allotted them to make representations, and then, often when they had finished arguing their case, would object to one of them with the question: "But, is it fair?" This, for him, was the key point.[66]

65 N. ANDRADA HERRERO, *La equidad como elemento..., op. cit.*, pp. 273-275. J. CASTÁN TOBEÑAS, *La formulación judicial del Derecho: (jurisprudencia y arbitrio de equidad)*, Madrid, Reus, 1954, pp. 55-56. A. GALLARDO RUEDA, under "equidad", in *Nueva Enciclopedia Jurídica*, F. Seix Editor, VIII, pp. 631-634. K. M. HOLLAND, "The Courts in the United States", in J. L. WALTMAN – K. M. HOLLAND, *The Political Role of Law Courts in Modern Democracies*, New York, St. Martin's Press.

66 A. GARAPON, "Peine fixe v. individualisation: analyse d'un clivage culturel", in *Justices. Revue Générale de Droit Processuel: Justice et Équité*, January-March, 1998, 9, pp. 137-151. On the United States Supreme Court, see, CH. E. HUGHES, *La Suprema Corte de los Estados Unidos*, 2nd. ed., México, Fondo de Cultura Económica, 1971. M. HALE, *The History of Common Law*, London, W. Strahan – M. Woodfall, 4th ed., 1779. K. L. HALL, – W. M. WIECEK, – P. FINKELMAN, *American Legal History. Cases and Materials*, New York-Oxford, Oxford University Press, 1991. T. G. HANS-

1.4. *The Scottish System of Sources*

Scotland has an independent and separate legal system, although from 1707 to 1800 it was part of Great Britain, and later a part of the United Kingdom of Great Britain and Ireland (from 1921, Northern Ireland).[67] Many Scottish people may not realize that, though the English and Scottish legal systems are different, this does not make the Scottish system a relic of barbarism or an example of irrationality.

One prevalent characteristic of Scottish law has always been its unitary spirit. There have never existed distinct bodies of principles for common law and for equity, nor for civil law and commercial law, nor are there differing administrative procedures for any of the aforementioned. Thus, while England developed various jurisdictions – King's Bench, Common Pleas, Exchequer, Chancery, Admiralty, and so on – Scotland only had one Court of Session. This had civil jurisdiction. It also had a High Court of Justice, with criminal jurisdiction. There was also a weak Court of Admiralty, but a Court of Chancery never existed. Further, in Scotland, there was no Council or Chancellor – ancient institutions – nor any other body to interfere with the course of justice should there be unjust acts or acts contrary to good faith.

In England, equity was – and to a certain extent, still tends to be – a body of rules and principles comprising an "appendix or addendum" to the general rules of law. In Scotland, by contrast, equity was and remains the fundamental idea explaining and justifying a great number of principles and rules found within the general rules of law.

It is crystal clear, therefore, to anyone who has encountered the ideas and principles of Scottish equity, that it is not in its essence any copy of the English Chancery model of equity. English law found no reception in Scotland. The adoption of a series of equitable principles in Scotland comes from their ultimate source in natural justice in its widest sense. That is, from its being "naturally" right, just and reasonable. What is certain, from the literature and the practice, is that Scottish equity never

FORD – J. F. SPRIGGS, *The Politics of Precedent on the U.S. Supreme Court*, Princeton, Princeton University Press, 2006. A. TUNC – S. TUNC, *Le droit des Etats – Unis d'Amerique, Sources et Techniques*, Paris, Presses Universitaires de France, 1955.

67 See, on the subject, J. C. GARDNER, *Judicial Precedents in Scots Law*, with an Introduction by Lord MacMILLAN, Edinburgh, W. Green & Son, Limited, 1936.

stemmed from the doctrines, principles and rules developed and applied by Courts of Chancery, nor from abstract, general ideas about "justice" and "fairness", but rather from the application by Scottish Courts of the idea of natural justice, and the principles resulting from that application.

The content of equity in the Scottish legal system is similar to that of the Anglo-American: the idea of applied justice, of "actual justice and fairness", of which the late John Rawls of Harvard University spoke so much. This idea is the basic principle of equity in both systems.

In Scotland, for its part, the common law system has developed more slowly and did not give rise to any rigid system of procedural actions. It became rather a more informal system as a consequence of the influence of Canonical law and the resurgence of Roman law. Both tried to remedy injustice or damaged interests when and where they occurred. The fact that, from the very beginning, in Scotland, an equity jurisdiction should have existed, inherent in the Court of Session – and later, in many aspects, spreading to the lower Courts – raises doubts as to whether the Scottish have gained or lost by not having any separate jurisdiction.

As pointed out, it is quite clear that Scottish equity does not derive from the English Chancellor's equity, but is rather influenced by the Roman law idea of an "equitable" law, under the influence of the Roman Praetor. Still, it might also be noted that, especially since 1800, the influence of the House of Lords (now the Supreme Court) played its part. The House was the Highest Court of Appeal common to both England and Scotland. Further, the tendency to look to the works and cases of English law in the search for assistance regarding issues where original, native Scottish principles are absent has led to a certain parallelism and, in a way, to the integration of English solutions.[68]

2. Distinction between "Jurisprudence" – Science of Law – and "Case Law" – a Judicial Phenomenon

It should be made entirely clear that what we are concerned with is the concept equating to what is understood in Continental law as *jurisprudencia*, and not the Anglosaxon term "jurisprudence". The latter is – as in

68 D. M. WALKER, "Equity in Scots Law", in R. A. NEWMAN (ed.), *Equity in the World's Legal Systems, op. cit.*, pp. 187-203. T. B. SMITH, *The Doctrine of Judicial Precedents in Scots Law*, Edinburgh, W. Green, 1952. "Legal Precedent", in *Dictionary of the History of Ideas. Studies of Selected Pivotal Ideas*, vol. III, USA, Charles Scribner's Sons Publishers, 1973.

Roman law – a synonym of science of law, or general theory of law, these terms being used in a wide sense and incorporating Philosophy and History of Law, and referring to the collection of knowledge used by the jurist in carrying out their role.[69]

Despite there having been attempts to formalize the knowledge of law as a science, by authors including Thomas Hobbes, Jeremy Bentham, and John Austin, a traditional understanding of "jurisprudence" which approximates it to "Philosophy of Law" prevails. In English, the distinction between law as a collection of legal rules and knowledge of law as a collection of legal propositions is not clear. The expression "legal doctrine" refers more to the legal rules themselves than to science of law as a collection of legal propositions as in French – *Science du droit* – or German – *Rechtswissenschaft.* In Anglosaxon countries, the judge does not limit himself to *praxis* – interpreting and applying the law – but considers scientific doctrine, of theoretical character. Without a clear separation of legal science/legal philosophy/legal history, philosophical works such as *A Theory of Justice* by John Rawls or *The Concept of Law* by H.L.A. Hart constitute classics of legal thought, forming part of the training of jurists and academics alike. This situation owes itself to the lack of real existence of a legal dogma, given the limited importance of legislative law, the importance of which in relation to common law is comparable to that of regulations in relation to legislation in Continental systems. This is a consequence of the idea dominant in the Anglosaxon world that "natural law is an integral part of the common law", and that "judges do not create law, but only declare it".[70]

3. Differences between Common Law and Continental Legal Systems

While the present section deals with common law systems in general, we must add the caveat that it is basically inspired by English law.[71] Given

69 See, E. BODENHEIMER, *Jurisprudence. The Philosophy and Method of Law,* Cambridge – Massachusetts, Harvard University Press, 1974.

70 J. A. MARTÍNEZ MUÑOZ, *El conocimiento jurídico, op. cit.*, pp. 276-277.

71 See, on the subject, C. M. SCHMITTHOFF, "Die Englische Equity", in *Festschrift für Ernst von Caemmerer zum 70 Geburstag,* Tübingen, pp. 1049-1066; G. B. ADAMS, "The Origin of English Equity", in *Columbia Law Review,* 16, 1916, pp. 87-98; J. ADAMS, *The Doctrine of Equity,* 8th. ed., Philadelphia, Johnson, 1890. W. ASHBURNER, *Principles of Equity,* Lon-

that it forms the basis of the other common law systems, what is attributable to English law is – to a great extent, and transatlantically – also attributable to the others.[72]

don, 1902, 2nd ed., by Browne Butterworth, London, 1933. (1rst. ed. 1902). H. BALLOW, *A Treatise of Equity,* Dublin, S. Cotter, 1756. CH. N. BARNEY, *Equity and its Remedies,* Boston, Jackson, 1915. G. T. BISPHAM, *The Principles of Equity,* 9th ed., New York, Banks Law Publ. Co., 1915. New York, Baker, 1931. 11th ed. I. J. BLACK – E. TWEED, *Equity in a Nutshell,* London, Sweet & Maxwell, 1951. V. BLACK, "Legal Equity ad its Misuse", in *Vera Lex,* 11, 1, 1991, pp. 8-10. M. D. BLECHER, "Equitable Delimitation of Continental Shelf", in *American Journal of International Law,* 73, 1979, pp. 60 ff. Y. Z. BLUM, "The Role of Equity in International Law", in A. MORDECHAI RABELLO (ed.), *Aequitas and Equity..., op. cit.,* pp. 229-239. E. E. BLYTH, *An Analysis of Snells Principles of Equity: with Notes Thereon,* London, 14th ed., Stevens & Haynes, 1929. (6th ed. 1898). BRADY, "Equity Without the Equity Lawyers", in *Acta Juridica,* Cape Town, 1978, pp. 125-134. Z. CHAFEE, *Some Problems of Equity,* 1950. *Cases and Materials on Equity,* Brooklyn, Foundation, 1958. 5th ed. 1967. *Book Review*: H. G. HANBURY, *Modern Equity: The Principles of Equity,* Ithaca, New York, Cornell Law Quarterly, 1945. L. B. CURZON, *Equity,* London, Macdonald & Evans, 1967, (2nd ed. 1974. 3rd. ed. 1979). DE FUNIAK, *Handbook of Modern Equity,* Boston – Toronto, 1956. Sir R. EVERSHED, *Aspects of English Equity,* Jerusalem, Magnes Press, The Hebrew University, 1954. A. H. EVERTON, *What is Equity About?,* London, Butterworths, 1970. *Id,* "Equitable Interests and Equities – In Search of a Pattern", in *Conv.* 40, 1976. G. E. GARDNER, *A Review on Laws and Equity for Law Students: a Handbook for Law Students,* New York, Baker, Voorhis. 1895. M. GARSIA, *Equity in a Nutshell,* 3rd. ed., London, Sweet and Maxwell, 1941. H. G. HANBURY, *Essays in Equity,* Oxford, Clarendon Press, 1934; *Id,* "The Field of Modern Equity", in *Law Quarterly Review,* 45, 1920, pp. 12 ff. Also in *Essays on Equity,* pp. 23-54; *Id,* "The Place of Equity in a Curriculum of Jurisprudence", in *Essays on Equity,* pp. 55-68. H. G. HANBURY – R. H. MAUDSLEY, *Modern Equity,* 13th ed. by J. E. MARTIN, London, Stevens and Sons, 1989, 6th ed. (1952). K. A. HARDY, "Equity in Court Dispositions", in *Evaluating Performance of Criminal Justice Agencies,* Beverly Hills, 1983, pp. 183-210. HAYNES: *Outlines of Equity,* Cambridge, Macmillan, 1858.

72 See, P. D. FINN (ed.), *Essays in Equity,* Sydney, Law Book Company, 1985. S. G. FISHER, "The Administration of Equity through Common Law Forms", in *Law Quarterly Review,* I, 1885, pp. 445-465. Reedited in Association of American Law Schools: *Selected Essays in Anglo-American Legal History,* 3 vols, Boston, 1907-1909. G. GOLDSMITH, *The Doctrine and Practica of Equity: or a Concise Outline of Proceedings in the High Court of Chancery,* 5th. ed., London, 1867; P. M. HORSFIELD, *Equity in a Nutshell,* London, Sweet

Western legal culture is divided into two large sectors which are very different from one another.[73] On the one side, there are the countries of the European Continent, while the Anglosaxon world is on the other. The differences between them principally lie in a differentiation of sources. These may be outlined as follows:[74]

3.1. The Distinct Influence of Roman Law

The countries of the European Continent had received Roman-Byzantine law in the 17th and 18th centuries – the "Reception" phenomenon. This occurred particularly in relation to the works of the Emperor Justinian – the *Code*, the *Digest* and the *Instituta*, completed in the series of *Novelas* and published between 529 and 534 A.D. These countries, in the heart of their universities, worked out a common legal science with its own methods, schemata, and vocabulary, via the work of the Glossators and the Post-glossators and, more recently, the Pandectists, who bestowed on the discipline – best known as Legal Dogmatism – the greatest degree of systematization and conceptualization.

When contrasted to the eminently Roman character of Continental legal systems, the slight influence of Roman law on the formation of English law is highlighted. Roman Law studies in England have traditionally been confined exclusively to the Universities. Those studies remained on the purely academic plane, with no direct influence on the legal system. As evidence, we might cite the fact that in England it has never been de-

and Maxwell, 1960; C. HOWELLS, *Equity in a Nutshell,* London, Sweet and Maxwell, 1966; G. W. KEETON, *An Introduction to Equity,* 5th ed., London, Pitnam, 1961, (1rst. ed. 1938; 2nd ed. 1948; 4th. ed. 1956). *Equity,* Milton, Professional Books, 1976, 2nd ed., "The Study of Equity Today", *Jubilee Lectures of the Faculty of Law University of Sheffield,* pp. 59-81.

73 M. RHEINSTEIN, "Common Law and Civil Law. A Comparison", in *Pennsylvania Bar Association Quarterly,* 12, 1, 1940, pp. 7-19. A. ROBLES ÁLVAREZ DE SOTOMAYOR, *El precedente judicial anglosajón y la jurisprudencia española,* Madrid, Instituto Editorial Reus, 1948. Also in *Revista General de Legislación y Jurisprudencia,* XV, 183, May 1948, pp. 508-561.

74 See, on the subject, M. BACHI, "I poteri del giudice in un sistema di codice, di 'judge made law' e di equità", in *Rivista Internazionale di Filosofia del Diritto,* 1952. A. DE COSSIO Y CORRAL, "La concepción anglosajona del Derecho", in *Revista de Derecho Privado,* XXXI, April 1947. F. J. MARTÍN MAZUELOS, "Principios del Derecho inglés", in *Documentación Jurídica,* 17, January-March, 1978.

manded of judges or lawyers that they possess a law degree. Both kinds of legal professional have been trained by practising at the bar, judges being chosen from among the most prestigious barristers as the culmination of a brilliant professional career. English law – with its procedures, positive rules, institutions, and so on– was English, not Roman, the common law being virtually consolidated in the 17th century.

Though already in the days of the Glossators – the first scientific elaborators of Roman law in the University of Bologna (1100-1250) – Roman law was also taught at Oxford. The body of jurists was at that time organised as a guild of lawyers, and this body ensured that future jurists would be trained on the basis of national law – whereas, on the Continent, law was only developed on the basis of Roman law. England resisted this movement because it already had a body of lawyers schooled in national law. The same occurred with the European Codification phenomenon, at the end of the 18th and start of the 19th centuries. England proved alien and indifferent to codification since, by this time, it had practically already consolidated its own common law.

3.2. The Influence of Legal Codes on the Continent compared with Case Law Character of the Anglosaxon System

Continental countries, constituted as Nation States mainly during the 16h and 17th centuries, possessed a basically legislative structure, written law being the main and almost exclusive source of law in the normative hierarchy of their legal systems – insofar as general norms emanated straight from State power. At the end of the 18th and the beginning of the 19th centuries, codification occurred in all these systems – a phenomenon coming after the reception of Roman law. Codification was a decisive factor for the unification of the respective national laws, and was fundamentally inspired by earlier ideas of rational natural law, the French Encyclopaedists, and the Doctrine of Nationalities. It favoured the dogma of the law's omnipotence. Using the codification technique, the nations proceeded to order and systematize the legal norms of the different branches of private law into Codes. These were organic wholes of systematized norms, with a logical internal structure, as opposed to collections, the latter merely being juxtaposed aggregations of norms. This gave the law stability, unity, coherence – an absence of antinomy – and "plenitude" – an absence of legal gaps. This latter was achieved by such methods as "self-integration".

In contrast to this legislative character of the Continental systems, traditional Anglosaxon legal systems, headed by English law, are based upon case law. The promoters of law in these systems are the courts and judiciary rather than the legislator. It is said that, while Romano-Germanic systems make up a law of "University Chairs", common law systems are a law of judges. For them, the case is more important than the rule. In the former systems, law proceeds by *deduction*, descending from the abstract legal principle to the specific case. In the latter, by contrast, law ascends by *induction*, from the specific case to the general legal principle.[75]

To designate the decisions of judges as opposed to normative law, Roscoe Pound coined the expression "law in action" and contrasted it to "law in the books". One of the characteristics of the Anglosaxon system is the overridingly practical perspective it adopts, with consequent difficulties in terms of systemisation. Common law is not presented as a normative system from which can be derived determined subjective rights, as much as a "system of actions" which may provide jurisdictional value.[76]

3.3. *The Rationalist, Rule-based and Formalistic Conception of the Continental Systems Compared with Anglosaxon Realism and Empiricism*

The reigning idea in Continental systems is a rationalist, normativist and formalist conception of the world, in contrast to the empiricism and realism of the Anglosaxon system. Generalisation and theory are predominant in the first system, while in the Anglosaxon system casuism and a practical spirit are a crucial point. As far as tradition is concerned, common law appears as a conflict resolution technique, consisting of applying principles taken from legal experience and conserved in collections of case law. It is carried out in the spirit of solidified Anglosaxon custom, addressing issues and resolving problems "when and where they occur", rather than "anticipating" solutions via universal, abstract formulae, as is done in Continental systems.

75 F. M. CALVO VIDAL, *La jurisprudencia ¿Fuente del Derecho?, op. cit.*, p. 17, in reference to M. FAIRÉN, "Aportaciones a la doctrina de las fuentes del Derecho y la interpretación", in *Revista de Derecho Notarial*, 21-22, July-December, 1958, pp. 234-250.

76 F. M. CALVO VIDAL, *La jurisprudencia ¿Fuente del Derecho?, op. cit.*, pp. 94 and 97-98.

3.4. The Evolution of and Respect for Tradition in the Anglosaxon System Compared with the Continental Revolutions

Within the Continental family, law is marked by change, by rupture, in the shape of revolution. The English legal system, by contrast, shows great historical continuity, without any important rupture in its trajectory. It demonstrates a kind of continous evolution.

A proof of this respect for tradition in England is the veneration of and regard for precedents. These are frequently and continually cited by judges, constantly re-evaluating old case law, while on the Continent, as time passes, older case law starts to lose its value.[77] Judge Holmes' comment comes directly from this reverence for tradition. Referring to the common law, he said: "In law, a page of history is worth more than a page of logic".

3.5. A "Procedural" Law compared with a Law of "Rules"

It is said that Anglosaxon law presents itself as a system of actions within which "remedies precede rights". It is not a law of norms, like the Continental system, and the legal norm in the Anglosaxon system does not possess the imperative, general and abstract character of illuminist law – in keeping with the interest in the specific common to the Anglosaxon mentality, as indicated by the phrase "comment is free, but facts are sacred".

3.6. A Social Organisation Model Based on Individual Initiative and Free Enterprise Compared with the Interventionist and State-centred Continental Model

Social freedom, particularly in the USA, plays an important part in the system. It is easier than in Europe to remain at the margins of political and public life, taking advantage of many extra-official forms of conflict resolution, such as arbitration. Individual initiative is of great significance in the country of "great opportunities", as a key part of the American Dream, meaning that – for example – an immigrant or African-American might reach the heights of leading the country. The model of social

77 See, A. T. KRONMAN, "Precedent and Tradition", in *The Yale Law Jornal*, 99, 1990, pp. 1029-1068.

organisation of the Continental Codes is more interventionist and State-based. The State protects the individual in many facets of life.

3.7. *An Open and Incomplete Law Compared with the Plenitude, Completeness and Closed Nature of the Continental Systems*

In its codified version, the Continental legal system seeks to provide in and of itself a response to any question that may arise. In contrast, the Anglosaxon model has a more favourable approach to the existence of gaps in the legal system, which allow the judge faced with a new case to propose new solutions without rigidly sticking to the law – while at the same time respecting precedent.

3.8. *A Casuistic System Compared with the Pre-established and Preconceived* a Priori *Ideas of the Continental Systems; An Inorganic Doctrine without Codes; The Case Method*

Continental law has a systematic structure with concepts developed *a priori* in accordance with a preconceived plan devised by a rational legislator, according to the rationalist and learned European model. As opposed to this, the Anglosaxon system does not correspond to a pre-established scheme, cases being resolved instead as social problems arise, in a pragmatic and specific – casuistic – manner, similar to the Roman and Medieval models. Abstract concepts are less numerous in the Anglosaxon system than in the Continental one. Therefore, Anglosaxon doctrine is inorganic – there are no codes systematically setting out the sources of law. Even agreements and handbooks often adhere to this lack of a "plan". Nevertheless, while there may not be codes, there are chronological collections in the United Kingdom and Great Britain, and in the USA there is uniform legislation.

The casuistic method means, with a touch of humour, that it has been possible to state that the English judge when passing judgement "presents his excuses to the loser and their advisers... the losing party truly knows why they have lost, and the jurists reading the judgement know why it has been passed... looking for the support of the parties and of public opinion, and furthermore demonstrating that the solution is equitative, opportune and socially useful". This judge-audience dialogue, in which the judge decides, but at the same time wishes to convince the parties to whom the judge shows great respect, is in contrast to the Continental model. Taking the example of the French system, and above all the Cassation Court, it can be stated that in said system the judgements are based on very formal grounds and argumentation is rejected. Even if it is necessary to respond to all the grounds of the claim, the entirety of the arguments advanced will not be addressed.

As a final point, English casuism is demonstrated in the "teaching method". Apart from the traditional magistral classes, the "case method" is followed. This system can be found implemented in the North American Universities, and since 1915 it has become generalised in those universities, taking Harvard and Yale as models.[78]

3.9. *Disregard of the Separation between Public and Private Law – a Key Issue in Continental Law*

English law does not distinguish between businesspeople and non-businesspeople. Neither is there a clear distinction between substantive and procedural law, and nor is there a differentiation between public and private law.[79]

4. Main Differences between Anglosaxon Precedent and Continental Case Law

There exist a series of characteristics which distinguish Anglosaxon precedent from Continental case law. These are, basically, the following.[80]

4.1. *Provenance of Precedent from any Jurisdictional Body regardless of Hierarchical Rank*

We might argue that an initial difference between Continental case law and Anglosaxon precedent lies in their origin. While the existence of case law in Continental systems requires the decision to emanate from a hierarchically superior court, Anglosaxon precedent may come from any judge or court, regardless of their hierarchical position.

78 J. A. MARTÍNEZ MUÑOZ, *El conocimiento jurídico, op. cit.*, pp. 278-282.

79 J. A. MARTÍNEZ MUÑOZ, *El conocimiento jurídico, op. cit.*, pp. 263-266.

80 See, on the subject, W. FRIEDMANN, "A Re-Examination of the Relations between English, American and Continental Jurisprudence", en *The Canadian Bar Review*, 20, 3, 1942, pp. 175-211.

4.2. One Single Ruling sufficient for Judicial Precedent

From the perspective of the number of decisions required to create case law, the Spanish system of case law of the Supreme Court requires more than one decision. This is not the case in the Anglosaxon countries, where one decision will suffice to create a judicial "precedent". It should be noted that, in the Spanish Constitutional Court, one judgement also suffices to create case law.

4.3. Precedent as the Main Source of Anglosaxon Law

It is worth questioning whether precedent is binding. In this area, the governing principle is that of *stare decisis* or *stare decisis quieta non movere* – "abide by what has already been decided and do not modify what exists". Nonetheless, this rule does allow for exceptions where the previous decision is clearly contrary to reason, and even more so should it be opposed to "divine law". The doctrine of the law is the following: precedents and rules must be followed unless the result would be absurd or unjust.[81]

English judicial law, case law such as decisions or judgements of the courts, has characteristics entirely distinct from those of Continental case law. English case law is true law. Judgements are more than a source of law – they are its principal source, although this is more from the perspective of the volume of judgements than in a qualitative, hierarchical sense. As a result of this, the phrase "judge made law" makes perfect sense in the context of Anglosaxon law. On the other hand, taking Spanish law as an example of a Continental system, the task of the case law of the Supreme Court is to act as a complement to the law – not to be an authentic source of law in itself.

4.4. The System of Dispersed Jurisdiction Compared with Concentrated Jurisdiction

According to Aragón Reyes, the Spanish Constitutional Court adheres to what has been described as the European model of constitutional justice. The North American model is "diffuse", in that the control of constitutionality is attributed to all judicial bodies, and with effects limited to the "specific judicial conflict", as if one considers a rule to be unconstitutional,

81 See, M. L. MARÍN CASTÁN: "Consideraciones sobre el Derecho inglés como prototipo...", *cit.*, p. 171.

this only causes the rule to be inapplicable in relation to the instant case. In contrast, the European model (also known as the Kelsenian model, by dint of the undeniable authority that the extraordinary jurist exercised in relation to it) is drawn up by way of a special court – the Constitutional Court – distinct from the bodies that exercise ordinary jurisdiction. This Constitutional Court has a monopoly – "concentrated" jurisdiction – in relation to declarations of unconstitutionality, its judgements being furthermore endowed with general effects – *erga omnes*. This implies that, instead of non-application of a rule in the instant case, a determination that a rule is unconstitutional will mean its annulment. Precisely due to the fact that this type of control involves a purification of the system, the Constitutional Court appears in part to be a "negative legislator".[82]

5. Current Harmonisation of Statute Law and Case Law Systems

We are currently witnessing a gradual convergence of the codified and case law systems. On one hand, case law today plays a more active role in Continental Europe, while on the other, in the common law countries, the rule of precedent is no longer so strictly applied as in the past. As a result, we are experiencing a progressive assimilation of the two models.[83]

There is no doubt that today, in the legal systems based on precedent, legislation is gaining in importance, while at the same time, in the systems of written law – the Continental ones – the use of precedent is becoming more frequent. This ever-increasing convergence between the two paradigms means that, currently, precedent does not possess a binding and irrefutable force in the Anglosaxon systems – but neither is it irrelevant in the Continental ones. Consequentially, the theoretical studies of precedent in the Anglosaxon legal culture focus more on the scope than the strength of precedent – and, in relation to Continental systems, there are heated debates regarding the status of precedent as a source of law.[84]

Nonetheless, the differences between the Anglosaxon and Continental forms of judicial organization continue to be considerable – as

82 M. ARAGÓN REYES, under "Tribunal Constitucional", in *Enciclopedia Jurídica Básica*, IV, Madrid, Civitas, 1995, p. 6691.

83 F. M. CALVO VIDAL, *La jurisprudencia ¿Fuente del Derecho?, op. cit.*, p. 102.

84 L. MORAL SORIANO, *El precedente judicial, op. cit.*, pp. 15-16.

much in the context of theory of sources as in the legal culture. We should therefore consider it a methodological error to adopt a doctrine such as that of Anglosaxon precedent, which is foreign to the Continental system, to explain a phenomenon of the latter system such as reference to previous decisions. Precedent would be every previous judgement with relevance to the resolution of future cases. A theory seeking to justify and explain the use and value of Continental precedents should not be a copy, not even an adaptation, of Anglosaxon theory.[85] For this reason, we dedicate the following section of this study to what is known as Continental case law, with its peculiarities and specific characteristics as opposed to Roman *iurisprudentia* as much as Anglosaxon precedent. We shall refer in particular to the Spanish model.

The fact is that, despite the convergence between Anglosaxon precedent and Continental case law noted above, something continues to differentiate the two: case law continues to be seen as a mechanism to ensure control over the uniform application of law – especially via annulment – while precedent is better described as a technique of legal argumentation.[86]

85 *Ibid.*, pp. 17-19.

86 *Ibid.*, p. 185.

Chapter 4

Continental Case Law

There is a third meaning of the term case law, which is the French or Roman-Germanic *jurisprudence*. It relates to case law as a judicial phenomenon, as a collection of the judgements of the courts or, speaking with more precision, of certain courts. This meaning of case law is the one which prevails in Spanish law. We will refer specifically to Spanish law in this section, where we consider the requirements, keynotes, and legal value of this conception of case law.

1. Concept and Main Requirements of Case Law in the Spanish Legal System

We can define case law in Spanish law as "the *eadem ratio decidendi* in a collection of judgements emanating from the Supreme Court or the judgements of the Constitutional Court on the interpretation and application of legal rules". Breaking down this definition, it is useful to identify the following essential notes and requirements regarding Spanish case law.

1.1. The Provenance of Case Law

First, it is necessary to examine which judgements and decisions create case law. The answer is that only the legitimate judgements of a hierarchically superior court can do so.

In Spain, prior to the enactment of the Constitution of 1978, in a "wide and inappropriate" sense case law was understood as being able to emanate from "any judge or court upon issuing a judgement". However, and despite the breadth of this conception, in a "strict or technical" sense the Spanish doctrine before 1978 restricted the concept of case law to constant and uniform opinions provided by the Supreme Court, case law being focused on this court and therefore precedents emanating from the other jurisdictional organs of the State being rejected. The creator of case law was only one court, superior to all others: hence the "Supreme Court".

Following the Spanish Constitution of 1978, the matter became complicated. In its "strict and technical" sense, case law remained only that which was established by reiteration of the Supreme Court when resolving questions posed to it in accordance with the established system of sources. But together with this understanding, another form of case law came to prominence: the "constitutional" case law comprising the doctrine established by the Constitutional Court when tackling the questions placed before it. Effectively, alongside "judicial" case law, it was now fitting to speak of "constitutional" case law. Case law is no longer solely that of the Supreme Court, but also emanates from the Constitutional Court – which, furthermore, will prevail in relation to matters concerning interpretation of fundamental rules, given its binding character.

Regardless of the above, in a technical sense judgements of the "inferior" courts will not constitute "case law". Nor will those decisions or resolutions of other administrative bodies, which in Spain include those of the *Dirección General de lo Contencioso* (Secretariat for Disputes), *Dirección General de los Registros y del Notoriado* (General Department of Registers and Notaries Public) and so on, regardless of their quality.

Case law from both the Supreme Court and the Constitutional Court refers to the "general central scope". But the Constitution establishes a second innovation in relation to case law, also including according to a key part of the doctrine a case law of "autonomous scope". This is that of the Higher Courts of Justice of the Autonomous Communities, the fruit of the establishment of said Communities by the State Magna Carta. The Higher Courts of Justice occupy a similar position to the Supreme Court within their respective territorial jurisdictions, even if the fact that their judgements can be appealed to the Supreme Court for a final appeal for annulment suggests they do not exactly establish case law. The only exception is provided by disputes regarding "provincial civil law" institutions existing in their territory. Only within this limited scope can the "case law" of the Higher Courts of Justice be appropriately labeled as such.[87]

However, the issue does not end here. Today, following the 1978 Constitution, it is appropriate to speak of even more "case laws" – of a true "superimposition of case laws". We must remember that we have referred above to the "internal" Spanish jurisdiction – central (Supreme Court

87 See, A. DE LA OLIVA SANTOS, "El Tribunal Constitucional como última instancia jurisdiccional", in *Revista de Derecho Procesal Iberoamericana*, 2-3, Madrid, 1987.

and Constitutional Court), and autonomous (Higher Courts of Justice of the Autonomous Communities). But the "international" aspect cannot be forgotten.

At a European level, to which Spain is party, there are two further instances of case law being produced. First we have the European Court of Justice, whose decisions in terms of application and interpretation of Community law bind the member States, prevailing even in relation to domestic laws or conflicting judgements of national courts. In this sense, the Supreme Court can no longer be considered supreme in relation to those questions the ultimate jurisdiction over which has been transferred to another, supranational, authority.[88] This authority, on occasion, will not even apply the original Spanish law, but instead that which is established by international Treaty.

Also at the European level, in the area of human rights, it is necessary to mention the European Court of Human Rights in Strasbourg.[89] Similarly, in The Hague, an International Criminal Court has been established. This Court aims to put on trial individuals alleged to have committed international crimes who are not prosecuted by their own States, with the ultimate goal of removing criminal immunity for Heads of State who may have committed crimes against humanity and seek to avoid facing justice by use of the principle of national sovereignty.

88 A. CARRETERO PÉREZ, "El Tribunal Constitucional, el Tribunal Supremo y los Tribunales Superiores de las Comunidades Autónomas", in *El Tribunal Constitucional,* I, Dirección General de lo Contencioso del Estado, Instituto de Estudios Fiscales, 1981, pp. 603-627. *Id.* et R. LÓPEZ VILAS, "Las menciones a jueces y tribunales en el Código Civil", in *El Centenario del Código Civil en el Tribunal Supremo, Ciclo de Conferencias organizado por la Presidencia del T. S.*, Madrid, 6 and 7 June, 1989, Madrid, Ministerio de Justicia, 1989. L. MORAL SORIANO, "Los precedentes del Tribunal Supremo: el acercamiento de la jurisprudencia a la teoría de los precedentes", in *Revista del Poder Judicial,* 57, 2000, pp. 119-154.

89 See, on the subject, L. ORTÚZAR ANDÉCHAGA, *Derecho y jurisprudencia en la Unión Europea,* Navarra, Aranzadi, 2003. M. C. ORTEGA CARCELEN, "Análisis del valor de la jurisprudencia en el Derecho internacional", in *Revista Española de Derecho Internacional,* 2, July-August 1988.

1.1.1. The Supreme Court; Appeal to the Highest Instance (Appeal for Cassation)

A. *History of the Supreme Court and Appeal to the Highest Instance (Appeal for Cassation)*

The *Consejo de Castilla* tends to be cited as the historical precedent for the Supreme Court. This entity was formed by King Juan I in 1385, and did not possess a judicial function upon its creation, though by way of later reforms – particularly that of the Catholic Kings in 1480 – it became a Higher Court. Despite this, the *Consejo de Castilla* did not manage to create a unified judicial doctrine, and neither was it the only Higher Court.[90]

Things changed with the *Cortes de Cádiz*, within which the Supreme Court took shape – in articles 259 and 261 of the Constitution of Cádiz of 1812. The Royal Decree of 24 March 1834 consolidated the existence of the Supreme Court, and following many constitutional detours during the 19th Century, we arrive at the Organic Law of Judicial Power of 1 July 1985,[91] which was partially modified as recently as November 2009.

The terms *casar* ("annul", or "quash") and *casación* ("annulment"), in their purest sense, were already in use in Spanish judicial practice. The precedents of the *recurso de casación* ("right of appeal/cassation") are: 1. *Fazañas* – deeds – judgements handed down *ex bono et aequo* by the Courts of Castilla, Aragón and Navarra, according to codes of laws. 2. *Partidas* – Title 26 of the Third *Partida*. 3. The *"Novísima Recopilación"*, which regulates the extraordinary appeals of "secondary appeal and evident injustice" against high court decisions. But we find the first authentic precedent in the Royal Decree of 4 November 1838, which regulated "appeals for nullity". We have to wait until the Royal Decree of 20 June 1852, concerning "Tax Jurisdiction and prevention of the crimes of contraband and fraud" to find the right of cassation named as such in a normative text.[92]

90 See, M. C. ENRÍQUEZ SALIDO, *Pautas para el análisis del léxico de la jurisprudencia del Tribunal Supremo*, Madrid, Civitas, 2005.

91 See, J. F. LASSO GAITE, "Aportación a la Historia del T. S.", in *Revista General de Legislación y Jurisprudencia*, LIX, 227, 1969.

92 See, on the subject, J. B. HERZOG, *Le droit jurisprudentiel et le Tribunel Suprême en Espagne, Essai sur les conditions de creation du droit par la jurisdiction de cassation*, Touluse, Impr. F. Boisseau, 1942. J. L. HALPERIN, *Orígenes de la noción moderna de jurisprudencia. Una obra jurídica del Tribunal de Casación bajo la Revolución Francesa*, Madrid, Marcial Pons, Ediciones Jurídicas, S.A., 1990.

B. *Main Purpose of Cassation*

The right of cassation has come about with the aim of preserving the integrity of legislation, leaving unlawful judgements without effect (reversing or annulling them), and avoiding divergences and contradictions among decisions of different tribunals regarding the same question (taking into account the diversity of places, times and circumstances). Its aim is to achieve uniformity of case law, which in turn is sought in order to guarantee definitively "judicial security". In the current Spanish State, comprised of Autonomous Communities, if the various Higher Courts of Justice have the right to annul, it will only be possible to unify case law in the areas in which these territorial entities cannot enact regulations.[93]

C. *The Various Chambers of the Supreme Court*

In order for judgements to create case law, they must emanate from the appropriate chamber of the Supreme Court according to the issue at hand and as established by article 1.6 of the Spanish Civil Code and the Supreme Court Judgements of 8 March 1935 and 5 May 1970, among others. The Supreme Court today comprises five chambers: the first, civil chamber; the second, criminal chamber; the third, contentious-administrative chamber; the fourth, social chamber; and the fifth, military chamber. When the matter relates to the constitution, the Constitutional Court is the competent body.

D. *Evolution of Concept of "Legal Doctrine" as a Basis for Cassation; Effect of the Reform of the Rules of Civil Procedure of 2000*[94]

The origin of "Legal Doctrine" is not French, but must be looked for in Spanish legislation. Initially, doctrine which was admitted by the courts was given the name Legal Doctrine, as seen, for example, in the Law of

93 See, L. DIEZ PICAZO Y PONCE DE LEÓN, "Fuentes de Derecho. Valor de la jurisprudencia", in *Anuario de Derecho Civil,* XI, Anotación a la sentencia del T. S. de 1 de febrero de 1958. *Id,* "Reflexiones sobre la jurisprudencia del Tribunal Supremo", in *Revista de Derecho Privado,* 1964, pp. 925-936. *Id, Estudios sobre la jurisprudencia civil,* Madrid, Tecnos, 1979. *Id,* "La jurisprudencia", in vol. I, *El poder judicial, en las Jornadas de la Dirección General de lo Contencioso del Estado,* Madrid, Centro de Estudios Fiscales, 1983, pp. 267-284. *Id,* "La doctrina de las fuentes del Derecho", in *Libro Homenaje a Jaime Guasp,* Granada, 1984, pp. 187-202.

94 Translator's note: the Spanish term "doctrina legal" refers to formal, published commentaries on the law, written by eminent legal scholars. "Legal

Civil Trial of 1855. Following the creation of the Supreme Court, Legal Doctrine could only arise from its decisions.

It is therefore worth distinguishing two stages in the evolution of the concept of Legal Doctrine: in the first stage, it was created by the case law "of the courts" – not of the Supreme Court, as such entity did not yet exist. The second phase saw the Supreme Court enjoy a monopoly over the creation of Legal Doctrine.

Since the appearance of the expression in 1838, the concept of Legal Doctrine has evolved. It was initially connected with *ley*, a fruit of legislation, to give it a greater firmness. The legislation was contained in the Codes and the Legal Doctrine in the commentators and in practice. This connection should not, however, cause confusion between the two notions:

- Legislation emanates from the legislative power; Legal Doctrine from the legislation itself, from the opinions of writers, and from the natural order.
- Legislation is in written form; Legal Doctrine is not necessarily so.
- Legislation is a formal source of law, as opposed to Legal Doctrine.
- Legislation has an absolute, *a priori* character, which is later applied to a specific case or context; Legal Doctrine is developed *a posteriori* and in a more abstract form, as a result of a specific case or context.

The concept of Legal Doctrine might also be confused not with that of legislation, but that of case law. Certain commentators distinguish the concepts of Legal Doctrine and case law, such as Federico de Castro, José Luis de los Mozos and Andrés de la Oliva.[95] Others, such as Ogayar,[96] Prieto Castro and Domínguez Rodrigo, argue that there is no substantial difference between the concepts. Finally, a third group of writers – such as Martín-Granizo – maintain that the equivalence or otherwise of these concepts is an irrelevance.

doctrine" in this sense is capitalised in this text, and should not be confused with "case law" or any "doctrine" emanating from judgements themselves.

95 A. DE LA OLIVA SANTOS, "La jurisprudencia en el nuevo Título Preliminar del C. C.", in *Anuario de Derecho Civil*, XXVIII, 2, 1975, pp. 441 and 445 ff.

96 See, T. OGAYAR Y AYLLÓN, *Creación judicial del Derecho*, Madrid, Real Academia de Jurisprudencia y Legislación, 1975. *Id*, "Las fuentes del Derecho en el Novísimo Título Preliminar del Código Civil", in *Libro Homenaje a Ramón Mª Roca Sastre*, I, Madrid, Universidad Complutense de Madrid, 1976, pp. 607-656.

On seeing this doctrinal controversy, one might conclude that the true meaning of the expression "Legal Doctrine" ought to be reserved for the principles that may deserve such label, or for the opinions of jurists that are given force of law by state legislation. In short, Legal Doctrine would be that which takes the legislation as a starting point and is established by the Supreme Court in the interpretation and application of that legislation. *Legislation gives existence to Legal Doctrine, and jurisprudential interpretation is what creates it.* Legal Doctrine depends, then, as much on legislation as it does on case law.

The reform of the Law of Civil Trial of 6 August 1984, regarding right of cassation insofar as it was referred to in Legal Doctrine, implied for some the "death of genuine right of cassation", with its essence – the defence of legality – being lost. The law is not even mentioned in the regulation of right of cassation. "For that reason", some said, "a requiem will need to be said for right of cassation, to thank it for services rendered".[97]

The new formula utilized for cassation is broader, given that it speaks of "rules" and in this manner attaches to legislation, but also to custom and general principles of law, and even other infringed norms or rules of the legal order as understood in a wide sense – it incorporates all jurisprudential rules.

As far as Legal Doctrine is concerned, this genuinely Spanish term is replaced by the more current "case law". For some writers, this change lacks any significance beyond the mere terminology. For others, though, the issue in a decentralized State such as Spain is more complicated. Someone needs to unify such a State, and hence there is a danger in introducing case law without specifying from whom it is to come.[98]

The reform of the Law of Civil Trial of 2000 and its consequences in this area will be considered in the later section 5.1.2, in the final part of this book.

97 L. DIEZ-PICAZO, "Constitución, Ley, Juez", in *Revista Española de Derecho Constitucional, cit.*, pp. 13-15.

98 F. M. CALVO VIDAL, *La jurisprudencia ¿Fuente del Derecho?, op. cit.*, pp. 234-249.

1.1.2. The Constitutional Court – Main Functions

A. *Introduction: the North American Model of Dispersed Jurisdiction Compared with the Austrian Model of Concentrated Jurisdiction*

Constitutional jurisdiction is but one of the mechanisms for the protection and guarantee of the Spanish Constitution.[99] Before the Spanish "Magna Carta" of 1978, the Republican Constitution of 1931 had established a Court of Constitutional Guarantees. The mission of the Constitutional Court is to invalidate any inferior rule to which it is opposed, or simply to annul such rule. In this way, the content of the text of the Constitution is protected at the same time as a rule of the legal system is eliminated.[100]

99 See, F. LLORENTE HURTADO, "Poder judicial y justicia constitucional", in Various Authors, *El poder judicial*, II, Dirección General de lo Contencioso del Estado, Madrid, Ed. Instituto de Estudios Fiscales, 1983. P. LUCAS VERDÚ, "Política y justicia constitucionales. Consideraciones sobre la naturaleza y funciones del Tribunal Constitucional", in Various Authors, *Tribunal Constitucional*, II, Madrid, Instituto de Estudios Fiscales, 1981, pp. 151 ff. J. NICOLÁS MUÑIZ, "El Tribunal Constitucional y las fuentes del Derecho", in *Revista Vasca de Administración Pública*, 10, II, 1984, pp. 73-89. A. NIETO, "El precedente judicial", in *Libro Homenaje al profesor Juan Roca*, Murcia, Universidad de Murcia, Secretariado de Publicaciones, 1989. *Id*, "El precedente judicial en la doctrina del Tribunal Constitucional", in *Estudios Jurídicos en honor de D. José Galbaldón López*, Madrid, Trivium, 1990. *Id*, *El arbitrio judicial*, Barcelona, Ariel, 2000. F. TOMAS Y VALIENTE, "Poder judicial y Tribunal Constitucional", in *Poder Judicial*, 11, 1989 (especial), pp. 13-41. *Id*, *Escritos sobre y desde el Tribunal Constitucional*, Madrid, 1993. J. P. URÍAS MARTÍNEZ, *La cuestión de inconstitucionalidad*, Madrid, 1996. A. TORRES DEL MORAL, *Principios de Derecho constitucional español*, 3rd. ed., Madrid, 1992.

100 See, on the subject, E. GARCÍA DE ENTERRÍA, "La posición jurídica del Tribunal Constitucional en el sistema español: posibilidades y perspectivas", in *El Tribunal Constitucional*, I, Madrid, 1981, pp. 21-129; also in *Revista Española de Derecho Constitucional*, Centro de Estudios Constitucionales, 1. 1, January-April 1981, pp. 35-131. *Id*, *La Constitución como norma jurídica y el Tribunal Constitucional*, 3rd. ed., Madrid, Civitas, 1985. *Id*, "Un paso importante para el desarrollo en nuestra justicia constitucional: la doctrina prospectiva en la declaración de ineficacia de las leyes inconstitucionales", in *Revista de Derecho Administrativo*, 61, 1989, pp. 5-17.

Constitutional justice can correspond to a series of models.[101] Sometimes, the power to defend a Constitution will be vested in political bodies, such as a parliament. On other occasions the judicial bodies will be entrusted with the defence of a Constitution – as is presently the case in Spain. In turn, this second situation has two variants: the North American system, and the European one – very particularly, that of Austria.[102]

The North American system presents a "diffuse" or "dispersed" framework of constitutional justice, in which all courts are competent to protect the constitution, via the mechanism of judicial review.[103]

101 A. WEBER, "La jurisdicción constitucional en Europa Occidental: una comparación", in *Revista Española de Derecho Constitucional,* 6, 1986, pp. 47-83.

102 On Constitucional justice, see: M. A. APARICIO PÉREZ, "Dos cuestiones interesantes en nuestra jurisdicción constitucional; control de las leyes anteriores y de la jurisprudencia", in *El Tribunal Constitucional,* Madrid, 1981, I, pp. 555-574. *Id,* "Algunas consideraciones sobre la justicia y el poder judicial", in *Revista Jurídica de Cataluña,* 4, 1983. *Id,* "Algunas consideraciones sobre el Tribunal Constitucional", in *Revista Jurídica de Castilla-La Mancha,* 1, 1987, pp. 27-53. M. ARAGÓN REYES, "Dos cuestiones interesantes en nuestra jurisdicción constitucional: control de las leyes anteriores y de la jurisprudencia", in *Jornadas de la Dirección General de lo Contencioso del Estado sobre el Tribunal Constitucional,* I, Madrid, Instituto de Estudios Fiscales, 1981, pp. 555-574. J. AROZAMENA SIERRA, "Valor de la jurisprudencia constitucional", in *La Constitución española y las fuentes del Derecho,* I, Madrid, 1979, pp. 253-279. L. ARROYO ZAPATERO, "Jurisprudencia constitucional en materia penal", in *Cuadernos de Política Criminal,* 17, 1982, pp. 385-405. S. DOMÍNGUEZ MARTÍN, "Visión constitucional de la jurisprudencia", in *Boletín del Ministerio de Justicia,* 1.155, 1979, pp. 5-14. *Id,* "Análisis crítico sobre la juridicidad del Tribunal Constitucional español", in *El Tribunal Constitucional,* Madrid, 1981, pp. 737-795. L. DIEZ PICAZO Y PONCE DE LEÓN, "Constitución y fuentes del Derecho", in *La Constitución española y las fuentes del Derecho,* I, Madrid, 1979, pp. 653-665. *Id,* "Constitución, ley y juez", in *Revista Española de Derecho Constitucional,* 15, September-December, 1985. *Id,* "Tribunal Constitucional y Poder Judicial", in "Constitucionalidad. Derecho comunitario europeo y jurisdicción ordinaria", in Various Authors, *División de poderes e interpretación (hacia una teoría de la praxis constitucional),* edited by LÓPEZ PINA, Madrid, Tecnos, 1987.

103 See, on the subject, E. ALONSO GARCÍA, "Los efectos formales de la declaración de inconstitucionalidad en el sistema constitucional norteamericano", in *Revista Española de Derecho Constitucional,* 6, 1982, pp. 209-257. *Id, La interpretación de la Constitución,* Madrid, 1984. *Id,* "El control por

The Austrian model, on the other hand, is one of "concentrated" constitutional protection, in the hands of a single, *ad hoc* court – the Constitutional Court. This is the Kelsenian model, on which the Spanish Constitutional Court is also based.[104]

el Tribunal Constitucional del sistema español de fuentes del Derecho a través del artículo 24 de la Constitución", in *Revista Española de Derecho Constitucional*, 24, 1988, pp. 191-211.

104 On constitutional case law, see, L. AGUIAR DE LUQUE, "El Tribunal Constitucional y la función legislativa: el control del procedimiento legislativo y de la inconstitucionalidad por omisión", in *Revista de Derecho Político*, Madrid, Universidad Nacional de Educación a Distancia, 24, summer 1987, pp. 9-30. F. J. EZQUIAGA GANUZAS, *La argumentación en la justicia constitucional española*, Bilbao, Instituto Vasco de Administración Pública, 1987. K. LOWENSTEIN, *Teoría de la Constitución*, 2nd. ed., Barcelona, Ariel, 1983. F. PERA VERDAGUER, "Fuentes del Derecho, jurisprudencia y constitucionalidad", in *Jornadas de la Dirección General de lo Contencioso del Estado, sobre « La Constitución española y las fuentes del Derecho »*, III, Madrid, Instituto de Estudios Fiscales, 1979. 1981, pp. 1607-1628. *Id*, "El T. S. y el nuevo ordenamiento constitucional", in *Jornadas de la Dirección General de lo Contencioso del Estado sobre el Poder Judicial*, III, Madrid, Instituto de Estudios Fiscales, 1983. X. PIBERNAT DOMENECH, "La sentencia constitucional como fuente del Derecho", in *Revista de Derecho Político*, Universidad Nacional de Educación a Distancia, Madrid, summer 1987, 24, pp. 57-85. L. PRIETO SANCHÍS, *Ideología e interpretación jurídica*, Madrid, 1987. *Id*, "Notas sobre la interpretación constitucional", in *Revista del Centro de Estudios Constitucionales*, 9, 1991, pp. 175-198. R. RUIZ DE LA PEÑA, "El Tribunal Constitucional", in *Estudios sobre la Constitución española de 1978*, Zaragoza, Ed. M. Ramírez, Libros Pórtico, 1979. J. J. SANTAMARÍA IBEAS, *Los valores superiores en la jurisprudencia del Tribunal Constitucional: libertad, justicia, igualdad y pluralismo político*, Madrid, Dykinson, 1997. J. M. SANTOS VIJANDE, *Doctrina y jurisprudencia del Tribunal Constitucional. Su eficacia respecto de los tribunales ordinarios*, Granada, 1995. G. TRUJILLO, "Juicio de legitimidad e interpretación constitucional: cuestiones problemáticas en el horizonte constitucional español", in *Revista de Estudios Políticos*, 7, 1979, pp. 145-158. T. S. VIVES ANTÓN, "Tribunales de Justicia y jurisprudencia constitucional", in *La libertad como pretexto*, Valencia, 1995, pp. 237-243, also in *Poder Judicial*, 2, June 1986, pp. 9-13. *Id*, "Valoraciones ético-sociales y jurisprudencia constitucional", in *La libertad como pretexto*, Valencia, 1996, pp. 171-174. G. ZAGREBELSKY, "La Corte constitucional y la interpretación de la Constitución", in Various Authors, LÓPEZ PINA (ed.): *División de poderes e interpretación (hacia una teoría de la praxis constitucional)*, Madrid, Tecnos, 1987. J. A. XIOL RÍOS, "El precedente judicial en nuestro Derecho, una creación del Tribunal Cons-

B. *Nature of the Spanish Constitutional Court*

One of the questions that falls to the Constitutional Court as established in the Spanish Constitution is whether or not it belongs to the judiciary[105] – put another way, there is a question mark over its nature. To argue in relation to the judicial or legislative nature of the Constitutional Court involves a degree of importance in the sense that whether or not the Court is considered an integral part of the judiciary will determine whether it is only accorded judicial powers. If the answer to this question is negative, the question arises whether the Court also has other functions – even legislative ones – in which case it should be considered a naturally political body. There are other writers who even attribute to the Constitutional Court a mixed nature, *sui generis* or special, which is both judicial and political in essence.[106]

a. Jurisdictional Nature

Those who argue in favour of the Constitutional Court being viewed as a naturally judicial body base their argument on the fact that, like any other court, the Constitutional Court requires some exterior impulse in order to act, while political bodies are able to act by their own initiative. Further, the decisions of the Constitutional Court take the form of legal judgements; the rules regarding conflicts are the same as for members of the judiciary; and the Court is bound by and must hence make determinations in accordance with the law and the Constitution. Its function is to resolve political conflicts, but using legal criteria and methods, with rigorous legal reasoning as a basis. Its function is bound up with the in-

titucional", in *Revista Poder Judicial*, 3, September 1986, pp. 25-40. *Id*, "El principio de igualdad en la aplicación de la ley", in *El principio de igualdad en la Constitución*, Madrid, 1991, pp. 278 ff. *Id*, *El precedente judicial y otros estudios sobre el proceso administrativo: técnicas de evitación del proceso contencioso-administrativo*, Madrid, Colegio Nacional de Registradores de la Propiedad y Mercantiles de España, 2005.

105 See, on the subject, J. A. MARÍN, *Naturaleza jurídica del Tribunal Constitucional*, Barcelona, 1998.

106 See, M. GARCÍA PELAYO, "El 'status' del Tribunal Constitucional", in *Revista Española de Derecho Constitucional*, Centro de Estudios Constitucionales, 1.1, January-April 1981, pp. 11-34. F. FERNÁNDEZ SEGADO, *La jurisdicción constitucional en España*, Madrid, 1984. J. DE MIGUEL ZARAGOZA, "Sobre las funciones latentes del Tribunal Constitucional", in *Boletín de Información del Ministerio de Justicia*, 1238, 5 May 1981.

terpretation and application of a previously existing rule: the Constitution.

b. Political Nature

In favour of the Spanish Constitutional Court being political in nature are the following arguments: the "act of impulse" which propels the Court to act is of political character, and even if the procedure is formally legal, political considerations cannot be discounted. As opposed to other courts, its members are selected in a specific fashion, it not being an indispensable requirement that they be judges, for example. While the personnel of the ordinary judiciary are recruited by way of specific examinations and tests – *oposiciones* – which aim towards their political neutrality – the appointment of constitutional judges (articles 127 and 159 Spanish Constitution) depends on political agreements. Its ultimate function of defending the Constitution, along with the matters on which it passes judgement, identifies it as a body with clear political characteristics.[107]

c. "Mixed", Special, *Sui Generis* and Complex Nature

As is always the case, there is no shortage of mixed, intermediate and conciliatory standpoints between the two extremes. Exemplars of these viewpoints include Óscar Alzaga, Pérez Tremps,[108] Aparicio Pérez, López Guerra, Serrano Alberca, Ureta, and the Constitutional Court itself in judgements such as those of 31 March 1981 or 50/1984, 5 April – on its third legal ground. According to this doctrine, while it may be clear that the Constitutional Court undertakes a political role, it is no less obvious that the Court is bound by law. The two jurisdictions – constitutional and ordinary – are not exclusive but complementary.[109]

107 M. MARTÍNEZ SOSPEDRA , "El Tribunal Constitucional como órgano político", in Various Authors, *El Tribunal Constitucional, vol. II, Jornadas de la Dirección General de lo Contencioso del Estado,* Madrid, Instituto de Estudios Fiscales, 1981, p. 1821.

108 P. PÉREZ TREMPS, *Tribunal Constitucional y Poder Judicial,* Madrid, Centro de Estudios Constitucionales, 1985. *Id,* "Constitución, Ley Orgánica del Poder Judicial y jueces ordinarios", in *Documentación Jurídica,* 45-46, January-June, 1985, pp. 23-41.

109 See, F. M. CALVO VIDAL, *La jurisprudencia ¿Fuente del Derecho?, op. cit.,* pp. 185-187. J. ALMAGRO NOSETE, *Justicia Constitucional (Comentarios a la Ley Orgánica del Tribunal Constitucional),* 2nd. ed., in cooperation with P. SAAVEDRA GALLO, Valencia, 1989.

C. *Relations between the Constitutional Court and the Supreme Court and other Judicial Authorities: A Question of Hierarchy or Jurisdiction?*

The exercise of jurisdictional authority in all types of process corresponds exclusively to the various courts, culminating in the Supreme Court – the summit of judicial power, and the superior jurisdictional organ in all cases except where constitutional guarantees are at stake.[110]

The Constitutional Court and the Supreme Court, we can therefore see, are not linked to each other by any kind of subordination or hierarchical relationship. To the contrary, they are distinguished by reason of their different areas of competence. The Constitutional Court guarantees the Constitution, being the court of last instance in this respect and therefore exercising a monopoly over the declaration of unconstitutionality of legislation.[111]

It is worth enquiring to what point the Spanish *recurso de amparo* ("appeal for legal protection from judicial decisions") constitutes a "third instance" or "super-instance" – and to what extent the scope and reach of such appeal moves in wholly "different" circles to those attributed to the ordinary judicial organs.

The Constitutional Court does not evaluate facts or evidence, and it therefore seems that the *recurso de amparo* could not be considered a "new instance" – this was stated in judgements passed on 30 January 1981 and 23 March 1982. Its function is limited to determining whether the rights or freedoms of the claimant have been infringed. This would not indicate a third instance in which the court undertook a general review of the facts proven and the law applied in the judicial resolution at hand.

110 See, A. DE LA OLIVA SANTOS, "Tribunal Constitucional y jurisdicción ordinaria: causas, ámbitos y alivios de una tensión", in *Id* – I. DIEZ-PICAZO GIMÉNEZ, *Tribunal Constitucional, jueces ordinarios y derechos fundamentales*, I, Madrid, 1996, pp. 19 ff. I. DE OTTO PARDO, "La posición del TC a partir de la doctrina de la interpretación constitucional", in *El Tribunal Constitucional*, Madrid, 1981, III, pp. 1939-1945. *Id, Derecho constitucional. Sistema de fuentes*, Barcelona, Ariel, 1987. 2nd. ed. 1988. *Id, Estudios sobre el Poder Judicial*, Madrid, Secretaría General Técnica del Ministerio de Justicia, 1989.

111 See, R. ALONSO GARCÍA, "El Tribunal Constitucional y la eficacia temporal de sus sentencias anulatorias", in *Revista de Administración Pública*, 119, May-August 1989, pp. 255-268. E. ÁLVAREZ CONDE, "La posición constitucional del Poder Judicial", in *Jornadas sobre el Poder Judicial, de la Dirección General de lo Contencioso*, IEF, I, Madrid, 1983.

The Judgement of the Constitutional Court of 27 March 1984 confirms this perspective. For its part, in its Judgement of 18 May 1981, the Constitutional Court considered that it would represent an infringement of the principle of exclusivity of judges if the Constitutional Court were to evaluate the manner in which the Supreme Court – or other courts – applied and interpreted legislation. The authority of the Constitutional Court extends to acting as the guardian of the Constitution, and not to providing a further instance to review the way in which legislation has been applied. Further judgements by the Constitutional Court – on 23 January 1981, 30 March 1981, 29 January 1982 (second legal ground), and 24 April 1982 – all follow a similar line of argument.[112]

D. *Place Occupied by Case Law Established by Constitutional Court Rulings and Orders*

Article 161.1.a) of the Spanish Constitution states:

> *The Constitutional Court has jurisdiction over the whole Spanish territory and is entitled to hear: A) Appeals against the alleged unconstitutionality of legislation and statutes having the force of legislation. A declaration of unconstitutionality of a legal provision having the force of legislation, and that has already been applied by the courts, shall also affect the case law doctrine built up by the latter, but the decisions handed down shall not lose their status of* res judicata.

While the rule may not be especially clear, it does seem evident that a direct appeal of unconstitutionality against case law itself does not exist. Appeals against unconstitutionality are only available in relation to legislation and statutes having the force of legislation.

Another controversial piece of legislation is article 40.2 of the Organic Law of the Constitutional Court, modified by Organic Law 24 May 6/2007, by virtue of which:

112 See, on the subject, CONSEJO GENERAL DEL PODER JUDICIAL, *La posición constitucional del Tribunal Supremo,* Discurso de Apertura de los Tribunales, Madrid, Consejo General del Poder Judicial, 1995. CONTROL CONSTITUCIONAL DE LAS JURISDICCIONES: EL TRIBUNAL CONSTITUCIONAL FRENTE A LOS PROCESOS, Miraflores, Perú, Gaceta Jurídica, 2006. F. HERRERO-TEJEDOR, "El Tribunal Constitucional y el sistema de fuentes", in *Repertorio Aranzadi del Tribunal Constitucional,* 1, March 2000, pp. 17-34.

> *In all cases, the case law handed down by the courts of justice regarding legislation, statute or acts judged upon by the Constitutional Court shall be understood as being corrected by the doctrine deriving from judgements and judicial orders made in constitutional proceedings.*

In light of this, it is worth enquiring as to the value of the judgements of the Constitutional Court. Does this Court in fact possess the power to create rules?[113] The problem stems from the fact that, while the resolutions of an ordinary court only have effect with respect to the specific case, *inter partes*, those of the Constitutional Court, at least insofar as they relate to appeals of unconstitutionality, have effect in relation to all cases, *erga omnes*. This is seen in article 164.1 of the Spanish Constitution, *in fine*:

> *The judgements of the Constitutional Court... which declare the unconstitutionality of legislation or of a statute with the force of legislation, and all those which are not limited to the acknowledgement of an individual right, shall be fully binding on all persons.*

Article 38.1 of the Organic Law of the Constitutional Court states the same point. For this reason, it has been said of this superior body that it is a "negative legislator" – Kelsen – in the sense that its decisions can repeal rules passed by a legislative power. Unconstitutional legislation is not rendered null and void, but is voidable, with *ex nunc* effects – from the time of the decision towards the future, but not retroactive.[114] Nonetheless, when the Constitutional Court nullifies a rule, it does not only act in the manner of a negative legislator. It is also acting positively, in the sense that the nullification will give rise to another rule. It is for this

113 See, L. LÓPEZ GUERRA, "El Tribunal Constitucional y el principio 'stare decisis'", in Various Authors, *El Tribunal Constitucional*, II, Madrid, Instituto de Estudios Fiscales, 1981, pp. 1437-1550. *Id*, "Jurisdicción ordinaria y jurisdicción constitucional", in *La aplicación jurisdiccional de la Constitución*, G. RUIZ-RICO RUIZ, Valencia, 1997, pp. 27-59. F. LÓPEZ MENUDO, "El principio de irretroactividad de las normas en la jurisprudencia constitucional", in *Estudios sobre la CE. Homenaje a García de Enterría*, Madrid, 1991, pp. 455-508. A. LÓPEZ PINA (*et al.*), Edition and Preface of *División de poderes e interpretación (Hacia una teoría de la praxis constitucional)*, Madrid, Tecnos, 1987.

114 F. M. CALVO VIDAL, *La jurisprudencia ¿Fuente del Derecho?*, *op. cit.*, pp. 187 ff.; esp. pp. 202-203.

reason that the grounds for the judgement and the basis for specific votes (where applicable) must be very seriously considered, since in exercising a form of constituent power without *potestas*, the acceptance of the rule will depend in great measure on those grounds. Consequentially, the validity and legitimacy of such rule will also be at stake, unless good reasons are given for ignoring the opinion of the Court and choosing another, different, opinion.

On occasion, the Constitutional Court can take a further step when hearing an appeal, and explain to the legislator how a specific institution must be regulated in order that it complies with the Constitution and therefore be declared constitutional. In this case, the high court becomes a supreme interpreter not only of the Constitution, but also of ordinary legality. These are called "interpretative judgements", which can be placed apart from those declaring legislation constitutional or not. [115] Rather than establishing unconstitutionality, these interpretative judgements exclude some or all but one possible interpretations, leaving a single one – that which conforms to the Constitution.

Yet the position of the judgements of the Constitutional Court within the system of sources is not equivalent to legislation, neither in a formal nor a substantive sense.[116] Its primary characteristic consists in being "similar to legislation". The standpoint of not considering constitutional case law to be a source of law is based on article 117 of the Spanish Constitution, the first section of which establishes that judges and magistrates are "subject only to the force of legislation". In the same context, the fourth legal ground of the Constitutional Court Judgement of 1 June 1981 merits mention. In accordance with a system of separation of powers, according to these writers, a judicial law is not possible bearing in mind the Constitution. The Constitutional Court is a supreme interpreter, but

115 See, F. J. DÍAZ REVORIO, "Interpretación constitucional de la ley y sentencias interpretativas", in *Repertorio Aranzadi del Tribunal Constitucional*, 2, April 2000, pp. 15-40. F. J. EZQUIAGA GANUZAS, "Diez años de fallos constitucionales (sentencias interpretativas y poder normativo del Tribunal Constitucional)", in *Revista Vasca de Administración Pública*, 31, pp. 117-141.

116 See, on the subject, R. BOCANEGRA SIERRA, *El valor de las sentencias del Tribunal Constitucional*, Madrid, Instituto de Estudios de Administración Local, 1982. *Id*, "Sobre el alcance objetivo de las sentencias del Tribunal Constitucional", in *Estudios sobre la Constitución. Homenaje al profesor Eduardo García de Enterría, vol. I, El ordenamiento jurídico*, 1991, pp. 509-536.

is not a legislator. Given that the Court is not bound by its judgements, those judgements can only provide guidance, and not bind, hence allowing for changes in case law. Furthermore, if a judge or court disagrees with an interpretation handed down by the Constitutional Court, it can utilize the technique of a "question of unconstitutionality" in order to force a new hearing concerning the legislation in question, thereby making the previous interpretation itself subject to the re-consideration of the Constitutional Court. Not having the status of a source of law does not mean that constitutional case law does not possess an unquestionable authority deriving from the organ from which it emanates, the highest interpreter of the Constitution, whose decisions are not susceptible to appeal. But it remains necessary to differentiate the *auctoritas* that the decisions of the Court may have from an authentic normative *potestas* which would be binding.

However, this point of view is not one which is shared by all writers. Some argue that judgements of the Constitutional Court do in fact have the value of an authentic source of law. As the Constitutional Court is the supreme interpreter of legislation, and as this legislation contains vague and ambiguous formulations, it is argued that the interpreter of the constitution therefore has the responsibility to establish *de facto* the meaning of that legislation. It is necessary to distinguish, within the group of writers who hold this view, between those placing the Constitutional Court on the same hierarchical level as the Supreme Court – such as M. Aragón Reyes, P. Elizalde Aymerich,[117] and F. Rubio Llorente[118] – and

117 P. DE ELIZALDE Y AYMERICH, "El Tribunal Constitucional y la jurisprudencia", in *Jornadas de la Dirección General de lo Contencioso del Estado sobre el Tribunal Constitucional,* I, Madrid, Ed. Instituto de Estudios Fiscales, 1981, pp. 859-899.

118 See, F. RUBIO LLORENTE, "La Constitución española como fuente del Derecho", in *La Constitución española y las fuentes del Derecho,* I, Madrid, 1979, pp. 51-74. *Id,* "Sobre la relación entre el Tribunal Constitucional y el Poder Judicial en el ejercicio de la jurisdicción constitucional", in *La forma del poder. Estudios sobre la Constitución,* Madrid, 1997, pp. 431-462; also in *Revista Española de Derecho Constitucional,* 4, Centro de Estudios Constitucionales, January-April 1982. *Id,* "La jurisdicción constitucional como forma de creación del Derecho", in *La forma del poder. Estudios sobre la Constitución,* Madrid, 1997, pp. 463-504; also in *Revista Española de Derecho Constitucional,* 22-24, January-April 1988, pp. 9-51. F. RUBIO LLORENTE – M. ARAGÓN REYES, "Enunciados aparentemente vacíos en la regulación constitucional del control de constitucionalidad", in *Revista*

those who would place the judgements of the Court immediately below the Constitution itself but above all other sources of law – such as J. De Esteban and J. Pérez Royo. The latter is based on the argument that "while the Constitutional Court is not bound by the actions of the legislator, the legislator is bound by the judgements of the Constitutional Court".[119]

In conclusion, it would be worth asking whether "too much has been asked of the constitutional judge. Has he not been transformed into a power that controls the other powers of the State, thereby transgressing the fundamental principle of the separation of powers?... as a humble attempt to re-establish equilibrium in the face of the normal increase of power that has been experienced by the legislature and the executive in recent decades".[120]

1.1.3. The Higher Courts of Justice of the Autonomous Communities; Territorial Jurisdiction

Cassation, via the case law of the Supreme Court, as an instrument of control and unification of interpretation, is all the more important in an autonomous State, given that the Higher Courts of Justice of the various Autonomous Communities hand down disparate and contradictory opinions. The Supreme Court in this environment has the responsibility to provide the correct interpretation of the law and to ensure unity of interpretation.[121]

The Spanish Constitution of 1978 selected an autonomous State as the organizational form. This necessarily gives rise to questions regarding the constitutional relationship between the Supreme Court and the Higher Courts of Justice of the Autonomous Communities.

The Supreme Court is established in article 123.1 of the Constitution as "the highest judicial body in all branches of justice, except with regard

de Estudios Políticos, 7, 1979, pp. 161 ff. *Id*, "La jurisdicción constitucional", in *La Constitución Española de 1978. Estudio sistemático*, directed by A. PREDIERI and E. GARCÍA DE ENTERRÍA, Madrid, 1984, pp. 831-886.

119 See, J. PÉREZ ROYO, *Las fuentes del Derecho*, Madrid, Tecnos, Colección Temas Clave de la Constitución española, 1984; there is a 3rd. ed.

120 F. M. CALVO VIDAL, *La jurisprudencia ¿Fuente del Derecho?*, *op. cit.*, pp. 210-217, esp. p. 216.

121 See, A. PÉREZ GORDO, *El Tribunal Superior de Justicia de las Comunidades Autónomas (Perspectivas procesales para el desarrollo de la previsión constitucional)*, Barcelona, Bosch, 1982.

to provisions concerning constitutional guarantees", with "jurisdiction over the whole of Spain".

The Higher Courts of Justice of the Autonomous Communities are located in article 152 of the Constitution, wisely placed in Title VIII – dedicated to the Territorial Organisation of the State – rather than in Title VI, which concerns Judicial Power. According to article 152, the Higher Courts are the heads of Judicial Power in the territory of each Autonomous Community, and "without prejudice to the provisions of article 123, successive proceedings, if any, shall be held before judicial bodies located in the same territory of the Autonomous Community in which the Court having jurisdiction in the first instance is located".

The Higher Courts of Justice are defined in the Constitution as bodies "of" the State "in" the Autonomous Communities, as highlighted by the Supreme Court in its famous Judgement 38/1982 of 22 June 1982.

With an eye to the future, the aims of reducing procedural costs and bringing justice closer to the citizen and the point of conflict require that the last instance of a process lie in the Courts of Justice of the Autonomous Communities. The objective would be to locate cassation – in its current sense – in the Civil Chamber of said Courts of Justice, meaning that the civil process would end in those Courts – though perhaps a different criterion should continue to be applied in relation to criminal jurisdiction. This idea is a consequence of the need to extend the remit of the Higher Courts of Justice and, correlatively, to reduce the currently unmanageable workload of the Supreme Court.

When *Derecho autonómico* ("autonomous law") is applied, the Higher Courts have a clear case law function, providing the final fixing of doctrine, since in relation to their decisions in this area, the Supreme Court cannot become involved or review cases. In other words, with respect to autonomous law, the Higher Courts are judicially akin to Supreme Courts.

The fact is that, currently, the Higher Courts are already exercising functions of cassation with respect to autonomous law but also in matters of *Derecho estatal* ("State law") – the new Law of Civil Trial has given the Courts the right to consider appeals of cassation in cases of extraordinary procedural infringements by lower courts. In light of this, the option of opening state cassation to the Higher Courts is gaining widespread acceptance. This option was initially subject to mistrust in some quarters due to perceived problems of constitutionality. However, today, the constitutionality of such option is widely accepted by doctrine and institutions alike. The basic argument would be that the constitutional position of the Supreme Court remains guaranteed and satisfied given that the power to "unify" doctrine where there is either a contradiction between judgements of the Higher Courts, or between a Higher Court judgement and a Supreme Court judgement, would remain vested entirely in the Supreme Court.

A remodeling as outlined above would involve locating in the Higher Courts an extraordinary appeal of cassation, which would allow for an initial unification of case law doctrine – fixed in each Autonomous Community – with the availability of a second appeal to the Supreme Court for purposes of unification of doctrine or control of interpretation. The Supreme Court would, wherever possible, ensure the sought-after uniformity in terms of the final interpretation of legislation.

A further area of controversy is the "preliminary ruling", not new or unknown to the Spanish legal system, appearing analogous to rulings on constitutionality and preliminary rulings at a European level. The issue here is that the Higher Court of Justice who wishes to derogate from the doctrine of other Higher Courts or the Supreme Court itself may consider this very ruling, which has obligatory force when issued. They may therefore think of the issuing of preliminary rulings as a system complementary to the appeal for unification of case law doctrine.

The above relates to the issue of the "horizontal and vertical binding effect" of case law. The "horizontal" effect refers to courts being bound by their own precedents, or by precedents established by other courts of the same hierarchical level. In this case, it seems that the requirement of continuity has the same intensity at all hierarchical levels, with "all" courts being subject to their own precedents. Nonetheless, there is no lack of commentators prepared to argue that the strength of the binding force of precedent should be greater in the case of courts of cassation.

But more important in the area with which this section is concerned is the issue of "vertically" binding case law, in the context of the territorially decentralized European judicial organization. This is relevant in terms of the extent to which the case law of the Supreme Court can be binding upon lower courts and the degree of removal of those lower courts from the precedents of the Supreme Court.[122]

122 See, on the subject, G. VIDAL ANDREU (dir.), *Poder judicial y estado compuesto: relaciones entre el Tribunal Supremo y los Tribunales Superiores de Justicia*, Madrid, Consejo General del Poder Judicial, 2005.

1.1.4. The European Courts

A. The European Court of Human Rights of Strasbourg

The European Court of Human Rights, based in Strasbourg, has as many members as there are States in the Council of Europe. The Convention requires that candidates for judicial posts "shall be of high moral character and must either possess the qualifications required for appointment to high judicial office or be jurisconsults of recognized competence". Further requirements, not expressly contained in the Convention, are the conflicts regime and an age limit. The mandate of the judge lasts for nine years, and judges enjoy immunity against all legal proceedings related to the oral or written opinions they provide and actions they take in the exercise of their role as judges.

In order for a case to be heard before the Court, the European Commission of Human Rights must have confirmed that agreement cannot be reached freely and within the time limits set. Only the Commission and the contracting States can submit an issue for consideration – not the private person who raised the case before the Commission. While this person does not have access to the proceedings as a "party", they may, via the Commission or their own declarations if called as a witness, provide the Court with their perspective regarding the case in dispute.

For a State to place a claim before the Court, one of the following circumstances must be applicable: 1) the victim is a national of that State. 2) The State in question has brought the case before the Commission. 3) The instant claim is against the State in question.

Few of the procedural rules of the Court are contained in the European Convention, meaning that the Rules of the Court must be principally borne in mind. In relation to the structure of judgements, there are three main sections: 1) description of the facts and actions before the Court. 2) Considerations of law. 3) The decision.

The objective of the judgements of the Strasbourg Court is to determine whether a decision taken or measure ordered by a judicial authority or any other authority of a contracting Party is partially or totally in conflict with obligations derived from the Convention. In principle, once an infringement has been declared to exist, the infringing State is required to remedy it. Only if the State fails to remedy the infringement or does so in an imperfect fashion will the Court be entitled to grant, if appropriate, "equitable satisfaction" to the injured party. The granting of said satisfaction, in the majority of cases, occurs in a new judgement.[123]

B. *The European Court of Justice of Luxembourg*

The European Court of Justice exhibits a series of characteristics which clearly separate it from international trials. It has general jurisdiction – its task being to guarantee the respect of law – and is not tied to specific disputes, enjoying total independence in choosing the sources on which it bases its interpretation of the Treaties, as opposed to the classical international court, which "accepts the imperfections and lacunae in the law to be applied". Its jurisdiction is obligatory, not requiring previous submission by States. In certain cases, private parties have access to the Court in addition to States and Community organs. The judgements of the Court do not only bind the member States, but also possess direct binding force by themselves in the entire Community territory, with no need for the State to act as an intermediate – even if, in fact, adequate channels to guarantee compliance do not always exist.

Due to these characteristics, it can clearly be affirmed that the Court of Justice is a genuinely autonomous and supreme judicial power. In contrast to other institutions such as the European Parliament, which remains far from comparable to the internal organs of a State, the European Court of Justice exercises the functions of a Constitutional Court. On the basis of the Treaties, it can annul the normative acts of the Communities, the executive acts, and make declarations regarding non-compliance and omissions in relation to any subject, thereby guaranteeing the distribution of powers and the internal equilibrium in the heart of the Communities. At the same time, it has functions characteristic of a Court of Administrative Justice – hearing compensation claims, staff complaints, etc. – and of an International Court, as the member States can go to the Court in order to resolve differences concerning the interpretation and application of Community law. But above all, the Court possesses co-ordination functions with regard to the national jurisdictions, via the technique of preliminary rulings. The Court acts here with its own sole jurisdiction, and not as a court of appeal or cassation for the national courts. In turn, its jurisdiction is exclusive, as the disputes sub-

123 E. GARCÍA DE ENTERRÍA – E. LINDE – L. I. ORTEGA SÁNCHEZ MORÓN, *El sistema europeo de protección de los derechos humanos*, Madrid, Civitas, 1979, esp. pp. 123-135.

mitted to the Court remove, by operation of law, part of the jurisdiction of judges and courts.[124]

C. The International Criminal Court

The desire to create a forum to judge persons suspected of having committed crimes with international repercussions, which in the case of the person being found guilty would lead to punishment, has existed for a long time. The goal was achieved with the creation of the International Criminal Court on 17 July 1998. The number of ratifications of the Statute of Rome (which created the Court) provides evidence of the warm welcome accorded to the idea of such a court. The whole world – even the most optimistic – had thought that decades would pass before the Treaty of Rome was ratified by a sufficient number of States. But four years proved long enough, and the Treaty came into force in April 2002.

The characteristics of the International Criminal Court are:[125]

- Its *independence* (free of State pressure).
- Its *permanent character* (as opposed to *ad hoc* courts created to consider specific conflicts or disputes).
- Its *aim of universality* (this being more an aim than a reality, as it is clear that in order for the Court to be able to exercise its universal and automatic jurisdiction, it would be necessary for the State to which the accused national belongs, without need of a posterior declaration, or the State in which the alleged crime took place, to be party to the Statute of Rome or to cede jurisdiction to the Court in the specific case).

124 R. FALCÓN Y TELLA, *Introducción al Derecho Financiero y Tributario de las Comunidades Europeas*, Madrid, Civitas, 1988, pp. 40-42.

125 On the Criminal Court of Justice, see, F. FALCÓN Y TELLA, *Nuevos retos de los derechos humanos*, Preface by C. FARALLI, Madrid, Difusión Jurídica y Temas de Actualidad, 2006. Reviews on *Economist & Jurist*, 104, Año XIV, October 2006, pp. 34 and 126. Also by: – M. Á. NOGALES NAHARRO, in *Anuario de Derechos Humanos, Nueva Época*, Instituto de Derechos Humanos, Facultad de Derecho, Universidad Complutense de Madrid, 25 Aniversario, vol. 7, t. 1, 2005, pp. 499-508. – M. E. PÉREZ MONTERO, in *Foro, Revista de Ciencias Jurídicas y Sociales*, 1, 2006, pp. 499-510. – J. M. CARABANTE MUNTADA, in *Persona y Derecho*, 2009. Translation into English: *Challenges for Human Rights*, by H. SHNEIDER, revision by the author, Boston – Leiden, Martinus Nijhoff Publishers, 2007. Translation into French: *Nouveaux défis des droits de l'homme*, by N. BREGAIN, revision by D. RENS and the author, Genève, Editions Diversités, 2007.

- Its threshold of *competence*, limited to the most serious crimes, which are the following:
  a) The crime of *genocide* (article 6).
  b) *Crimes against humanity* (article 7).
  c) *War crimes* (article 8). The incorporation in this section of war crimes committed during a civil, non-international conflict stands out as one of the finest achievements of the Statute, given that it is in this area, rather than in international conflict, where the greatest violence occurs, making it of critical importance to fight against impunity and prevent the excuse of State sovereignty being used for protection in this area.
  d) The crime of *aggression*. Initially, there was a debate regarding the possibility of sanctioning the crimes of terrorism[126] and drug trafficking, although with agreement not being reached in this respect, it was decided that these crimes would continue to be regulated by way of Treaty, as had previously been the case.
- Its *complementary* character, since the creation of the International Criminal Court does not seek to replace the obligations of all States to exercise their criminal jurisdiction against those responsible for international crimes. Therefore, if the States comply with their conventional obligations to prosecute or extradite those accused of violations of Conventions, the investigation and punishment of serious crimes will not reach the Court. The Court will only hear cases where the State involved does not carry out investigations itself.
- Its *lack of retroactivity* (article 24). On the other hand, there is no limitation period for crimes falling within the remit of the Court which occur in the future (but not those of the past) (article 29).
- The exercise of its *jurisdiction over persons and not States* (in relation with the idea that those who commit crimes are persons, rather than States), "persons" here being understood as natural persons. These persons are as much the material and intellectual "authors" of the crimes as the accomplices and accessories that in some way collaborate in the committing of the crime. In the case of genocide, the person liable will be a direct, public instigator, or whoever takes an important step towards committing the crime, even though they may not actually carry it out. There is no exclusion from personal

126 M. ÁLVAREZ DORREGO, *La Corte Penal Internacional: hacia la inclusión en el Estatuto de Roma del crimen de terrorismo*, Buenos Aires, Fabián J. de Plácido, 2004.

criminal liability on the grounds of holding public office, being a Head of State or Government, or forming part of a national Parliament. These circumstances will not even lead to a reduction in any penalty (articles 27.1 and 27.2).

- Its *legal personality.* Situated in the city of The Hague, the International Criminal Court is a permanent institution, permanently empowered to exercise its jurisdiction over persons in relation to the most serious international crimes.

But every silver lining has its cloud, and not all States have been prepared to participate. The United States, self-styled "conscience of the world", brought about the creation of other Criminal Courts such as those of Yugoslavia and Rwanda. But it has rejected the International Criminal Court, classing it as a "monster to annihilate" and hoping that it suffers a similar fate to the old League of Nations. [127]

1.1.5. Value of Rulings by the General Department of Registers and Notaries Public

The following all lack the quality of case law in any strict sense: judgements handed down by the General Department of Registers and Notaries Public (*Dirección General de los Registros y del Notariado*); the opinions of writers and jurists – in contrast to Roman law; and doctrine established by State attorneys (Supreme Court Judgement of 27 June 1898).

The Rulings of the General Department of Registers and Notaries Public cannot be cited in cassation processes (Supreme Court Judgement of 24 January 1928). Nonetheless, without being an obligatory source of case law, and it only being obligatory to take such Rulings into account when classifying the Registrars, such Rulings are traditionally considered an "informative source", the authority of which emanates from their frequent doctrinal wisdom (Supreme Court Judgements of 28 December 1956 and 30 January 1957). The strength of the Rulings' arguments added

127 F. FALCÓN Y TELLA, *Nuevos retos de los derechos humanos, op. cit.*, pp. 53-54. P. G. LAUREN, "Nuevos retos para los derechos humanos. El futuro a la luz del pasado", II Jornadas Internacionales "Nuevos retos de los derechos humanos", Instituto de Derechos Humanos, November 2003, Facultad de Derecho de la Universidad Complutense de Madrid. Translation into Spanish from "New Challenges for Human Rights: The Future in Light of the Past", by F. FALCÓN Y TELLA, *Anuario de Derechos Humanos, Nueva Época,* Instituto de Derechos Humanos, Facultad de Derecho, Universidad Complutense de Madrid, 5, 2004, pp. 369-386, esp. pp. 372-375.

to their authority, which acquired a real importance and was recognized by the case law of the Supreme Court (Judgements of 22 April 1987 and 29 January 1996). Sadly, following a series of Rulings which have proven difficult to classify, the prestige of the Rulings is currently at a low level.[128]

1.2. *Reiteration of Rulings*

In order for the Spanish Supreme Court to provide case law, there is a need for a degree of habit in terms of the way in which a particular issue is resolved. A certain "custom" is necessary – rulings must be reiterated. Here, we encounter the quantitative aspect of the case law requirements of the Supreme Court. A single judgement will not constitute case law, but two will suffice. Various judgements of the Supreme Court establish this requirement, including those of 10 February 1886, 27 October 1930, and 11 December 1953. In these judgements, though, it is also made clear that the fact that a ruling has yet to be reiterated does not imply that it be devalued or disregarded, given that it may constitute the first ruling in a series – it could be a starting point, in other words an antecedent.

As far as the Constitutional Court is concerned, a single judgement is in fact sufficient to create case law.

1.3. **Ratio Decidendi** *Compared with* **Obiter Dicta**; *The* **Ratio** *and Similar Concepts in Law*

Referring to the requirement of habituality or reiteration in a qualitative rather than quantitative sense, decisions of the Spanish Supreme Court must be "substantially identical" to constitute case law. [129] Decisions must be identical, with a uniformity of opinion in terms of the resolution of the issue. This requires both "situations" and "solutions" to be essentially identical – that the grounds on which a case is resolved be the same.

The Sentences of the Supreme Court of 12 April 1954 and 5 November 1970 deal with "analogous" cases. That of 31 January 1930 deals with "identical" cases. In reality, there is no contrdiction between the two adjectives used, given that cases must be "analogous" – that is to say, similar – on a factual level, and "identical" in their essence, in the *ratio* – those

128 An example of this is "Resolución de 14 de febrero de 2007 (BOE de 1 de marzo)".

129 See, on the subject, H. H. A. COOPER, "Ratio Decidendi", in *The New Law Journal*, 118, 1968, pp. 1180-1181.

points on which the judgement depends. This is known in full as *eadem ratio decidendi*. The part of the judgement that is not a circumstantial consideration – *obiter dicta* – will be *ratio decidendi. Obiter dicta* decorate judgements. The key is the decision and the part of the considerations on which it is based – the grounds, the decisive reason for the decision – rather than any remaining incidental reasons. Article 4.1 of the Civil Code refers to this *eadem ratio* as the grounds for analogy.

In the following part, we will turn to the diverse meanings of and concepts related to *ratio*.

1.3.1. The *De Facto* Assumption, Legal Consequence and *Ratio* as Elements of the Law; Historical Development of the Concept of *Ratio*

The structure of the legal norm is quite simple. It consists of three elements: the "*ratio*," the legal consequence, and the factual situation. The ratio fits in to the values plane – the plane of idealism. The legal consequence corresponds with the plane of what ought to be – the plane of logic. And the factual situation corresponds with the plane of what is – the factual plane. This is an instance of three-dimensionalism in the world of law. The view of the legal norm as a hypothetical judgment was originally put forth by Zitelmann – in disagreement with Thon – followed by Kelsen, with whom the idea reached its greatest articulation.

When we say that the legal norm is a hypothetical judgment, we are expressing the relationship that exists between a *hypothesis* and a *thesis* – between a *factual situation* and a *legal consequence*. The first has the form of "if A" – for instance, "if you kill someone." The latter idea has the structure of "should be B" – for instance, "you should be punished by being sent to prison." The link that unites these two elements is imputation. Imputation functions as a part of *legal norms*. It arises in the world of *what ought to be*, what the Germans call "*Sollen*." Linguistically the relevance of imputation can be found in *prescriptive, preceptive, or imperative* propositions – propositions that "*make a person do something*". One can use these as the basis to speak of *justice or injustice, validity or invalidity, and effectiveness or ineffectiveness*.

Opposing this type of connection one can find the so-called *relationship of causality*. This relationship unites a *cause* with its *effect*. It has the form of "if it is A, it is B," and falls in the factual, or "*what is*," plane – what the Germans call "*Sein*." It is typical in the *laws of physics* and *the laws of nature*. Its articulation gives rise to *descriptive* propositions – propositions that "*make one know*". From this link one can surmise the *true or false* nature of something.

The difference between imputation and causality lies in the fact that in the first, the link between the factual situation and the legal consequence is not borne of necessity, but rather is *arbitrary* or *conventional.* In this fashion, imputation becomes suitable for those who form the political community. On the other hand, in the relationship of causality the link between cause and effect is necessary, because things could not be any other way. If this were not the case, if we could not test and empirically prove causality, then the laws of physics would lose their character. For instance, according to the law of gravity, if we jump in the air, we eventually will fall back down towards Earth. This is a law of physics, of necessary character, to which there are no exceptions. On the other hand, if one person kills another, he or she can be punished by time in prison. However, depending on the culture, that person could also be dealt with by capital punishment or another type of sanction. And on an island where cannibalism is common practice, such a person may not be punished at all. It is a juridical law, and as such a conventional law. This is so because members of a specific society have agreed it will be this way. But such a result does not mean that there are not other possibilities in other legal contexts.

The laws of physics are necessary. If they cannot be scientifically confirmed, it is necessary to reformulate such laws. Columbus' discovery of America proved that the Earth was round. In turn, this reformulated the theory describing the Earth as a flat planet, beyond which monsters lived. When Galileo Galilei demonstrated that the Earth revolved around the sun, and not vice versa, the geocentric vision of the universe changed to become a heliocentric conception.

We can demonstrate the necessary and inexorable nature of the laws of physics with an example from the world of science. One afternoon, after returning home from her laboratory, the two-time Nobel Prize winner (once on her own and another time with her husband) Marie Curie asked her daughter for the physics homework she had been assigned in school. Madame Curie's daughter explained to her mother that the teacher had asked them why Archimedes' principle did not hold true in the case of fish. Archimedes' principle establishes that all bodies submerged in a liquid occupy a volume of liquid equivalent to the volume of the submerged body. In other words, if we fill up a container with liquid to its top, and later we place a body in the container, the water spills over the top of the container.

"How did you answer?" Madame Curie curiously asked her daughter. Her daughter replied: "some school children said that when you place a fish in a full fishbowl, the water doesn't spill out because the fish has scales, because fish blow out bubbles, and thousands of other imaginative answers." "But you, how did you answer?" the mother asked her daughter. "I simply tested what was said by trying it out with the fishbowl we have at home and seeing what happened. And I saw that it was not true what the teacher wanted us to believe. The water spilled over just the same when I placed a fish in the fishbowl."

Why does this happen? To repeat: because in the world of the laws of physics and of nature, for every cause there follows a necessary and inexorable effect which can be foreseen. It would be unthinkable to scientifically confirm that two plus two equalled five. There are no exceptions to the rule, or else the rule would have to be reformulated. In science, two plus two equals four. This type of rule is not applicable to juridical laws, which are of an arbitrary and conventional nature. In the law, two plus two is not always four, but rather, the interpretation and the legal argumentation can alter the result. We all know, in this respect, how important it is in the realm of the law to have a good lawyer who will fight effectively for our interests.

A. *The Greek* **Logos**

The term *ratio* has deep doctrinal roots. However, in various doctrines the term has been employed with different meanings. Historically, in Greece, *ratio* was used in the same fashion as the term *logos.*

B. *Appearance of the Term* **Ratio** *in Roman Law with a Different Meaning: The Arithmetical and Geometrical* **Ratio** *of Mathematical Content – Proportionality*

Even in ancient Rome, despite the Latin origin of the word "*ratio*," the term was not widely used in any legal sense. Later on in Roman law, the term grew in importance. Its meaning at that point, however, was still different from its current meaning, and corresponded more with a cultural meaning rather than a legal one. At that stage, the term ratio was used as a synonym for proportion (for instance, the "*ratio*" of 12/6=8/4=4/2=2).

C. *The Middle Ages*

It was in the Middle Ages, with the commentators, when the term acquired its modern meaning, tied to the law – *ratio legis* – and reason, as a synonym for *rationabilitas.* Initially the term was used by commentators as a synonym for *causa legis,* but later the commentators began to link the notion of a lawsuit to legal transactions, and "*ratio*" was reserved for the law.

a. The Glossators and Devotion to the Letter and Literal Interpretation

The Commentators or Post-glossators contributed enormously to the theory of *ratio* as a mode of interpretation, and they did so in a manner very different from their predecessors, the Glossators.[130] The difference between these two Medieval schools – the Glossators and the Post-glossators – is shown in two regards: with respect to the material object to be interpreted, and with respect to the formal object, their method, their point of view or the focus through which they carried out their interpretation.

The Glossators – Cino de Pistoia, Placentino, Acursio, Azón, and so on – had as their object of study Roman texts, especially Justinian's *Corpus Iuris*. During the Middle Ages, this was considered a sort of common law – as opposed to the recently created statutory law of the growing cities. It was a kind of "Bible of Law", the closest thing to what would later be the Codification of the Modern Era. A comparison is often made between the *Corpus Iuris Civilis* and the Napoleonic *Code*, insofar as their similar importance for their respective historical epochs is concerned.

b. The Post-glossators or Commentators and Use of Logical Interpretation in Search of the *Ratio*

For their part, the Post-glossators interpreted Roman law, though in an indirect fashion, by way of the analysis of the Glossa of their predecessors, the Glossators.[131]

The Glossators gave priority to the letter of the law in their interpretive method, limiting themselves to making annotations or marginal notes on legal texts. That is, they made Glossas, what we would today consider a literal or grammatical interpretation of texts. This emphasis on the "*corpus*" of the law – as opposed to its intention ("*animus*") or to its soul ("*anima*"), to its spirit, in a word – was turned upside down by the Post-glossators, who gave greater importance to the spiritual element over the material, thus carrying out what in modern legal parlance would be seen as a logical or teleological interpretation of the norm. The Post-

130 See E. M. MEIJERS, "Le conflit entre l'équité et la loi chez les premiers glossateurs", in *Tijdschrift voor Rechtsgeschiedenis*, 17, 1941, pp. 117-135, also in his *Études d'Histoire du Droit, vol. IV, Le droit romain au Moyen Âge*, II part, Leyden, Universitaire Leyden, 1996, pp. 142-156.

131 See, A. ROTA, "La concezione irneriana dell'aequitas", in *Rivista Internazionale di Filosofia del Diritto*, III S., 26, 1949, pp. 241-257.

glossators put the law's *ratio*, its *intentio* or the *mens legislatoris* before the *littera* or the *mens legis*. Should there be a conflict between the two elements, the material and the spiritual, the Post-glossators gave priority to the latter. Here, Bartolo de Sassoferrato's example stands out. He held, for instance, that capital punishment, foreseen for all who spilt blood in the Communal Palace, should not be applicable when this came about because a doctor was attempting to save the life of a patient.[132]

1.3.2. The *Causa Legis* in Transactions compared with the *Ratio Legis* in Law

As a preliminary measure, it is worth defining legal acts as "*legal voluntary licit facts*." The step from fact to legal act comes about in the following way: the facts may be indifferent or relevant to the law. The latter are called "legal facts." In turn, legal facts may be natural or voluntary. The latter are the "legal acts." The legal acts, for their part, are divided into illicit or licit. Within the second class we can highlight so-called "legal acts."

Following this, a legal act may be defined as "a licit legal fact, constituted at least by a declaration of private will, protected by the law, which recognises it as a basis for the production of effects that said law may order to take place, in league with what, according to such declaration, may be classified as desired ends." It is precisely these "*ex voluntate*" effects which comprise the distinguishing characteristic of legal acts.

1.3.3. The *Ocassio Legis* Compared with the *Ratio Legis*

The *ratio legis* constitutes the essence, the heart, of the legal rule, as opposed to the *ocassio legis*, which represents the circumstance, the accessory and the non-essential of a precept.

1.3.4. The *Anima Legis* Compared with the *Animus*

One must distinguish between the notions of *anima legis* and *animus legislatoris*. The first alludes to the soul of the law, to its spirit—as opposed to the letter of the law, or its *corpus*. *Animus legislatoris* refers to something

132 P. G. CARON: *"Aequitas" romana, "misericordia" patristica, ed "epicheia" aristotelica nella dottrina dell "aequitas" canonica (Dalle origini al Rinascimento)*, Milano, Giuffrè, 1971. Review by F. D'AGOSTINO, in *Rivista Internazionale di Filosofia del Diritto*, 48, 1972, pp. 123-124, esp. pp. 74-81; BARTOLO DE SASSOFERRATO: "In primam Codicem Iustinianeum partem, tit. De legibus et constitutionem principem", lex prima "Inter aequitatem", 7-10.

less objective and more subjective—the intention, will, or purpose of the legislature.

Both *voluntas legis* and *voluntas legislatoris* in principle refer to the goal of the law, the "what for", the intention. However, there also exists what could be denominated the "because" of the law – its basis, essence, or underlying principle. This is referred to as the *anima* or the soul of the law. Case law is related to both these things. It is arguably more connected with the *animus,* since this is more subjective, than with the more objective *anima,* for reasons already given. Overall, however, it concerns both because both make up the essence of *ratio,* as opposed to the letter or *corpus.*

What interests us here is simply differentiating between *animus* and *anima.* Though both allude to whatever is not the letter, the "*corpus*", and though in the discourse of jurists they are often handled as equivalents, in good, technical jurisprudence, *animus* is intention, aim; *anima* is soul or spirit.

1.3.5. The *Ratio Legis* Compared with the *Ratio Legislatoris*

This section investigates a type of argument used by the judge-interpreter in law, by way of psychological argument. Via this argument, the meaning of the will of the law-maker is attributed to a norm. That is, one tries to establish the will of the specific legislator who enacted the law. The problem is how to find this "legislator's will". Any psychological investigation would in fact be impossible, even more so than usual, since we normally deal not with an individual person but with an assembly. Therefore, it is necessary to analyze the documents where this "legislator's will" might have been set out. Preparatory works are doubtless the most important thing here. What is more open to doubt is whether or not we should include preambles and outlines of motives which might also reveal the legislator's will. A preamble and an outline or declaration often precedes the legislation itself. In those documents, the legislator explains the principles which have guided him, the end pursued or, in general, the motives leading to the enactment of that particular regulation rather than another.

There are some arguments suggesting it is not possible to know the legislator's will. For instance, in Parliaments, as they are collective organisms, it is only fictitiously that we can speak of a single legislative will, since various ideological stances co-exist therein. The Parliamentary vote is frequently the fruit of trade-offs between leaders of certain groups with representation in Parliament, rather than the true expression of the original will of the legislator. Technical, legal specialists are involved in the drawing up of the preparatory works and drafts, and these are not legislators. Their intervention is, however, decisive in the construction of the bill. Even amongst parliamentarians themselves, some may not know the detail of the bill yet vote for it in any case, out of pure routine. Whatever the case, not all parliamentarians are experts in the question being ruled on. Furthermore, as a consequence of Parliamentary debates, bills may include arguments stemming from all kinds of opinions. Finally, it can be argued that if the legislator had a definite and certain will, then he would make it crystal clear.[133]

No matter how difficult it may be to discern the legislative will, and while we may have to content ourselves with imagining a hypothetical will, this hypothetical will is what must be pitted against the will of the law – *ratio legis* – which is fixed once and for all in the text of the law and which is more objective, and less susceptible to debate. However, it must often be said that the judge, as interpreter of the law, attempts to verify the true meaning and extent of the law – that is, theories of the objective will of the law. In our view, what he is looking for is in reality the will of the subject who created the law. This, it is supposed, should correspond to the interpretation and application of the law – that is, theories of the subjective will of law.

If we invoke a musical metaphor, we might say that, once the disc being made has been recorded, the margin of appreciation is less broad than the singer and the studio might have hoped for. At first, there was a simple score and it had to be interpreted. The recorded disc here is the law. Of course, the result is open to evaluation and opinion: "I like it", "it is melodious", and so on. Still, the further the process of production moves, the more decisions have gone into it, and the arbitrary margin left open to interpretation lessens. This is similar to what takes place regarding the legislator's and the law's will. While the former – be it historical or the hypothetical or presumed will supposed to exist at the moment of the law's application – is somewhat subjective and so open to opinion, the latter is much less so, being more objective.

Regarding *voluntas legis* and *voluntas legislatoris*, it is interesting to note how, historically, there has been an evolution with respect to the prevalence of the one over the other. While the Glossators limited themselves to delving into the literal tenor of the law, the early Commentarists

133 FRANCISCO JAVIER EZQUIAGA GANUZAS, *La argumentación en la justicia constitucional española*, Thesis, Instituto Vasco de Administración Pública, Bilbao, 1987.

assumed that the spirit or *ratio legis* should be the criterion of interpretation, rather than the letter of the law. At that time, this *ratio* was identified with the subjective will of the legislator. Hence, they spoke of *ratio seu mens* – reason, or mind. However, later, in the 15th and beginning of the 16th centuries, the Commentarists considered the substantive or essential content of the law through the objective prism of the search for the law's final aim, rather than as a matter of the subjective profile of the legislator's personality and intellect. They then began to speak less of *mens legislatoris* and more of *mens legis* or *voluntas legis*.[134] That is, they shifted from giving priority to the *animus*, or intention, of the legislator to awarding it to the *anima*, or soul, of the law.

1.3.6. The "Historical *Ratio*" Compared with the "Presumed or Hypothetical *Ratio*"

One must also differentiate between a *historical ratio* of the law and a *hypothetical ratio*. The first corresponds to the moment in which the law is pronounced. In other words, it corresponds to the will of the specific legislators that developed that law. The hypothetical ratio is that supposedly possessed by the historical legislature which enacted the law by placing itself in the specific circumstances of the moment in which said law would be applied. The historical ratio is the true *ratio* which existed at the moment in which the law was created. The hypothetical ratio, however, "pretends" to know the law in order to adapt that law to the reality existing at the time of application. The two *ratios* may not coincide.

Still, many problems arise when one tries to determine the historical will of the legislator. Firstly, the will might have ceased to exist. Moreover, it may prove a contradictory will. Additionally, and here case law has much to say, it is very probable that any such will no longer corresponds to the demands of present-day, social reality. The development of the theory of hypothetical legislative will developed, in part, due to this issue. The hypothetical will is the intention the legislator would have had if he had taken into account the situation which was going to arise. That is, it is a will one believes the legislator would have had when considering the application of the norm, not its creation.[135]

134 P. G. CARON, *"Aequitas" romana...*, *op. cit.*, p. 100.

135 See, A. A. AARNIO, "On the Truth and Validity of Interpretative Statements in Legal Dogmatics", in A. A. AARNIO – R. ALEXY – A. PECZENIK, "The Foundation of Legal Reasoning", in *Rechtstheorie*, 12, 1981, pp. 423-448, esp. p. 435.

1.3.7. The *Corpus* Compared with the *Ratio* and the "Criteria for Interpretation"

Case law finds its most comfortable setting within the terms of *ratio*, in contrast to the letter of the law, or the *corpus*. With the latter, we move upon a formal rather than an essential plane. It is when the spirit transcends the letter that we find we must adjust the parameters of each. Case law plays an important role here.

Ratio thus conceived, as *ratio legis* in a broad sense, may have the following meanings:

a) The sense of finality – *animus*; either in the subjective sense of the legislator's goal – *voluntas legislatoris* – or in the objective sense of the end at which the law aims – *voluntas legis*. Here, we are dealing with the "what for" of things.
b) The meaning of the principle serving as foundation for the law, that is, the *anima legis* or *medulla legis*, in contrast to the *occasio legis*. Here, we consider the "because" of things.
c) In a third sense, *ratio legis* is conceived of as the content of the law. This is neither the "what-for" nor the "because", but rather the "what" of law. One seeks out protected legal interests, taking into consideration the logical construction of the norm together with the surrounding environment within which it will operate.

Meanings a) and b) both have to do with teleological interpretation. As regards the third meaning – protected legal interests – this is more correctly linked to sociological interpretation. Case law is connected to interpretation, whether teleologically or sociologically, depending on whether the emphasis is final-value or fact-specific. In both cases, an attempt is being made to adapt abstract justice to a concrete, real case, contrasting principles and data and values and facts, and "adjusting" them within a judicial interpretation.

Three elements may be distinguished in the interpretation of the law: the purpose or goal sought by the law (this is the *anima*, *ratio* or spirit of the law); the object upon which it is carried out (the *corpus* or textual body of the law); and the means which the interpreter uses in their task (the interpretation criteria).

1.3.8. The *Opinio Iuris* in Custom

The concept *opinio iuris* is related to that of *ratio*.

Alongside the written law, we will now examine other sources of law such as custom. Custom is a type of norm, as with written laws and general principles of law, but is distinguished by its origin in the people, in society, and by its form, in arising from spontaneous creation out of facts – *ex factis*. It can be said to differ from written law because the latter has its origin in the state, a political organization imposed on the people – or demographic element – and is by nature reflexive and written. It differs from the general principles of law in the sense that these principles have a mixed and eclectic nature, dealing sometimes with written principles – the case with the so-called positive principles – and other times with idea-based principles – so-called natural principles.[136]

136 See, on the subject: R. ALEXY, "Reschtsregeln und Rechtsprinzipien", in *A.R.S.P.*, Beiheft NF, 25, 1985, pp. 25 ff. J. AUSTIN, "Sobre la utilidad del estudio de la jurisprudencia", translation into Spanish and Introduction by F. GONZÁLEZ VICÉN, Madrid, Centro de Estudios Constitucionales, 1981. J. J. AVILA, "Principios jurídicos y positivismo jurídico de Carrió", in *La Ley*, 141, p. 1062, Buenos Aires, 1971. F. BACON, "Sur la legislation et la jurisprudence", in *Archives de Philosophie du Droit*, 30, *La jurisprudence*, 1985, pp. 351-362. G. BALLADORE PALLIERI, "I principi generali del Diritto riconosciuti dalle nazioni civili nell'art. 38 dello statuto della corte permanente di giustizia internazionale", Memorie del'Istituto Giuridico, Torino, 1931. A. BARATTA, "Le fonti del diritto ed il diritto giurisprudenziale", in *Materiali per una Storia della Cultura Giuridica*, 1980, 1, XX, pp. 189-211. N. BOBBIO, *La consuetudine come fatto normativo*, Padova, Cedam, 1942. *Id*, "Principi Generali del Diritto", in *Novissimo Digesto Italiano*, XXI, fasc. 1-2, vol. XIII, 1966, pp. 3-32. E. BODENHEIMER, *Jurisprudence*, Harvard University Press, Cambridge – Massachusetts, 2nd ed., 1974. E. E. BORJA, "La naturaleza de los principios generales del Derecho", in *Revista del Colegio de Abogados de la Plata*, 1962. A. BRADNEY – V. FISCHER – J. MASSON – A. NEAL – D. NEWELL, *How to Study Law*, London, Sweet and Maxwell, 1986. E. BULIGYN, "Sentenza giudiziaria e creazione del Diritto", in *Rivista Internazionale di Filosofia del Diritto*, 1967, pp. 164-180. Translation into Spanish, La Ley, 1966. P. CABANILLAS GALLAS, "Consideraciones sobre los principios generales del derecho". Discurso leído en la Real Academia de Jurisprudencia y Legislación el 2 de mayo de 1977, Madrid, Real Academia de Jurisprudencia y Legislación, 1977. M. CAPPELLETTI, "Reflessioni sulla creativitá della giurisprudenza nel tempo presente", in *Rivista Trimestrale di Diritto e Procedura Civile*, 1982, pp. 774-792. *Id*, *Giudici legislatori?*, Milano, Giuffrè, 1984. B. N. CARDOZO, *La naturaleza de la función judicial*, Buenos Aires, Ed. Arayú, 1955. A. CARTHY, "L'impact de Dworkin sur la philosophie du Droit anglo-americaine", in *Droit et Societé*, 2, January 1986, pp. 7-14. G. R. CARRIO, *Principios jurídicos y positivismo jurídico*, Buenos Aires, Abeledo-Perrot, 1970. *Id*, "Judge Made Law Under a Civil Code", in *Louisiana Law Review*, 41, 1981, pp. 990 ff. *Id*, "Sobre la administración de justicia y el derecho de la jurisdicción", in *Anuario de*

Derechos Humanos, 5, 1988-89, pp. 41-53. B. CLAVERO, *Los derechos y los jueces*, Madrid, Cuadernos Civitas, 1988. M. COCA PAYERAS, *La doctrina legal. (Estudio de su naturaleza y contenido, así como de la incidencia ejercida sobre ella por la doctrina jurisprudencial del Tribunal Supremo)*, Barcelona, Bosch, 1980. V. CRISAFULLI, "A proposito dei principi generali di diritto e di una loro enunciazione legislativa", in *Jus*, I, II, 1940, pp. 193-214. *Id*, "I principi costituzionali dell' interpretazione ed applicazione delle leggi", in *Scritti in Onore di Santi Romano*, vol. I, Padova, Cedam, 1940, pp. 663-703. *Id*, "Per la determinazione del concetto dei principi generali del diritto", in *Rivista Internazionale di Filosofia del Diritto*, 1941, I, II, pp. 41-63; III, pp. 157-181; IV-V, pp. 230-264. L. B. CURZON, *Jurisprudence*, Plymouth, Macdonald and Evans, 1979. L. DE ECHEVARRIA, "Riflessioni sulla funzione della giurisprudenza", in *Studi in memoria di Mario Condorelli*, III, pp. 147-160. Milano, Giuffrè, 1988. G. DEL VECCHIO, *Los principios generales del Derecho*, Barcelona, Bosch, 1978. (Italian version "Sui principi generali del diritto", in *Archivio Giuridico*, 1921, LXXXV), 2nd. ed., translation into Spanish by J. OSORIO MORALES, preface by DE DIEGO, 3rd. ed. 1971. DOMINGUEZ DE ANDRADES, "Sentido e valor da jurisprudença", "O raçao da sapiença" 30-X-53, University of Coimbra, 1973. L. M. DOMINGUEZ RODRIGO, *Significado normativo de la jurisprudencia: ¿Ciencia del Derecho o decisión judicial?*, Madrid, Ministerio de Justicia, 2 vols, 1984. K. J. EDDEY, *The English Legal System*, London, Sweet and Maxwell, 1987. J. ESSER, *Principio y norma en la elaboración jurisprudencial del Derecho Privado*, Barcelona, Bosch, 1961. Translation into Spanish from the first ed. in German (1956): *Grundsatz und Norm in der Richterlichen Fortbildung des Privatrechts*, by E. VALENTÍ FIOL. There is a 3rd. ed. of 1974. F. J. EZQUIAGA GANUZAS, "Los juicios de valor en la decisión judicial", in *Anuario de Filosofía del Derecho*, 1984, pp. 33-59. E. GARCIA DE ENTERRIA, *Reflexiones sobre la ley y los principios generales del Derecho*, Madrid, Civitas, 1984. GARCIA VALDECASAS, "Los principios generales del Derecho en el nuevo Título Preliminar del Código Civil", in *Anuario de Derecho Civil*, XXVIII, II, 1975. E. L. GARGAGLIONE, "Los jueces crean derecho como profecía", in *Notas de Filosofía del Derecho*, 5, 1969. P. GERARD, *Droit, égalité, ideologie. Contribution a l'étude critique des principes generaux*, Bruxelles, Publications des Facultés Universitaires Saint Louis, 1981. F. GIZBERT-STUDNICKI, "How Many Theories of Truth are Needed in Jurisprudence?", in N. MACCORMICK – S. PANOU – L. LOMBARDI VALLAURI, *Conditions of Validity and Cognition in Modern Legal Thought*, Wiesbaden, Franz Steiner, 1985, pp. 153-161. J. IGARTUA SALAVERRIA, "Sobre 'principios' y 'positivismo legalista'", in *Revista Vasca de Administración Pública*, 14, 1986, pp. 23-41. *Id*, "Unica solución correcta y principios jurídicos indeterminados", in *Reason in Law, Proceedings of the Conference held in Bologna 12-15 Dec. 1984*, Milano, Giuffrè, 1988 vol. II, pp. 321-332. H. KELSEN, *Dio*

In addition to their distinct origin and form, custom can be distinguished from written law in terms of its different validity, since while legislation is repealed in accordance with considerations stipulated by itself or another piece of legislation, custom only disappears due to disuse, by *desuetude* – a phenomenon opposed to custom or *consuetude* – when, in a repeated and general manner, it is no longer observed in practice.

Both custom and legislation have their advantages and disadvantages. The principal virtue of legislation is the great *certainty and juridical security* that it generates, given its written, codified character. The principal virtue of custom is the opposite, being its great *adaptability* to social changes, its dynamic and flexible character.

In modern States, and differing from what has occurred in certain historical ages – for example, in the Middle Ages or with the Historical School of Law – legislative law *predominates* over custom or customary law. The reason for this primacy lies in the fact that sovereignty currently resides in the people who express the national will through the laws of Parliament, which acts as the direct representative of the people and is elected by universal, direct and secret suffrage. Today in Spain, this su-

e Stato. La giurisprudenza come scienza dello spiritto. Translation and introduction by A. CARRINO, Napoli – Roma, Edizione Scientifiche Italiane, 1988. M. VAN DE KERCHOVE, "Jurisprudence et rationalité juridique", in *Archives de Philosophie du Droit,* 30, *La jurisprudence,* 1985, pp. 207-244. A. K. R. KIRALFY, *The English Legal System,* 7th. ed. London, Sweet and Maxwell, 1984. E. LALAGUNA, *Jurisprudencia y fuentes del Derecho,* Pamplona, Aranzadi, 1969. S. LEADER, "Le juge, la politique et la neutralité. A propos des travaux de Dworkin", in *Droit et Societé,* 2, January 1986, pp. 23-41. G. MORANGE, "Une categorie juridique ambigue: les principes généraux du droit", in *Revue de Droit Publique et de la Science Politique en France et à l'Étranger,* 1977, 4, pp. 761-778. T. OGALLAR Y AYLLON, *Creación judicial del Derecho. Discurso de recepción (contestación por Antonio Hernández Gil),* Madrid, Real Academia de Jurisprudencia y Legislación, 1975, pp. 43 ff. M. C. ORTEGA CARCELÉN, "Análisis del valor de la jurisprudencia en el Derecho Internacional", in *Revista Española de Derecho Internacional,* 2, XL, 1988, pp. 55-89. E. PATTARO, "La completezza degli ordinamenti giuridici e i principi generali dell'ordinamento giuridico dello Stato", in *Materiali per una storia della cultura giuridica,* XVIII, 1988, pp. 145-161. J. PUIG BRUTAU, *La jurisprudencia como fuente del Derecho,* Barcelona, Bosch, 1979. Various Authors, *La Motivation des Decisions de Justice,* directed by CH. PERELMAN and P. FORIERS, Bruxelles, Bruylant, 1978. G. ZACCARIA, "L'obiettivitá del giudice tra esegesi normative e politica del diritto", in *Rivista di Diritto Civile,* XXV, 1979, pp. 610 ff.

premacy of the written law is reflected in article 1.3 of the Preliminary Title of the Civil Code, according to which custom will only prevail in the absence of legislation.

We are now presented with the question of what the requirements are for customs thus configured. The Civil Code does not indicate this. Before, it said nothing; and now, its Preliminary Title having been reformed, it says little: only in article 1.3 does it demand that custom not be contrary to ethics or public order. One must supplement this deficiency of information with what is established in doctrine and case law. Even though this is not overwhelming in this regard, it is usually considered that there are three necessary requirements for the existence of custom law: use, *opinio iuris*, and rationality—to which the majority of legal systems add a fourth: that of not being contrary to legislation.

1. Use – *usus* – is the external and material element of custom. It is the repetition of acts which are "external, uniform, generalized, lasting, and of predictable continuity." By nature, the acts which constitute custom should be external—perceivable by the senses—and uniform—with a substantial identity; reaching their subjective scope, they have to be generalized for the majority of people. By duration, even though an initial period of validity is not required, it is thought that they should be lasting and of predictable continuity.
2. The *opinio iuris seu necessitatis* – the binding character – is the spiritual or internal element of custom. This consists of considering the previous element, use, "as a legal custom," with a generalized will "that it is law or that there is necessity that it should be", that is, a will to "legally" regulate behaviour in question according to use. In other words, the use should not be simple courtesy, but rather a norm of obligatory observance, legal custom. This is the requirement that distinguishes between mere "social uses" (acts of courtesy, rules of decorum – for example, giving a tip in a restaurant), which are not legally binding, and customary law, with which compliance is of an obligatory and coercive nature.
3. Rationality. In addition to the previous requirements, in order for custom to exist, rationality of use is required. It is understood by this that it "*may not be contrary to the public morality or order.*" As previously stated, this is the only requisite demanded by the Civil Code.

4. Finally, in the greater part of autonomous territories as well as in common law, a fourth requisite is required – that the custom not be contrary to legislation.[137]

137 On customary law, see: ALCALA-ZAMORA Y CASTILLO, "Derecho consuetudinario y función judicial", in *Estudios Jurídicos,* 1934, pp. 842 ff. *Id,* "La prueba del Derecho consuetudinario", in *Revista de Derecho Privado,* 1934, pp. 145 ff. *Id,* "Ensayo de diferenciación entre la jurisprudencia y los 'usos forenses'", in *Boletín de la Universidad de Santiago,* 1933. J. ALMEDA Y ROIG, "La costumbre como fuente de Derecho", in *Revista Jurídica de Cataluña,* 1908, pp. 5 ff. C. E. BALOSSINI, "Consuetudini, usi, pratiche, regole del costume", Milano, Giuffrè, 1958. *Id,* "L'accertamento del diritto consuetudinario compito del giurista e del sociologo", in *La prassi amministrativa,* Milano, Giuffrè, 1963. *Id, La categoria del 'diritto dei privati' nei rapporti commerciali 'internazionali',* Milano, Giuffrè, 1968. N. BOBBIO, *La consuetudine como fatto normativo,* Padova, Cedam, 1942. COSTA, "Requisitos de la costumbre jurídica según los autores", in *Revista General de Legislación y Jurisprudencia,* 1881. *Id, El problema de la ignorancia del Derecho y sus relaciones con el "status" individual, el referéndum y la costumbre,* Discurso de recepción a la Academia de Ciencias Morales y Políticas, Madrid, Academia de Ciencias Morales y Políticas, 1901. V. CRISAFULLI, "Variazione sul tema delle fonti con particolare riguardo alla consuetudine", in *Scritti in memoria di Antonino,* Milano, Giuffrè, vol. III, 1967, pp. 253-278. FRANCESCHELLI, Under "Consuetudine" and "Desuetudine", in *Nuovo Digesto Italiano,* Torino, UTET. F. HERNANDEZ IGLESIAS, *El Derecho consuetudinario y la codificación,* Madrid, 1903. M. IGLESIAS, "¿Cabe el 'usus fori contra legem'?", in *Información Jurídica,* November 1950. J. LOIS ESTÉVEZ, "La costumbre ante los principios fundamentales de la política del Derecho", in *Revista General de Derecho,* Valencia, April/May 1948. V. MIECHI, *La forza obbligatoria della consuetudine considerate nelle sue basi sociologiche e giuridiche,* Perugia, Unione Tipografica e Cooperativa, 1899. L. MOUTON Y OCAMPO, *Derecho consuetudinario español y europeo,* Madrid, 1911. *Id,* under "Costumbre" and "Derecho consuetudinario", in *Enciclopedia Jurídica Española,* Barcelona, Seix. PAVONE LA ROSA, under "Consuetudine, f) Usi normativi e usi giudiziali", in *Enciclopedia del Diritto,* IX, 1961, pp. 513-31. PORTOLÉS SERRANO, *El Derecho consuetudinario a través de la codificación civil castellana,* thesis, Zaragoza, 1920. RAMÍREZ DE LA TORRE, "Ley y costumbre en la bibliografia inglesa", in *Revista Crítica de Derecho Inmobiliario,* 1926. I. VANNI, *Della consuetudine nei suoi rapporti col Diritto e colla Legislazione,* Dissertazione di laurea, Perugia Tipografia Santucci, 1877. P. VINOGRADOFF, *Custom and Right,* Oslo, Aschehoug, 1925. Instituttet for Sammenlignende Kulturforskning. Serie A. Vol. III. V. ZAGREBELSKI, *Sulla consuetudine costituzionale nella teoria delle fonti del diritto,* Torino, Giappichelli, 1970. F. ZICCARDI, "L'integrazione del

1.3.9. The *Ratio* in Legal Argumentation; Types

The expression *ratio* is well established by doctrine. Nevertheless, doctrine points to a great diversity of meanings. In studying the legal norm, we saw how *ratio* was one of the elements in play and how it had a triple meaning: that of finality or the "what for" of the norm, that of the grounds for or the "why" of the norm, and that of the object or the "what" of the norm.

There would even also be a fourth meaning of the term *ratio*, as *ratio decidendi*, the "reason for which it is decided" in the most literal sense of the expression, in the jurisprudential technical sense, as that which is not "*obiter dicta*" of the judgement.[138] This last meaning of *ratio* is the one applicable in legal argumentation.

Additionally, we believe that in legal argumentation, *ratio decidendi* arises between two cases: the factual situation of the rule, and an unregulated case (and not between the law and a case or only within the law), amongst which there exists a comparison of equality (analogy), superiority (*a fortiori* argument) or inferiority (*a contrario* argument). Lastly, it is worth highlighting how legal argumentation places *ratio* at an intermediary level between the factual (based on the events and facts) and the legal (based on legal consequences).

Basing ourselves on this three-dimensional division in planes (the factual, the legal-factual and the legal), we can distinguish a series of arguments.

On the *factual plane*, there is a triple possibility: a) That the factual situation of the rule and the real case requiring regulation are identical; b) That they are totally contrary; and c) That they are similar, or in other words, contain common points and different points. The first situation, where the two are identical, gives rise to "subsumption", which occurs when the case of reality falls completely within the normative circumstance. In the case of absolute contradiction, the theory of the exclusive general rule would enter into play in support of the dogma of completeness of the law. According to this theory, that which is not prohibited is permitted (*inclusio unius, exclusio alterius*).

contratto", in *Rivista Trimestrale di Diritto e Procedura Civile*, 1969, pp. 108-90.

138 See, G. W. PATON – G. SAWER, "Ratio Decidendi and Obiter Dictum", in *The Law Quarterly Review*, 63, 1947, pp. 461-485.

A. *The* Eadem Ratio *in Analogy*

The circumstance of similarity is that which admits the greatest number of possibilities. Therein it is necessary to bring into play the second plane of distinction; that of *ratio*. In this respect, the unregulated case may be a) identical; b) greater; or c) neither one nor the other, but lesser or contradictory with respect to the factual situation of the rule; we are facing the possibility respectively of: a) analogical argument, b) *a fortiori* argument, or c) *a contrario* argument.

With respect to the third plane of the differentiation, the legal, of the legal consequences, both in analogy and "*a fortiori*" argument and in subsumption, these are those established by the rule for the regulated factual situation. Meanwhile, in the theory of exclusive general rules and the "*a contrario*" argument, the opposite occurs. The legal consequences are anything but those established for the case already regulated.[139]

B. *The Major Ratio in the* A Fortiori *Argument*

The *a fortiori* argument may be of two types. The first is the so-called *a maiori ad minus* (from greater to lesser) argument, according to which he who has better grounds for the greater shall also have right to the lesser. As shown in the foregoing, it can be observed that the *a fortiori* argument in this first category is applied to advantageous classifications, permissive laws or positive prescriptions. An example of this would be the following: he who has the right to use hard drugs to cure certain diseases in certain cases because a law permits their use, that person having "better grounds", shall also have the right to use soft drugs although the law may be silent on the latter issue.

The second kind of *a fortiori* argument would be the inverse of the above, the so-called *a minori ad maius* (from lesser to greater) argument, applicable to unfavourable classifications, prohibitive laws or negative prescriptions. According to this, if the lesser is prohibited, the greater shall be prohibited due to greater grounds. For example, if a law prohibits the consumption of wine at certain hours of the day or in certain places, with greater grounds, although the law says nothing, alcoholic beverages

139 See, M. J. FALCÓN Y TELLA: "Papel de la 'ratio' en la argumentación jurídica. Ensayo de una nueva configuración teórica del argumento 'a contrario'", in *Revista de la Facultad de Derecho de la Universidad Complutense de Madrid*, 75, 1989-1990, pp. 259-283; *Id*, *El argumento analógico en el Derecho*, preface by J. ITURMENDI MORALES, Madrid, Civitas, 1991, esp. pp. 86-103 and 174-177.

stronger than wine shall also be prohibited during those hours and at those places.

C. *The Minor or Contrary* Ratio *in the* A Contrario *Argument*

It may seem strange to discuss similarity of cases in *a contrario* argument and to reserve contradiction for the "*ratio*" level. But in reality, there is nothing untoward if we bear in mind that even those which are contrary have in common that they are "extremes of the same genre." The foregoing can be graphically expressed with an example which, for greater explanatory clarity, we take from common language: "high" and "low." According to the classic interpretation, these are two categorisations for which the *a contrario* argument would be applicable, as these qualities are totally opposed and contrary. In this way, that established for the "high" *a sensu contrario* would not govern that established for the "low." However, in light of the explanations given, the situation would vary somewhat. This would also be considered a case of applying the *a contrario* argument, although not because high or low stature are contrary facts, but because similar facts ("high" and "low" have in common at least the fact that both adjectives measure stature) are essentially opposed. The two extremes, the lower ("low") and higher ("high"), belong to a single genre (stature). Contrary in fact (the theory of exclusive general norm therefore being applicable), would be, for example, "high" and "long," in that they belong to different genres, those of height and length respectively – or even more obviously, "high" and "horse," in that both do not even belong to the same genre, as the first is an adjective and the second a noun.

1.3.10. The *Ratio Decidendi* of the Judgement Compared with the *Obiter Dicta*; Fundamental Points of Law

Finally, there are those who speak of the *ratio decidendi*, which refers to the reason articulated by the judge at the moment of handing down a judgement. Judicial sentences are made up of two parts:

- The *obiter dicta*, which is what the court says before its holding: the factual records, and the legal rules or grounds to be considered.
- The decision, which contains the legally reasoned resolution —*ratio decidendi*, the result of applying legal rules to the facts of the case.

2. The Functions of Case Law

2.1. The Interpretation of Law

Interpretation is the intellectual process by way of which, starting from the language of the wording, the normative content of a law is obtained: from the "signifiers" – the wording – to the "signified" – the rules. Interpretation is a valid process for transforming laws into rules. The combination of laws is merely an indefinite number of interpretative possibilities, or of potential rules. Legal interpretation flows between two poles: the "case to regulate" and the "regulatory rule". Interpretation is an activity which aims to unite the one with the other, leading to a satisfactory result on both counts. The interpreter behaves in a circular fashion, starting from and returning to the case at hand in order to find a solution, and harmonizing the requirements of reality and those of the law.[140]

Wherever the judge applies a legal rule to a real case, it is an inescapable truth that they must either previously or simultaneously interpret that rule. The processes of application and interpretation are intimately and inseparably linked. Every legal rule requires interpretation in order for it to be applied – not only the obscure rules, in which this necessity is more clear-cut, but also the clear rules, since, faced with the aphorisms *in claris non fit interpretatio* and *clara non sunt interpretanda*, it is certain that in order to see something as "clear", a hermeneutical task must necessarily have been undertaken, though it may have been minimal. In the context of application/interpretation of legislation, we may sometimes encounter an event in which a literal or grammatical interpretation of a rule is insufficient, and a more in-depth interpretation is therefore required. It is appropriate to identify two interpretative phases, checking: 1) that the literal tenor is not sufficient. 2) That it is necessary to investigate the spirit, or *mens*, of the rule in order to apply it correctly to the instant case and ensure justice is done.

But application and interpretation going hand-in-hand does not mean that they are the same thing. The two notions should be distinguished. While the objective of interpretation is to determine what the legislation says, the aim of application is to see whether a case falls within the scope of a rule, with the aim of applying the corresponding legal effects.

140 F. M. CALVO VIDAL, *La jurisprudencia ¿Fuente del Derecho?*, *op. cit.*, pp. 84-85.

There are therefore differing steps in the process of application – in a wide sense – of a rule. First, it is necessary to consider whether the rule applicable to a case is valid – whether it has been created by a competent body in accordance with established procedure (decision as to validity). Next, the meaning of the applicable law must be clarified (decision as to interpretation). The proven facts of the case must then be considered (decision as to evidence). Fourth, we need to check whether or not the proven facts fall within the factual remit of the rule to be applied (decision as to subsumption, or application in the strict sense). Finally, the legal consequences of the proven facts must be investigated and legally classified (decision as to consequences).[141]

2.2. *The Application of Law*

As already indicated, there exists an indissoluble relationship between interpretation and application of the law, between "understanding of the rule" and "construction of the facts". This is based on the recognition of the analogous character of law, and the link which exists between "analogy" and "the nature of things" in the production of law via maxims of decision. To apply a rule does not only mean to understand it and subsume the case to that rule, but also to select the relevant elements – those which in essence constitute the *ratio* – from among the multiple possibilities, determining the major premise – interpretation – and the minor premise – application – of the legal syllogism.[142]

Aristotle highlighted the singularizing and individualizing role of case law, in that it required the application of an abstract law to a specific case, and the step to be taken from general justice to equity. In this double sense, we can speak of application. In relation to application of justice, we find ourselves in the realm of ethics; in relation to application of the legal rule, particularly that of legislation, we are in the realm of law – more specifically, in the realm of legal argumentation.

141 JERZY WRÓBLEWSKI, "Evaluative Statements in Law. An Analytical Approach to Legal Axiology", in *Rivista Internazionale di Filosofia del Diritto*, 1981, 4; J. IGARTUA SALAVERRÍA, *Teoria analítica del Derecho (La interpretación de la ley)*, Oñati, Instituto Vasco de Administración Pública, 1994, p. 14. J. IGARTUA SALAVERRÍA, *Márgenes y límites en la aplicación del Derecho*, Donostia, Librería Carmelo, Facultad de Derecho, 1992.

142 F. M. CALVO VIDAL, *La jurisrprudencia ¿Fuente del Derecho?, op. cit.*, p. 86.

Normally, when we speak of application of law by way of legal argumentation – for example, in the analogous argument, the *a fortiori*, the *a contrario* or, even, in the application of general principles of law – the product of such application is a maxim of decision, the result of providing the instant case with the legal consequence of the jurisprudential rule applied. In reality, in systems of Continental character such as the Spanish one – and in direct opposition to the legal systems based on the Anglo-saxon case law tradiction – this maxim of decision is not an authentic legal rule, since in Spain, at least in a formal sense, case law is not a source of law (with the caveats we will later encounter).

2.3. The Integration of Law

The expression "fullness of the legal system" – some prefer to speak of "completeness" – alludes to the need for every legal system to be complete, to contain all the necessary legal rules to offer a legal solution to any case arising in real life.

In fact, reality is much richer than any framework which seeks to capture it, as far-reaching as such framework may be. There is hence always the possibility of original cases, not foreseen by the rules but which may, nonetheless, require regulation. This gives rise to the phenomenon of legal lacunae and loopholes. And it is here that case law comes into play as a mechanism, among many others, assisting the dogma of fullness of the legal system, as a means employed by the interpreter of performing the conjuring trick of filling in the lacunae and closing the loopholes, ensuring that the legal system appears to be altogether "full", or whole.

Case law is not unconnected with the problems of fullness of law, in two senses at least: positively, when we use case law to verify the "full" character of the legal system; on the other hand, in a more negative sense, when we observe the existence of loopholes that break the dogma of fullness of law, particularly when we encounter "inappropriate" gaps, resulting from the lack of an adequate interpretation of a legal rule in the light of case law.

Within the first, positive aspect of case law, it is worthwhile to stress the theory based on the judge's obligation to provide a judgement. It is there that we best observe the role played by case law.

According to this theory, legal systems are complete, if not in an immediate or *a priori* sense – since the legislator is not perfect and may have omitted particular legal rules which are necessary, although they may not have appeared to be so – then, at least, following the interpretative intervention of the judge, who always has the obligation to provide a response. The courts cannot abstain from judgement on the pretext of silence, uncertainty or insufficiency of legislation, and would be liable if they sought to do so. This is the prohibition of *non liquet.*

2.4. The "Limited" and "Derived" Creative Function of Case Law

The judges and courts undertake a task of integration of the legal system, filling lacunae and closing gaps where the system suffers from the absence of specific rules at the time of responding to the multiple real cases which fall to be considered. In this "hole-filling" task, the judges themselves will occasionally construct the rules, even in Continental legal systems such as the Spanish one. Nonetheless, judicial creation when handing down judgements is "limited" and "derived".

Creation is "limited" because it only produces *inter partes* effects, not general *erga omnes* effects as in legislation (an authentic legal rule with general effect). Judgements resolve a particular case, but a judge confronted with a similar situation in future will not be bound in the Romano-French systems by the decision of a previous judge. On the contrary, legislation aims to act as a guide to general conduct for all cases falling within its factual ambit and arising after its promulgation.

Creation is "derived" because the judgement has "one foot" in the letter – or, at least, the *ratio* – of the law. Creation here is not free and original, but a slave to the legal rule which it serves. The grounds of judgements are hence extremely important, but are not required to be given except in terms of legal rules. Legislation remains stable until it is repealed, but in contrast, discrepancies can exist in case law, just as distinct lines of argument are employed in the application of a rule to reality. If judges limited themselves to declaring the will of legislation, conflicts in case law would be inexplicable. But questions regarding the existence of creation of case law, and "to what point and in what measure" it exists, are linked to the content of a later section of this book concerning the status of case law as a source of law.[143] We will consider these issues in that section.

143 See, G. BOEHMER, *El Derecho a través de la jurisprudencia. Su aplicación y creación*, translation and notes by J. PUIG BRUTAU – from *Praxis der Richterlichen Rechtsschöpfung*, Tubingen, J. C. B. Mohr (Paul Siebeck), 1952 – , Barcelona, Bosch, 1959. J. BOLANGER, "Notations sur le pouvoir createur de la jurisprudence civile", in *Revue Trimestrielle de Droit Civil*, LIX, Sirey, 1961. E. BULYGIN, "Sentencia judicial y creación de Derecho", in *La ley*, Buenos Aires, CXXIV, 1967, pp. 1.307 ff. G. PACCHINI, "I poteri creativi

2.5. *Other Functions*

Although the character of case law as a source of law is open to question and debate, no one would deny that, in practice, case law possesses an unquestionable degree of importance in all legal systems as an auxiliary and complement to those systems. We refer here to its functions of decantation and application of the general principles of law, of bringing legislation up to date, and even of acting as an "advance party" for a great number of institutions which first saw the light of day as a result of judicial creation, only later being established in legislation.[144]

2.5.1. The Function of Decantation and Application of the General Principles of Law

By way of case law, judges create general principles of law. These can fall into two categories: natural and positive law. The first are created by a process of deduction, from the abstract to the concrete, starting from a general idea such as that of nature (classical natural law), divinity (theological-medieval natural law), or reason (19th Century rationalist natural law).

Positive law principles, in turn, are classified as express or implicit. Express positive law principles feature in legislation in an explicit, patent manner. An example of such a principle would be that of good faith, according to which the legal text states: "good faith is presumed. Whoever alleges bad faith shall have the burden of proof".

With respect to implicit positive law principles, these are latent and not expressed in legislation, requiring a legal process or mechanism to become express – *analogia iuris,* by way of which a series of specific legal rules demonstrating a certain similarity and identity in terms of *ratio* are compared, with a general principle of law extracted via "induction". This general principle can then be applied to the specific case in need of regulation. Case law entrusts this work of creating legal principles to the judicial power.

della giurisprudenza", in *Rivista di Diritto Comerciale,* X, I, Roma, 1912, pp. 40-44. F. SOTO NIETO, *Cuestiones jurídicas (jurisprudencia creadora),* I, Madrid, Ed. Montecorvo, 1976. A. G. SPOTA, *El juez, el abogado y la formación del Derecho a través de la jurisprudencia,* Buenos Aires, Ediciones Depalma, 1976.

144 R. FISCHER, "El perfeccionamiento del Derecho por la jurisprudencia", translation into Spanish by M. NOVALVOS, in *Revista de Derecho Procesal-Iberoamericano,* 2-3, 1980.

2.5.2. The Updating Function of Law

It is said that legislation is deaf, while case law listens to man and provides solutions to his problems. Hence the large number of case law journals and collections – in Spain, these include *Aranzadi, Revista General de Legislación y Jurisprudencia, Revista Jurídica de Cataluña, Revista de Derecho Privado, Revistas La Ley, Colex, Praxis, Actualidad Civil, Anuario de Derecho Civil* and so on. The reason for this proliferation is the enormous importance of and immense interest in case law, not only for the practicing lawyer, but also for the theorists and scholars of law.

Case law performs the function of updating the law, reanimating it and adapting it to the requirements of the present, this being essential in order to maintain the continuous and necessary adjustments between social reality and law and avoid ideological lags between the two. Case law, in a patient and silent manner, adds new vitality to the old branches of the legal system. The legislator would find it impossible to amend, modify and change the law from day to day, as should be done, given that real life moves more quickly than the law can foresee. First, it is the fact, and then the law. This is where case law comes into play.

2.5.3. The Function of Forming and Creating Legal Concepts

Case law both forms and creates legal concepts, such as abuse of law, unjust enrichment, misuse of power, the principle of good faith, and so on. As such, it can be affirmed that although *de iure* case law (of the Supreme Court) is not considered a formal source of Spanish law in the strict sense, *de facto* it is greatly important and is imposed on all – lawyers have to bear it very carefully in mind, and must cite it if they do not wish to run the risk of their petitions being rejected.

3. Is Case Law, Especially that of the Supreme Court, a Source of Law in the Spanish Legal System?

The question of whether case law constitutes a source of law was first raised by writers in the 19th Century, and the debate reached its zenith in a famous lecture given by the American judge Oliver Wendell Holmes on "the path of the law". The controversy continues to this day.[145]

145 See, on the subject, E. R. AFTALIÓN – J. VILANOVA, "La jurisprudencia como fuente del Derecho", in *Revista La Ley*, Buenos Aires, 81, pp. 769 ff. J. ANGLADA VILARDEBO, "La jurisprudencia ¿fuente del Derecho?", in *Estudios de Derecho Civil en Homenaje al Profesor Castán Tobeñas*, IV,

Currently in Spain and the other similar Continental systems, a doctrinal argument regarding the legal value of case law – particularly that of the Supreme Court and other higher courts – is taking place. While some jurists emphatically maintain that, even in Continental systems, judges create law, others equally emphatically argue that this is not the case. The following section contains a synthetic review of the principal arguments advanced in favour of each doctrinal position – with the proviso that the section is particularly applicable to the case law of the Spanish Supreme Court.

Pamplona, Ediciones Universidad de Navarra, 1969, pp. 71-85. A. BARATTA, "La jurisprudencia y la ciencia jurídica como fuente del Derecho", in Various Authors, (BARATTA, GRIMA, RUBIO LLORENTE *et al.*), *Las fuentes del Derecho, Anuario de la Facultad de Derecho, Estudi General de Lleida*, Barcelona, 1983. S. BELAID, *Essai sur le Pouvoir Createur et Normatif du Juge*, preface by M. VILLEY, Paris, Librairie Generale de Droit et de Jurisprudence, Bibliotheque de Philosophie du Droit, directed by Ch. EISENMANN, H. BATTIFOL and M. VILLEY, vol. XVII, 1974. J. L. M. ELDERS, "Dans quelle mesure la jurisprudence et la doctrine sont-elles des sources de Droit?", in *Nederlandse Vereniging voor Rechtsvergelijkin*, 14, Deventer, Kluwer, 1974. A. GAMBARO, "Les reactions de la doctrine à la creation du droit par les juges en droit civil", *Journées Italiennes. Travaux de l'Association Henri Capitant*, XXXI, 1980. A. HERNÁNDEZ GIL, Discurso de recepción al nuevo académico D. Tomás Ogallar y Ayllón, on *Creación judicial del Derecho*, Madrid, Real Academia de Jurisprudencia y Legislación, 3 March 1975. Both lectures published by the Academia, Madrid, 1975. L. DE LA MORENA Y DE LA MORENA, "La jurisprudencia. ¿Fuente del Derecho?", in *Libro Homenaje al Profesor José Luis Villar Palasí*, 1rst. ed., Madrid, Civitas, 1989. G. MURILLO, "La jurisprudencia obligatoria", in *Problemas jurídicos de México*, Sección de Derecho Constitucional, México, Editorial Ius, Asociación Nacional de Funcionarios Judiciales, 1953. J. PUIG BRUTAU, *La jurisprudencia como fuente del Derecho (Interpretación creadora y arbitrio judicial)*, Barcelona, Bosch, s. f. E. LOUZAO, "La jurisprudencia. Su fuerza obligatoria", in *Revista de Derecho Privado*, 78, March 1920, pp. 74-77. J. B. VALLET DE GOYTISOLO, "Algunas consideraciones acerca de la ley y la jurisprudencia de los Tribunales como fuente del Derecho", in *Estudios sobre el Título Preliminar del C. C. Parte General. Vol. I*, Academia Matritense del Notariado, Edersa, 1977.

3.1. *Arguments in Favour of it Being a Source*

3.1.1. The Evolution of the Principle of Separation of Powers

Those who argue in favour of case law creating law base their standpoint on the historical evolution of the principle of separation of powers from its original formulation by Montesquieu, and argue that the role of the judge now incorporates a broader creative element. The judge, at least in cases where there is a lack of clarity or a gap in the legislation, is no longer limited to being the mouthpiece that speaks the words of legislation.[146]

3.1.2. Kelsen's "Stufenbau" Theory and Hart's "Open Texture" Theory; Problems Resolving the Improvement of Strict Legal Positivism and the Conception of Law as a Legal System

Additional grounds for considering case law to be a source of law are found in the theory of law such as the "normative pyramid" of Hans Kelsen, and the "open texture" of H.L.A. Hart.[147]

According to the first theory, the legal system has a graded or layered structure in the form of a normative pyramid (*Stufenbau*), in which judicial maxims are granted their place as "specific rules", even if it may be in the last layer of the pyramid.

The theory of Hart states that, together with "easy cases", legal systems also encounter "hard cases" and areas of semi-darkness, in which situations the judge would enjoy a greater creative freedom.

146 See, MONTESQUIEU, *Del espíritu de las leyes*, Introduction by E. TIERNO GALVÁN, translation into Spanish by M. BLÁZQUEZ and P. DE VEGA GARCÍA, Madrid, Tecnos, Colección "Clásicos del pensamiento", 1985. V. CANTOS, "¿Función automática o función creadora?", in *Revista Crítica de Derecho Inmobiliario*, 1917, September 1934, pp. 641 ff. M. CAPPELLETTI, "¿Renegar de Montesquieu? La expansión y la legitimidad de la justicia constitucional", translation into Spanish by P. DE LUIS DURÁN, in *Revista Española de Derecho Constitucional*, 17, 986, pp. 9-45. E. GRANDE, "Principio di legalità e diritto giurisprudenziale: un'antinomia", in *Sistema penale in transizione e ruolo del diritto giurisprudenziale*, Padova, 1997, pp. 129-146.

147 See, H. KELSEN, *Teoría General del Derecho y del Estado*, 2nd. ed., México, UNAM, 1979. *Id*, *Teoría pura del Derecho*, translation into Spanish by R. J. VERNENGO, México, 1993. H. L. A. HART, *The Concept of Law*, Oxford, Clarendon Press, 1967.

Along the same lines as the previous arguments, it may be asserted that today, strict legal positivism – which associated law exclusively with legislation – has been superseded. In its place would exist the conception of law as a system which admits other sources alongside legislation, such as equity and analogy – and if these are admitted, why not case law? The law contains holes and gaps, and when faced with them the judge has something to say and may create genuine rules in "hard" or "incomplete" cases, those rules having previously been non-existent, or at most implicit. Case law comes from the text, like fruit from the tree, but once away, fruit and tree – case law and legal rule – are different things. Gradually, the concept of the legal system is replacing that of the legal rule as the key to legality.[148]

3.1.3. The Infringement of Case Law as Grounds for Appeal to the Highest Instance (Appeal for Cassation)

Third, and now in the legal field, a further argument is put forward for case law constituting a source of law: the article of the Law of Civil Trial (after the reform of 7 January 2000) which appears to place case law on the same footing as a general legal rule as a ground of appeal for cassation. Article 477.3 states: "It shall be considered that an appeal for cassation may be admitted when the judgement subject to appeal is opposed to the case law doctrine of the Supreme Court..."

However, opponents of the theory that case law is a source of law argue that there is no indication that the infringement of case law provides a ground for appeal for cassation: case law is not autonomous, it is an application of legislation and refers to that legislation. The infringement of case law doctrine referred to would therefore be an infringement of legislation. The real source of law is not case law, then, but legislation interpreted via case law – legislation wrapped up in case law.

3.1.4. Association of Case Law with Other Sources of Law

The supporters of the argument that case law is an authentic source of law in Continental systems have on occasion based their stance on its relation

148 See, G. PECES BARBA, "La creación judicial del Derecho desde la teoría del ordenamiento jurídico", in *Revista del Poder Judicial*, 6, March 1983, pp. 20 ff.

to the "true" sources of law, and especially those of custom and general principles of law.[149]

A. Association with Custom, i.e. *Judicial Practice* – Usus Fori

Justification for the creation of law by case law has been offered on the basis of its assimilation to custom, either as a sub-class or a form of customary law, as "judicial custom". In this regard, case law has been denominated "forensic custom", *usus fori*, or *stylus curiae*. This viewpoint has been supported by the fact that, in Continental case law, a certain reiteration or repetition of the decisions of courts is required. This requirement can be assimilated with that of the "material element" which constitutes custom – practice reiterated by behaviour, or common use.

But if one wishes to see a form of custom in case law, all of the requirements for custom-based law need to be satisfied, and not simply the external or material element, but also the most important requirement – that of the "internal" or "spiritual", the *opinio iuris seu necessitatis*. This means the conviction that such common use is legally binding, that it constitutes authentic law and not a mere form of non-binding social courtesy. In this respect, the closest one can come to a positive affirmation is to say that while legislation may reign, case law "governs in fact" – or, to put it another way, that the importance and practical impact of case law is "like" that of a source. In this manner, there would be an opportunity – though it may simply be a "legal fiction" – to view case law "as if" it were binding law, even if it may not possess such character in a formal sense.

A potential criticism of the argument that case law can be recognized as having obligatory legal force by way of assimilation to legal custom would be that such conception does not correspond to the classical theory of customary law. The origin of customary law is popular, not judicial. It lies in the popular conscience rather than that of magistrates and legal professionals. The character and scope of customary law is general and abstract, not referring to singular, specific and particular cases. It comes about in a spontaneous and unthinking fashion without the need to provide grounds for its content, as opposed to case law which requires argument and explanation. Customary law is the fruit of a succession of specific facts, rather than a connection between facts and rules submit-

149 F. M. CALVO GARCÍA, *La jurisprudencia ¿Fuente del Derecho?*, *op. cit.*, pp. 118-126.

ted to interpretation. Finally, *opinio iuris* points to its binding character, which can only be considered a fiction to apply to case law.

B. Association with the General Principles of Law, as a Source of Said Principles

A second argument advanced with the aim of justifying Continental case law as a source of law emanates from the fact the judges create general principles of law via their judgements, which do constitute law.[150]

In effect, especially concerning general principles of law of an implicit positivist nature, case law by way of *analogia iuris* compares analogous legal rules, producing a general principle of law which makes patent what was previously latent. Equally, in the case of natural law principles, there is creation of law, of authentic general principles. On this occasion, however, creation is via a deductive rather than inductive method, starting from a general idea – nature, divinity or reason depending on whether we are considering classical, medieval or rationalist natural law – from which a general principle can be inferred within which specific cases can be subsumed.

But this argument also has its Achilles heel, namely that it is one thing to obtain a general principle of law as a "result or product" – inductive or deductive – of application of case law, but another thing to do so as an "activity or process". We will return to this idea later, in the section of the book referring to case law and analogy.

C. Association with Legislation[151]

Many writers seek to place case law among the sources of law in the sense that case law involves the creation of a special law, an individual or specific law or statute. Those three concepts are not exactly equivalent: although they have in common the reduced degree of generality of application of a rule, the reference is respectively to the *ratio*, the "subject" or the "object" of the rule.

150 See, A. GORDILLO CAÑAS, "Ley, principios generales y Constitución: Apuntes para una relectura, desde la Constitución, de la teoría de las fuentes del Derecho", in *Anuario de Derecho Civil*, XLI, II, April-June 1988.

151 F. M. CALVO VIDAL, *La jurisprudencia ¿Fuente del Derecho?, op. cit.*, pp. 126-138. R. ÁLVAREZ VIGARAY, "Las mutuas influencias entre la legislación y la jurisprudencia", in *Libro Homenaje a Ramón María Roca Sastre*, I, Madrid, Junta de Decanos de los Colegios Notariales, 1976, pp. 825-841. P. A. ESMEIN, "La jurisprudente et la loi", in *Revue Trimestrielle de Droit Civil*, January-March, 1952, I, pp. 17-23.

Others speak of case law as a source of law based upon the "tacit approval of the legislator" – or even claim an "express" approval based on the "additional provisions of the Civil Code".

a. Case Law as "Special", "Individual" or "Specific" Law

Some writers, including the Cuban Bustamante and Montoro, argue that case law creates "special" law. To properly understand this argument, we must take the preliminary step of examining the concept of special law. We understand this to mean that a small area of precepts is covered – for example, Mortgage Law or Water Law – and exists alongside general law. This is as opposed to so-called "exceptional" laws, which are singular and cover an exception, such as a privilege, replacing and colliding head on with the general rule from which they derogate.

In accordance with the above, the argument could be advanced that it is not beyond the realms of sanity to consider case law to be special law, given that "various" judgements exist, satisfying the quantitative element, and that the law is not repealed but applied – "the law it's not judged, judgement is made according to the law". In other words, case law must agree with the law.

Others, such as Kelsen, argue that the legal system is not solely composed of general rules but also comprises "individual" rules – such as a judgement or contract – which have a value limited, respectively, to the parties in dispute – claimant and defendant – or to the contracting parties in the case of a contract. The difference between the general and the individual lies in the greater or lesser degree of generality with reference to the subjects of the rule: are there few or many?

The general/individual rule distinction should never be confused with the distinction between abstract and specific rules. In the latter situation, the question of greater or lesser degree of generality is concerned with the "objects" or "regulated actions", in the objective rather than subjective sphere, and the distinction depends on whether the regulation applies to all types of actions or one in particular. In the case of individual laws, generality is a requirement of the principle of equality before the law. In the context of specific laws, it is a reflection of the requirements of "legal certainty".

But as much in one as in another type of law, the processes of individualization and precision bring a touch of creation with respect to the general or abstract rule. They are not limited to automatically deducing what is already contained in the rules, but contribute additional content which converts individual and specific rules into rules distinct from their general or abstract origins, while retaining the same legal character. This is, at least, the Kelsenian perspective – but not necessarily that of other jurists such as Francisco Suárez, for whom the characteristic of generality is an essential and fundamental requirement of any legal rule. Against the author of *De Legibus*, the supporters of this argument claim that the judge is not limited to declaring but in fact creates new legal rules, those rules simply being individual or specific.

The criticism to be advanced in relation to the previous opinion is that, in the work of the judge, there is creation – but it is a derived form of creation, "with one foot in the law from which it stems", and a limited one – one which can never go so far that it contradicts legislation. Judges create law, but within the options permitted by legislation and not against them. Furthermore, except in legal systems like the Swiss or Anglosaxon where case law is a clear source of law, it is necessary to provide caveats regarding the meaning of the claim that judges create law.

b. The Legislator's Tacit Approval via a *posteriori* "Reception" or Prior "Delegation" of the Case Law Rule

According to the present argument, a "fiction" is created according to which the legislator will, in an assumed and implicit form, grant authority to case law decisions: if they are not formally authoritative, they do have practical authority. This is the opinion of Waline, who speaks of the implicit "reception" by the legislator of case law, of a "delegation" of a general rule. But the concepts of legislative reception and delegation are not entirely equivalent, although they allude to the same idea. Reception is *a posteriori*, while delegation is prior to the act. However, for the purposes of this section we can use them as synonyms and not in their technical sense, given that the key to the point is the absence of reaction on the part of those who hold the legislative initiative. This absence of reaction means that the legislators do not consider it possible to repudiate a case law interpretation of objective law. A worthwhile criticism, once again, would point to the "fictional" character of the argument.

c. The Legislator's Express Approval in the Additional Provisions of the Civil Code, by reference to the *Comisión de Codificación* (Council of Law Reporting)

Some writers, such as Manresa, base their argument that case law is a source of law on the expression recognition of such in the additional provisions of the Civil Code. The third of these provisions establishes that:

> *Taking into account information of progress made in other countries which may be of use in ours, and the case law of the Supreme Court, the Codifica-*

tion Commission will formulate and provide to the government, every ten years, the reforms it would be advisable to introduce.

According to this precept, case law would appear to serve to change legislation via the Codification Commission. Although it would not create law in itself, it would influence the later creation of law through the legislative channel.

This idea is rejected by Herzog, who argues that it involves a confussion between the concepts of source of "production" and source of "knowledge" of law. The third additional provision of the Civil Code, according to Herzog, merely affirms the documentary value of case law as a means of facilitating knowledge of the law.

3.1.5. The New Value of Case Law due to Progressive Importance of "Agreements Adopted by the Non-jurisdictional Meetings of the Supreme Court"

The panorama of sources of law may be seen to be altered in the future given the progressively increasing importance of a singular institution: the "agreements adopted by the non-jurisdictional sections of the Supreme Court".

This original, dynamic and quasi-normative figure appears to have been called to modify the traditional Spanish system of sources – the Romano-Germanic system, the *res iudicata* system, the system with more than two thousand years of history – with the introduction of a legislative reform in the making which will intentionally declare the doctrine of the Supreme Court to be "binding" upon all judges and courts in the jurisdictional system, under penalty of committing "prevarication".

Article 264 of the Organic Law of Judicial Power regulates these non-jurisdictional agreements, establishing that "*the Magistrates of the various parts of a Chamber will meet in order to unify opinions and co-ordinate procedural practice*", adding that "*in every case, the independence of the Sections shall be protected in the trial and resolution of the different proceedings they may hear*".

Interpreting the article cited, it is clear that the agreements are not and do not create case law; that they cannot be compared to judgements, court orders or judicial resolutions, and only have *ad intra* value; that the sections in which the agreements are adopted are mere meetings of Magistrates making up the Chamber or Section, and not Court sections; and that said sections are not equivalent to a normal trial in the exercise of jurisdiction.

It is the case that the "non-jurisdictional sections" are very swift in contrast to the slow process of development of case law. They introduce a new dynamism, being lively and brief, to the judicial creation of law – allowing the case law doctrine of a Chamber to be proclaimed following a single section – as opposed to the conventional process of consolidation of existing case law. Moreover, they cover a large *vis expansiva* and have an almost normative appearance compared with the strict and exclusive subjugation of the single judge to the "rule of law" (article 117 Spanish Constitution). It hence appears that, based on an agreement from a non-jurisdictional section, there may be incrimination and sentencing for conduct which is not explicitly set out in the criminal law – and not even established by the consolidated case law to date. This is against the principle of *nullum crimen sine lege.*

It should be noted that there is a problem with the new force of these agreements from non-jurisdictional sections. They are based more on *imperium* than *auctoritas*, being of a directing and pyramidal ("binding") type, as opposed to the old case law, which was and remains linked to specific cases and real life.

Moreover, in accepting the reform of the Organic Law of Judicial Power which is in course and will establish the "binding" nature of the doctrine of the Supreme Court, it may be affirmed that the Spanish legal system is abandoning the traditional system of sources, and doing so without the prior and obligatory reform of articles 1.1 and 1.6 of the Civil Code, articles 25.1 (*nullum crimen sine lege*) and 117.1 of the Constitution, and article 12.1 of the Organic Law of Judicial Power – and similarly ignoring the reiterated case law of the Constitutional Court.

A preliminary step in this sense was the much-criticised judgement of the Supreme Court of 11 December 2001. A judge contradicted the consolidated doctrine of the Supreme Court on the matter of calculation of prescription. The judge was found guilty of *delito doloso de prevaricación* (the willful crime of prevarication – article 446 Criminal Code). This assault on the current Spanish model of sources of law originates in the incomprehensible and ever increasing tension that dominates the relationship between the Supreme Court and the Constitutional Court.

The agreements adopted by the non-jurisdictional sections of the Supreme Court must be "internal, orientative" agreements to co-ordinate future procedural opinion – but they must not resolve cases as does a court. The agreements can be of use for the "unification of opinions and co-ordination of procedural practice", to resolve discrepancies in interpretation existing within the Court, as an essential and efficient instrument in the event of legislative crises and jurisprudential loopholes or discrepancies, to deal with the absence of consolidated case law doctrine – but not as an ordinary and natural mechanism for the creation of case law doctrine.[152]

3.2. *Arguments against it Being a Source*[153]

3.2.1. A Strict Interpretation of the Principle of the Separation of Powers and the Judge's Position

The supporters of the argument that case law is not a source of law base their stance on a strict interpretation of the principle of the separation of powers, according to which the plane of creation of law is separate from that of its application. While the legislature is competent to create rules, the judiciary is only empowered to strictly apply those rules by way of syllogism or subsumption. According to this reasoning the judge must limit himself to considering whether the proven facts – the so-called "results", or minor premise – fall within (can be subsumed) the grounds of law – "considerations" or major premise. By virtue of this syllogism, the judge must then hand down the corresponding decision or judgement without the interference of any stage of creation of law. Article 117 of the Spanish Constitution demonstrates the theory of subsumption in the Spanish legal system, speaking as it does of judges and magistrates who are independent, immovable and "only subject to the rule of law".

Traditional doctrine relies on the principle of separation of powers to deny case law the character of source of law, given that – at least in its classical version – for separation of powers to exist, the judicial power cannot be granted legislative functions. In the contrary case – if we allowed judges to hand down general rules – we would be in a situation of "usurpation of powers". The judge must never legislate: his decision can never constitute a general rule. In the sphere of case law, the principle of division of powers has been recognized by the Supreme Court itself, in judgements on 2 July 1926, 23 March 1972, 23 September 1988, and 3 January 1990, among others.

152 A. GARCÍA-PABLOS, "Relevancia de los cambios de criterio de la doctrina jurisprudencial y los Plenos no Jurisdiccionales del Tribunal Supremo", in *Cuadernos de Derecho Judicial*, VII, 2006, Nuevas posiciones de la dogmática jurídica penal. Consejo General del Poder Judicial. Escuela Judicial, pp. 183-213, esp. pp. 208-213.

153 See, on the subject, F. M. CALVO VIDAL, *La jurisprudencia ¿Fuente del Derecho?*, *op. cit.*, pp. 145-177.

It is important here to ascertain the position occupied by the judiciary among the powers of the State. Formerly, the idea was prevalent that the power of the judiciary was practically "null and void". Kelsen, among other writers, argued along these lines that the judicial function was immersed in that of the "executive". The celebrated phrase of Montesquieu, that the judge was "no more than the mouth that pronounces the words of the law", follows the same line of argument. With the French Revolution of 1789 the situation had changed notably, due to the separation between judicial and administrative authority. The judicial power was relegated to the litigious in its strict sense, lacking any initiative and weakened due to the principle of separation of the administrative from the judicial. The French Revolution gave birth to the omnipotence of legislation, seen as the product of reasoned creation. It was argued that the judge must limit himself to applying this legislation via exclusively logical-formal and syllogistic processes, abstaining from arbitrary decisions.[154]

This conception suffered a crisis when the 19th Century Codes – the French and the other European Codes in general – demonstrated the insufficiency of legislation in terms of offering an answer to all the cases that in reality came before the judge. Despite this realization, judges remained obliged to declare and provide a decision on all issues submitted to them, not being entitled to refuse to judge on the pretext of silence, uncertainty or insufficiency of legislation (prohibition of *non liquet*). The work of the judge could no longer be limited to applying and interpreting legislation via the technique of subsuming the fact under the rule, however – the judge also had to undertake the work of filling the holes existing in legislation, and resolving the contradictions that might arise. The judge could not be the simple *bouche de la loi*, and stopped being the automaton of the initial post-revolutionary period in France. This idea of judicial independence was faithfully reflected in the Spanish legal system, the evidence being the Constitution of Cádiz of 1812. Another clear representation of this idea can be found in article 117.3 of the current Spanish Constitution.

The Constitution of 1978 is effectively based upon the principle of separation of powers, establishing that:

> *Justice emanates from the people and is administered on behalf of the King by judges and magistrates members of the Judicial Power who shall be inde-*

154 *Ibid.*, pp. 27 ff., p. 34.

pendent, shall have fixity of tenure, shall be accountable for their acts and subject only to the rule of law (article 117.1).

And, related to the judges and courts:

> *The exercise of judicial authority in any kind of action, both in ruling and having judgements executed.....Judges and courts shall not exercise any powers other than those indicated in the foregoing subsection and those which are expressly allocated to them by law as a guarantee of any right* (articles 117.3 and 117.4).

In turn, the order of article 9 of the Constitution, guaranteeing that public authorities are subject to the Constitution, incorporates the judicial power as a part of its target.

But the judge is neither an automatic subsumption machine nor a legislator or creator of general rules. The judge is subject to legislation and must apply it to the instant case – but the truth is that legislation, however strict it may be, always leaves a margin of creative freedom. For that reason it can be argued that within the margins of uncertainty allowed by the general rule which is being applied, the act of judging creates a new rule – it is simply that in this instance, the rule is individual rather than general. What distinguishes the legislator from the judge is not so much the creative nature or otherwise of their decisions, as the fact that the judge intervenes at the behest of a party, must give reasons for their decision, and such decision will normally lack general effect.

3.2.2. The General and Abstract Nature of Statute Law and the Specific Area of Case Law Maxims for Isolated Cases

Legal rules are formulated with a high degree of generality and abstraction. They are potentially addressed to a universal audience, to the general population of a country and a particular time. To the contrary, judgements are specific decisions made in isolated situations, whose effectiveness is limited to the parties to the trial and, as the case may be, to the consequences for any third parties who may be involved. The legal rule is defined by its generality and abstraction according to the majority of doctrine, although there are those – such as Kelsen, as previously explained – who would recognize individual norms such as those derived from case law as also having legal character.

3.2.3. The Imperative Nature of Statute Law as a Source of Law compared with the Merely Persuasive, Non-binding and Merely Authoritative Value of Case Law

It may be argued that case law, rather than being considered a source of law, might be better viewed as a simple authority, of merely persuasive value. Case law must possess the quality of being non-binding, because the bodies who hand down judgements can change opinion in a later decision, while decisions at lower instance courts can be followed or not, without any liability being incurred. The lack of binding effect must be noted not only in relation to the courts, but also for "private" parties, who are only bound by authentic legal rules. The Supreme Court never binds third parties in its judgements. Rather, its sphere of effectiveness is limited to ensuring that lower courts uniformly observe the legal system and the principles of that system. The link between these courts is not legal or formal, but moral and indirect, and only properly emerges by way of appeal for cassation due to infringement of case law doctrine. In other words, the unsuitable decisions of judges can only, at most, lead to their "revocation" in the event that the decision is challenged.

The case law of the Supreme Court can only draw up the written law behind its decisions by way of reports to the Codification Commission, and, if the Commission accepts the proposed change and the change is approved by the legislative assembly, it becomes legislation, thereby becoming obligatory at the same time. In the meantime, its status is that of mere "authority". But until the preparative work for legislation is produced, the judgements of the Supreme Court do not create general rules that it is obligatory to observe. At most, they complement, explain, integrate, adapt and configure those general rules. The interpretation of the judge as expressed in case law can vary from literal to "declarative" interpretation, the proofreader or – in the extreme case – annulment, *interpretatio abrogans*, not applying a rule, suspending its application, which may amount to tacit repeal.

3.2.4. Inclination of Legislation in Principle towards Permanence, Stability and Coherence compared with Freedom to Vary Doctrine and Contradiction in Case Law

For the existence of a source of law – legislation, custom, or general principle of law – a certain inclination towards permanence and stability over time is often required. Although all that is human is temporary and will fade, and while there is no legal rule that has lasted or will last indefinitely, the principle of inclination towards permanence exists as much in the case of custom – where usage, or some external element, must be of foreseeable continuity – as in that of legislation. The exceptions are temporary and transitory laws, which have a fixed period of enforceability prior to being passed.

In contrast, as we will see when considering changes in case law, the Supreme Court can change case law in spite of its function being to unify doctrine. This is because, as it is not a source of law, it is not legally binding. This change in case law – which must be justified and not arbitrary – is not only possible but even advisable, given that to err is human and wisdom lies in rectifying mistakes. The evolution of law and its continuing adaptation to the changing circumstances of life, the avoidance of ideological lags and stagnation characteristic of legal rules when they are set in stone in Codes and Constitutions, are only possible in this manner.

Therefore, the case law of the Supreme Court is not a source of law since it can be varied, and, if it were truly a source of law, it would enjoy stability. Not even the Supreme Court can dictate rules of general character. Neither can it govern itself – it can never be bound by its own decisions. And this seems for the best. As it is not tied by its own, inevitable, errors, it is capable of making all the rectifications that prudence may advise.

It is said that the case law of the Supreme Court has a contradictory and changing mood, which stands in the way of it being a source of law. But this may, in a sense, be criticized. The same could be said of legislation, which can also change itself via the mechanism of repeal, or of custom, which can fall into disuse – *desuetude* – and nor legislation nor custom stop being direct sources of law as a result.

3.2.5. The Presumption of *Res Judicata* Compared with the Merely Exemplary Value of Case Law for all Cases Comparable with the One at Issue

The force of *res judicata* only applies to firm judgements which cannot be challenged. Only those judgements create law, but it is an *inter partes* law, between those involved in the litigation and not susceptible to challenge by those parties. The formal exception of *res judicata* prevents the grounds of an already resolved issue being considered again, as it cannot be resolved twice – *ne bis in idem*. On the other hand, the potential value of case law involves examining the grounds of a case, and appreciating whether it ought to be resolved in the same manner or if, in contrast, a different judgement is justified. This process bears no relation to the formal exception of *res judicata*.

It has been stated that if the judgement handed down in one case could be used in another, it would be an infringement of the rule that the presumption of *res judicata* can only take effect in another trial where the two cases coincide absolutely perfectly.

The relative value of *res judicata* has nothing to do with the exemplary value that case law offers for all comparable cases. The *res judicata* exception prevents a consideration of the basis of an already resolved case, while case law involves considering the basis of a case and evaluating whether it should be resolved in the same way as the precedent, or in a different manner.

In one situation – *res judicata* – the cases are identical, and there is no consideration of the basis of the subject; in the other – case law – the cases are similar, in terms of the *ratio*, and the basis is indeed considered: the new case is resolved.

3.2.6. The Creation of Objective Law by Legislation Compared with the Award of Subjective Rights by Case Law

We have previously argued that the principle of separation of powers, among others, prevents the judge handing down general rules, or objective law. What the judge will do is modulate legal relationships, granting subjective rights to one party and legal obligations to the other. We should not forget the double aspect of law – as *norma agendi*, objective law, and as *facultas agendi*, subjective rights. Subjective rights derive from objective law. The judge, when adjudicating upon the rights, is in reality bringing to fruition objective justice, distributing it among specific subjects, but not properly creating anything that was not in some form previously contained within legal rules, within objective law.

3.2.7. The Requirements of Legal Certainty

Legal certainty is another of the factors leading to the denial of case law of the Supreme Court being a source of law, given that legal certainty requires a certain permanence and stability which is characteristic of legislation, custom and general principles of law. This is only the case in a very limited sense when considering the case law of the Supreme Court, due to the possibility of changing that case law. Supreme Court case law is essentially mutable, dynamic and variable. It adapts well to change, but requires a certain maturity to create legal certainty and security – neither of which the law can do without. Law without order, without being fixed, does not work. The greatest injustice is disorder. At the root of this is the fear that the decisions of the judge derive from arbitrariness, the freedom in licentiousness. If in a specific case these requirements of security and certainty were to conflict with the principle of justice, "the judge must bow down silently before the rules of legislation" – he cannot consciously attack or violate legislation, or become a legislator. The judge is not a "knight errant" in search of the quixotic ideals of beauty and justice. Like Sancho Panza, the judge must remain tied to reality – in this case, to legislation. The judge must not display immobility and excessive automatism in the application of legal rules. But at the same time, it must not be forgotten that the judge is acting as a representative of the judicial power, independently, only subject to legislation and not to personal status, prejudices or private interests.

3.2.8. The Originating Value of Legislation Compared with the Borrowing Nature of Case Law

Doctrine of a sociological nature, particularly from France, indicates that case law is a sociological phenomenon: it is living law. The result of this is an affirmation, at least in Continental systems, that case law lives off other things, that it does not provide anything new or independent – but it is just as much an affirmation that case law takes from the other norms considered to be direct sources.

3.2.9. The Creative Nature of Legislation Compared with the Function of Mere Interpretation, Application and Integration of Case Law

Case law decisions have an essentially executive and declarative nature. They are limited to interpreting and applying law which already exists – though in truth, the integrative and, to an extent, creative roles of case law are ever more recognized, even if this creative role can never be spoken of as being originative or unlimited. It does not appear that the power to create legal rules rests in the courts. It is more the case that they apply existing legal rules, although there may be a certain "bonus" of originality. If the judges handing down case law were strictly subject to legislation, the law would stagnate as a result.

Sources create law. Case law interprets and applies what has already been created. *An interpretation can always come from a rule, but a rule can never come from an interpretation.* Case law also applies rules to real-life situations, but the idea is to apply the essence or *ratio* rather than the letter. It nonetheless plays an integrative role in the legal system, and, by way of appeal for cassation, it undertakes a "rectification" task in the production of law. The purpose of cassation is not only the defence of objective written law, but equally the achievement of legal unity and of case law interpretation – which constitutes its loftiest aim.

3.3. *Case Law and Equity*

Equity's function as the creator of law concerns the sources of law.[155] It is a matter over which opinions may clash, in part because the question varies according to each positive legal system, and in part because the expression "sources of law" is vague and equivocal.

In Spanish law, the creative function belongs to three material powers, via three sources or formal channels. These are: 1) Parliament, the House or Legislative Assemblies; 2) The People; 3) Judicial Power. The first, both national and regional, create legislation in a reflexive, written fashion. The second create spontaneous oral law via custom. The third, judicial law is the application of law, by way of which iusnaturalist or positivist general principles of law arise.

There is little more. Case law is not "formally" considered a source of law in the current Spanish legal system. The sources are set out in article 1 of the Preliminary Title of the Civil Code, after its reform of 31 May 1974. Nevertheless, it is true that, *de facto*, case law of the Constitutional Court plays a role as a source of law – or, at least, something very similar. To the case law of this Court – and, in fact, that of the Supreme Court – we would apply the aphorism "the law reigns, but precedent governs". On the other hand, looking at other legal systems, distinct from the Continental kind, we can see the enormous role precedent may play as an authentic, formal source of law. With Anglosaxon precedent, it becomes the most important source of law.

155 See, on the subject, M. J. FALCÓN Y TELLA, *Equidad, Derecho y Justicia*, Preface by J. IGARTUA SALAVERRÍA, Madrid, Editorial Universitaria Ramón Areces, 2005. Reviews: – *Foro. Revista de Ciencias Jurídicas y Sociales. Nueva Época*, Facultad de Derecho, Universidad Complutense de Madrid, 1, 2005, pp. 375-376. – *Otrosí. Publicación informativa del Colegio de Abogados de Madrid*, January 2006, p. 72. – T. GARCÍA-BERRIO HERNÁNDEZ, in *Foro. Revista de Ciencias Jurídicas y Sociales. Nueva Época*, Facultad de Derecho, Universidad Complutense de Madrid, 2, 2005, pp. 468-472. – J. M. CARABANTE MUNTADA, in *Revista de Estudios Políticos*, Nueva época, 133, July/September 2006, pp. 263-265. – I. RUIZ-GALLARDÓN, in *Anuario de Derechos Humanos, Nueva Época, 25 Aniversario*, Instituto de Derechos Humanos, Facultad de Derecho, Universidad Complutense de Madrid, 7, 2006, pp. 478-489. – J. M. CARABANTE MUNTADA, in *Persona y Derecho*, 55, 2006, pp. 518-521. Translation into English by P. MUCKLEY, *Equity and Law*, Boston – Leiden, Martinus Nijhoff , 2008.

This brief introduction to case law in the Spanish legal system is of interest, since equity in its typical form – as a legal argument applied in the argumentation of judges and Courts– results in the creation of "judicial maxims". Here, the judge tries to apply a rule in a just spirit, to provide an equitable solution to a real case, a case where the strict application of the law would give rise to injustice. That is, what stems from the play of equity is a judgement which in most cases would, in the end, be an "improper", *"sui generis"* or indirect source of material – though not formal – law. This occurs when the judgement is issued by a hierarchically superior court (the Supreme Court, the Constitutional Court, or the Regional Higher Courts of Justice, in their respective territories, and with their respective powers), is supported by at least one other judgement, and has an identical *ratio decidendi* in the finding. This is when a judgement constitutes case law. Even then, it is not a proper source of formal law.

Still, does equity then create nothing? In equity, there is creation. How could there not be if the judge makes a special, particular application of equity to law, beyond the letter of the law, though guided by the *mens legislatoris* – what the legislator would have wanted had he known of the specific case to which the rule was going to be applied? The judge thereby transcends the *mens legis,* even if he does not betray the essence, the *ratio* or spirit of the rule. Every choice made by a judge implies for the choice of a specific interpretation and a certain, specific application, which presupposes the discarding of other possible solutions. Further, as concerns interpretation in the strong sense, the judge does not limit himself to executing the law, but, rather, like the soloist or the orchestra's conductor, he confers his own particular vision of things as he reads the score—in this case, the text.

This is unquestionable: there is creation in equity. That creation, however, is not the creation of law, the decision maxim not even being an authentic, "formal" source of law when it constitutes case law of the Supreme Court or of the Constitutional Court. Thus, we arrive at a triple conclusion as to the possible creative function of equity in law:

1. There is creation in equity, via an interpretation-application-integration of the law, taking interpretation in the strong sense. This goes beyond the *corpus* of the rule to the *mens legis,* delving into the law's *anima* and the *mens legislatoris.*
2. The result or product of the application of equity is a decision maxim, or legal judgement which, when all necessary requirements are fulfilled, will count as case law.
3. At this time, case law in Spain is not a formal *de lege data* source of law. Though, *de facto,* its role in many cases is very similar to that of

> a true source, it can at most be considered an indirect or improper source. In our view, the question is clear in this regard, and furthermore, an exhaustive analysis would go beyond the subject of equity, which is what concerns us here, instead entering into that other question of whether case law does or does not constitute a source of law. Much has been written about this issue.[156]

What should be asked here is the question of whether equity, insofar as it implies a certain creation, might on its own be a source of law, without recourse to the case law to which it has ties. The value of certain anti-formalist trends of thought lies precisely in their having widened the sphere of traditional sources of law to take in other possible methods. So, to cite some examples, we might consider scholars' discussions on the role of other mechanisms, like analogy (especially its *analogia iuris* aspect), jurisprudence or contracts. There have even been times when a favourable view has been taken regarding equity being a source of law. Examples include the jurisprudence of the *prudents* in Rome – *iurisprudentia* or Roman legal science – or of the Glossators and Post-glossators, during the Middle Ages, both having important historical value. The same happened with analogy, which took on a very important role in the Historical School of Law and with the German Pandectists. As regards the remainder, nothing would necessarily prevent similar trends occurring in the future.

In our view, the correct thing to do is to bring together positivism and legalism to create a legal dogmatic investigation – using theory, abstract reasoning, and substance – informed by a more jurisprudential analysis. This is necessary because the role of a reflection concerning theory of law, from a legal philosophy perspective, is to tackle problems through general and abstract theory without anchoring them (at least, not overly or exclusively) to specific constraints of time and space. It does not deal with any specific positive law or any specific legal system, as would civil law or any other area of law approaching legal problems from a positivist perspective. Again, we see the clear interdisciplinary nature of the subject of equity, a true *mare magnum* of issues, where the most diverse approaches must be reconciled.

156 M. J. FALCÓN Y TELLA: *Lecciones de Teoría del Derecho,* Madrid, Servicio de Publicaciones, Facultad de Derecho, Universidad Complutense de Madrid, 1rst. ed. 2001, 2nd. ed. 2003, 3rd. ed. 2006, 4th. ed. 2009, p. 131 of the 3rd. ed.

Furthermore, and leaving aside the theme of equity's contribution to the creation of law via judicial maxims when these constitute case law, the writer would argue that equity also helps in legal production when judicial maxims do not constitute case law. This is because, simply in its function of applying pre-established law to specific cases, equity adapts itself to those cases and individualizes them, or softens the law for these cases and thereby creating an exception to strict law. It then gives rise to what are called individual rules, that is, those rules not addressed to the people as a whole but designed for a specific subject. This is the case with simple judgements which, though they do not go on to create case law, do have *inter partes* value – though not *erga omnes* value – for the issue being judged – *res iudicata*.

These judicial resolutions, the fruits of equity even if they do not qualify as case law, are truly individual rules, which some modern legal schools do consider authentic law. This is true of Kelsen's *Reine Rechtslehre*, which includes them at the bottom of the normative pyramid, the "*Stufenbau*", but at least within the same pyramid, that, for him, comprises the legal system. It is even true of the Swiss legal system or the "egologic theory" of law of Carlos Cossio, the La Plata professor. He holds this position in contrast to traditional legal theory as represented, for example, by Francisco Suárez, who maintains that generality is an essential and inexorable characteristic of all legal precepts.

Further, for those who follow Ronald Dworkin's line – opposing his teacher, H. L. A. Hart – the legal system is not the mere sum of primary and secondary rules, since there also exist "legal policies", "legal standards", "directives", "*Erfahrungssätze*", "maxims of experience", "valve concepts" or "elastic concepts". Here, the panorama of sources becomes much more complete.

In summary, as José Castán Tobeñas has already noted, there is in our legal systems something we might call legal "reconstruction", which is the role of judges. This sits together with the originative and "creative" or "constructive" function of positive law by way of legislation and the formal sources. Neither the one nor the other should be ignored.[157]

Not even *contra legem* equity can make us consider equity a source of law. *Contra legem* equity is the most radical form of equity, where the judgement is not limited to interpreting the law in accordance with the spirit (this being *secundum legem* equity), but goes on to resolve the case

157 J. CASTÁN TOBEÑAS, *La formulación judicial del Derecho…*, *op. cit.*, pp. 7-26, esp. p. 26. See also pp. 144-146.

through his "best knowledge and understanding", without the help of any positive rule, and not only in a vacuum (supplementary equity or *praeter legem* equity), which would not be so serious, but even going against the rule (derogatory or *contra legem* equity, seldom admissible). This is so because, as Lacruz Berdejo states, the judge here disregards sources – and he himself is not a source – so no trace is left which might serve in any case to act as precedent or hold authority for later judges. It should further be noted that *contra legem* equity is not a typical instance in the cases of equity considered here. Hence, we might assert that, neither as "*ius adiuvandi*", "*ius suplendi*", nor "*ius corrigendi*" is equity a source of law.[158]

Equity serves as a guide. It is not a norm but a directive. It is the lense through which we view the problem. The spectacles are not the eye – the vision – and nor are they the reality seen through them. A blind man would see nothing through spectacles. A table cannot appear as a tree no matter how many types of glasses and gradations are tried out. What spectacles can do is help us gain in precision and visual acuity, correct our myopia or visual defects – with their aid, we can focus on what would otherwise be too blurred. The same is true of an overly strict conformity to general, abstract justice. Equity lets us see the situation more clearly. There are no rules of equity. What appear to be such are other sources of law: a law which must be equitably interpreted for the specific case, a general principle of law, and the like. Still, equity is neither the law nor the general principle, though it does take both into account.[159] Equity represents the spectacles allowing us to focus on the object – the specific, real case requiring legal regulation – through which our eyesight passes – legislation, or another source of law to be applied.

We might draw out another conclusion which sums up the foregoing: equity is not a source so far as case law is concerned, since it is not case law; and equity is not a source in itself. Such a conclusion amounts to: *equity is not a source even though it manages sources* – laws, customs

158 See, J. L. DE LOS MOZOS, "La equidad", in *Estudios de Derecho Internacional Público y Privado*, I, Oviedo, 1970, p. 163. C. M. ENTRENA KLETT, *La equidad y el arte de juzgar*, Pamplona, Aranzadi, 1979, 2nd. ed., 1990, pp. 60-63.

159 J. L. LACRUZ BERDEJO (*et al.*), *Elementos de Derecho Civil, T.I, Parte General*, Madrid, Dykinson, 1998, pp. 70 and 72. See also A. SQUELLA and A. GONZÁLEZ, *Dos concepciones de la equidad*, Valparaíso, EDEVAL, 1981, pp. 19-21.

or general principles of law. The source, as the name indicates, is what creates, what originates, or gives life to, something which did not exist before. The process of application-interpretation of an already existing source is not itself a source. It is like a lift which goes up and down, bearing within it people and goods – these being in this case legislation, customs, general principles of law. When the lift goes down – when abstract justice is applied to the specific case – it is bearing a load. It did not create the load, it merely transports it, changing the load's position. The load has been created by someone – a person, another human being, or by something which made it. It is this person or thing which is the true source. Equity is the process which moves something from a greater to a lesser level of generalization, the something being the cargo in movement.

In the same way as we say that legislation, custom and general legal principles are sources of law, we also say that the source of law is not equity. Sources are: a result of a parliamentary process of development – legislation –; a social reiteration – custom –; or positivization – general principles of law –. The source, however, is the result, and not the process used to arrive at it. The interpretation-application process applied to legal rules is not the source – the equitably interpreted and applied legal rule is.

Another possibility,[160] both tentative and threatening – and doomed to fail too, in all probability – of ascribing to equity the characteristic of a source, might be to see equity as such in those cases where *the law refers to equity* – in a general way. This is unlikely, since, as we have already had occasion to point out, at least in Spanish law, no such reference is made. This is the same in article 1 of the Spanish Civil Code and in any other legal rule to which the character of a source of law is attributed. What appears perhaps easier, and does occur in Spanish law – when the law refers to equity in specific articles, with respect to specific matters – is where equity passes from being "well regarded" or considered as having "legal authorization" to being a source – or at least close to being one.

This, however, is at the very least debatable. It might be better characterised a situation where a legal rule is "re-sent" to equity, and this remission or "re-sending" is a recognized, foreseen process included in the legal system. It is in this sense not so much a source of law as a way of completing a rule which, in and of itself, is not complete or autonomous, but requires for completion support from that process to which it has been re-sent. The same happens with legal definitions or restrictive rules.

160 J. CASTÁN TOBEÑAS, *La idea de equidad…*, *op. cit.*, pp. 58-60.

The law would be like a limping man without his crutch or a deaf man without his hearing-aid. These devices help him to lead a normal life, but his life itself exists before these things. He might even be able to go on without them, though his life would then be poorer in terms of movement or auditory experience. This is because – as in the case of the law being sent back to equity – the nature of the originating source should be reserved for the law sent back, and not for the equity to which it is sent. Equity in itself, with no rule to which it may be applied, without legislation, would be the same as the crutch or the orthopaedic leg without the person who needs it. It would, in short, be useless. No matter how much a disabled person may say these aids have given him back his quality of life, and no matter how many times the law authorizes equity, the aids remain complementary in the first instance, as with the process of remission or re-sending to equity in the second.

Complementing is one thing; *completing* is another. A complement is like an accessory – a belt, some gloves. Something must already be in existence to be complemented. It takes something not yet whole, not yet finished, to be completed. Whether "completing" represents the best account of equity's role in the legal system is much debated. This debate occurred, for instance, in the preparatory works leading up to the definitive draft of article 1 of the Preliminary Title of the Spanish Civil Code in the Reform of 31 May 1974. The term would have given rise to the question of whether equity is an authentic source of law. It was ultimately decided that the expression "complement" would be better used. Scholars interpreted this as an unequivocal sign of the existence in the legislator of a will to take away from equity its character as a source of law. Similarly, a law remitted to equity seeks a complement through such a remission, especially at the legal application phase when the law is applied to the specific case. The law already existed in a complete state before the equity, precisely as the fruit of an earlier stage, that of the law's creation by Parliament.

It is a characteristic of equity that it offers a certain margin of freedom to the judge, a relatively broad discretional power. But it never permits this power to become arbitrary. The judge's arbitration must never be capricious or irrational, a situation which would allow him to base his decisions on his personal feelings or on the legislator's utopian ideals. The judge is not a free and absolute arbiter, but an arbiter bound by the law.

There are various restrictions on judicial freedom when a judge uses equity. On the one side, he must take into account the *circumstances of the case* to be decided. These must be decided and delineate the conditions for the decision, from the point of view of the facts. It is not so much a matter of deduction from the general rule, as it is a kind of induction from observing the specific case. Empiricism takes over the first plane. It is essential to consider the interests at stake in depth, and to take into account an average model of behaviour suitable for resolving the case. This is clearly seen in the American model of the judge. For him to complete his legal investigative work, a margin of freedom must be provided. This margin must not be so wide as to allow the judge to go beyond the bounds of legal certainty, nor must his decision give rise to later problems as it might be feared that contradictory, inharmonious, vitiated, subjectivism would create. Hence, as K. N. Llewellyn states, the law is what those who are in charge of its application do, and not what they say they do, nor what the books say they should do. So one must tread carefully, moving along the knife's edge: judges, for one part, must seek out the most just, and apt solution for the specific case, yet at the same time they must respect the law and provide grounds for their findings.[161]

In the distinction between discretional and arbitrary power, the practical issue which casts a shadow is the distrust of the judge as a human and the consequent need to limit his freedom of action to a minimum. This, in turn, relates to the question of the separation between the judge as real person and the judge as legal institution – a servant of the State, a mere automaton of his office. There inevitably exists the danger that the judge will interpret legal rules in some personal fashion, erring in their application to some specific case. However, holding this vision of the person and function of the judge might create an overly pessimistic perspective. It would concentrate too much on the negative aspects of the scene, making us forget the other positive points – for these certainly do exist.

Though the power of the judge is discretional, it is subject to certain limits. These derive from the social function he performs. Equitable justice links this social function directly to the person of the judge and has no need of legal syllogistic "mediation". The judge is not, as Montesquieu claimed, the mere mouthpiece of the law, pronouncing the words of the law in a logical-syllogistic deduction and acting formally and almost automatically. In law, there exists certain subjectivity and there is an impossibility of total, formal verifiability where equity's workings are concerned. We must never forget that, when employing equity, we are dealing with a strict legal judgement – since the law reverts to equity and,

161 J. CASTÁN TOBEÑAS, *La formulación..., op. cit.*, pp. 108-109, 151, 152-154 and 157-158.

in turn, equity constantly sends back laws – so we should never equate discretional power with arbitrary power, nor with "free law". Further, the use of equity must lead back to law, from which it draws its binding force and upon which it stands when coming into play.

The judge's subjective judgement finds both inner and outer limits. The internal limits derive from the internal logic of the argumentative process, which must ensure the equitable judgement is verifiable. External restrictions come from a series of directives that must be followed, such as those which are delineated by *constitutional rules.* These once again reveal the will of the legislator, and prevent the judge issuing his own personal or arbitrary judgements. The judge has the opportunity to put the spirit of the Constitution into practice and to make it operative. This should be the ordinary and not the extraordinary state of affairs, according to the extent that the Constitution itself has a programmatic reach, which – to a greater or lesser degree, directly or indirectly, depending on the type of legal system – binds the judge when applying the law.

The argument often advanced against the application of judicial equity which claims it to be an exercise of arbitrary judicial power does not really take into consideration the law's certainty, imposed as an idealist dogma by the Constitutionalist and Codificatory movements. Taken to an extreme, the dogma would result in a restrictive vision of reality. A more social and less individualist vision shows that trust in the law is not an absolute, nor a secure bulwark for freedom, and still less for equality, unless certain guarantees exist ensuring that the specific realities of life will be taken into account. Such realities change at an infinitely greater rhythm than does the law. Equity takes charge of this task, along with its main guardian, the judge, always watching over to ensure a system of guarantees regarding the constitutional rules of the democratic game. When carrying out its work, the legal organ should not pursue its own abstract ideal of justice, like a fabled knight seeking truth and beauty, nor should it use discretional power in any individualistic way, transforming it into arbitrary power. Neither should the judge convert himself into some sort of technician or mechanic who, when applying law, believes he should limit himself to considering only what is expressed in law. The judge, when using equity, will be bound by constitutional guidelines which, even if they do not define the grounds of equitable justice, do mark out the legal limitations of his task when he goes beyond them. They act, in brief, as a constant inspiration. The judge in his work must also make use of a series of qualities, such as proportion, balance, and harmony.[162]

Therefore, rather than speaking of judicial will, we should speak of the will of equity, in the manner understood when it was more closely tied to the Western Christian tradition. Equity is a form of justice, while arbitrariness is never an instrument capable of realizing justice. Equity is not arbitrary, but is rather arbitrating. An exception might come about in the case of so-called "cerebral" equity. There, as in "fitting laws", of which the Spanish writers of the Golden Age spoke, an arbitrary and capricious use is made of equity.

3.4. *Analogy and Resultant Maxims of Decision*

We should initially point to Greece, since it was there that the term "analogy" first appeared, although the Greek construction of analogy has more of a philosophical nature, in the metaphysical and mathematical sense. Here one may speak of *logos analogante* in order to designate that which, translated to Latin, is *ratio*. The analogical procedure in Greece was not called "analogy," but "procedure by similarity." Perhaps the finest indicator of analogy in Greece would be the Aristotelian concept of "paradigm," but in reality this construction is nothing more than the climax of an evolution already begun by Aristotle's predecessors, Socrates and Plato. These thinkers speak of analogy as the combination of induction and syllogism or deduction, but a historic evolution takes place according to whether emphasis is placed on the first (Socrates), on both (Plato) or on the second (Aristotle).

In the Middle Ages, with the Glossators and especially with the Post-Glossators or Commentators, a clear legal concept of analogy appeared through the creation of the concept of *ratio* (conceived as *ratio legis*), a concept of analogy which, although under terms which were still diverse (*a simile, a pari* or *a comparatis* arguments), was already identical to the current one from a logical perspective. On the other hand, outside of the strict legal framework, analogy had a metaphysical and teleological scope in the Middle Ages, through the already-mentioned construction of the "analogy of entity."

With the Renaissance, as from the mid-16th century, the expression or term "analogy" begins to appear in Europe, understood in the

162 F. GAZZONI, *Equità e autonomia privata,* Milano, Giuffrè, 1970, pp. 162-183 and 317-318.

interpretatio analogica sense as the elimination of the ability for a law to contradict another within a body of laws, coordinating the different rules by way of comparison. This was the stage at which the founding axiom of analogy was coined and popularised: "*ubi eadem ratio, ibi eadem iuris dispositio*" (where there is identity of reason, there must be the same regulation).

The later evolution of analogy is marked by its study principally on the cognitive plane, as a means of probable knowledge particularly linked to the rationalist trend, of primacy of reason, though this is also studied as "analogy of experience" in Empiricism and Kant. In the legal aspect, which is the more interesting for us, this is a decisive stage in the configuration of the modern and current concept of analogy, as well as the definitive consolidation of the term. This advance occurred, above all, thanks to the contributions of the Historic School of Law and the Pandectists, which made a qualitative leap possible with regards to analogy, introducing the idea that all laws are united in a logical system which completes itself with its systemic force. From there arose the expression *analogia iuris* as the means for filling in the gaps of the law, and as something different from *analogia legis*, a term which designates analogy by excellence. In turn, the role of the judge in interpretation of law becomes ever stronger.

The same complexity and superimposition of planes can be appreciated with respect to the function of the analogical argument. This is a controversial subject. In reality, it deals with a verbal question, wherein the different writers refer to different concepts using the same expression and, vice versa, to the same idea using different expressions. In our judgement, a series of functions co-exist, rather than oppose each other, in this matter. Worth highlighting here are the applicative function (deductive or syllogistic, in its "indirect" aspect, in applying the legal consequences of a rule to a case similar to that established for the rule), interpretative function (as inherent to all application) and creative function.

With respect to this last, the much-debated creative function, the writer is in favour of this, but with clarifications – analogy can be somewhat creative (of the *ratio legis*) by way of "logical principle", which underpins the rule, but through a process of induction, generalisation, abstraction and selection of essential points is configured as a separate entity, with a reach separate to that of analogy, different from the *de facto* assumption and the legal consequence.

Notwithstanding the above, this would be a *sui generis* creation, both due to the origin, since it relies on and is supported by the rule (in this sense, it is a derived creation, neither originating nor free), and to the result of the analogy, which is a decision maxim of the judge (and not a true legal rule). All it can give rise to is case law, which in Spanish law only "complements" the legal system as discussed. This hinders the argument that analogy is a source of law.

The assertions just made are valid for the *analogia legis*, or legislative analogy, this being the prevailing analogy in our times. Clarification is necessary with respect to the *analogia iuris*. The *analogia iuris* may be defined as the *"appeal to non-express and positive general principles of law."* In this context, instead of *ratio legis*, we have authentic general principles of law. There are two differences between analogy in its *analogia iuris* aspect and general principles of law. First, the first analogy is the recourse to the general principles of law, the process of its creation and application – the analogy is like a legal "service lift," while the principles represent the cargo, or the person in the lift. Second, the *analogia iuris* does not refer to all the general principles of law, but only to those which are positive and non-express. Natural principles and express positive principles are therefore excluded.

In *analogia iuris*, we also encounter the inductive/deductive double phase, as seen previously. In the inductive phase, there is also creation – more so than in *analogia legis*, since a real principle of law is created, a true general principle of law, with its own identity beyond the norm. Nevertheless, it remains debatable whether this would constitute a source of law. The source is not the *analogia iuris*, as a process, but the general principle of law which is created. The source is that which "is" law, not the "procedure" which creates law – as, in statute law, the source is the product obtained and not the legislative activity necessary for its production. At the deductive stage, in the *analogia iuris* the principle created would be applied to an unregulated case which would be subsumed therein, resulting in the production of a simple decision maxim: a judgement, but not a genuine legal rule.

The distinct theoretical configuration of the *analogia legis* and the *analogia iuris* means they can be found in different parts of the legal system: the first in article 4.1 of the Preliminary Title of the Civil Code, within Chapter II, concerning the application of legal norms; the second in article 1.4 of the same legal text, within Chapter I, referring to sources of law together with the general principles of law.

In this way, we arrive at the central requirement: the identicalness of the reason (*eadem ratio*). This would be the *ratio* as *ratio decidendi*, the reason for which a decision is made in legal argumentation. This is a *ratio* which arises in cases (the factual situation regulated by the analogous legal provision and the unregulated case) where there is similarity on a factual level. Here it may seem a contradiction to speak at the same time of similarity (as a situation partly the same and partly different) and identicalness (complete equality). But the apparent contradiction is dispelled in reality if we bear in mind that the similarity and identity are predicated of different entities: the cases and the reason, respectively. Even so, it is worth asking how identical reason may be superimposed onto the similarity of cases. The answer is simple: the cases are similar, or in other words, with certain specific points and certain points in common. What occurs is that the common points, the identical ones, are the essential ones – those which establish the *ratio* or essence. Therefore, similarity arises in terms of the entirety of the points of the case (the facts), and identicalness in the essential points (the reason). For example, if there is a notice at a train station which prohibits getting on the train with dogs, by analogy, getting on with bears would be likewise prohibited. A dog and a bear are circumstances which are only similar (since they possess characteristics which distinguish them with regards to size, appearance, etc.) but in the *raison d'être* of the prohibition, both are identical (both are animals which could cause damage). In this way, we see how the identicalness of reason is qualitatively different from similarity of cases, but the two remain perfectly compatible.

3.5. The Consideration of Case Law as an Improper, Material Source or Source of Knowledge of Law: "Legislation Reigns and Case Law Governs"

To determine the value of case law – the aim of this work – and to coherently answer the question of whether it can be considered a source of law in Continental systems such as the Spanish one, the definition we adopt of "source" needs to be clarified. Is it material or formal – is it a sociological, realist concept citing social forces as the answer to the question of what creates law, or a formal concept pointing to formal procedures and channels as the answer to the same question? [163] Only in the first sense would it be possible to answer in the affirmative regarding case law having the status of a source.

163 See, M. J. FALCÓN Y TELLA, *Lecciones de Teoría del Derecho, op. cit.*, p. 95 from the edition of 2006. L. RODRÍGUEZ RAMOS, "Hacia una teoría de las fuentes materiales del Derecho penal", in *Anuario de Derecho Penal y Ciencias Penales*, 1981, pp. 721-737.

It is also of use here, when considering case law as a source within the Spanish legal system, to apply the distinction commonly used in theory of law between source of "production" and source of "knowledge" of law. Sources of production are those which in the strict sense create, originate or produce objective law – which make law where previously it did not exist. In contrast, sources of knowledge of law are understood, as indicated by their name, as texts, documents and other media by way of which we obtain notice of the sources of production – for example, a Code or a Constitution, which provides access to legal material. In this sense, we might consider that case law – especially that of the Spanish Supreme Court – is more a source of knowledge than of production, given that its role is more that of "derived" creation – always having a foot in legislation – than originative.[164]

De iure, the issue is fairly clear. Case law of the Supreme Court is not a source in Spanish law – neither before nor after the reform of the Preliminary Title of the Civil Code. The reasons are the following. Case law does not create rules, but is limited to interpreting and applying them, while a true source of law does create rules. Article 1.1 of the Civil Code does not list case law among the sources of the legal system, and the list provided in said article is exhaustive. The function assigned to case law in the Preliminary Title of the Civil Code is that of a "complement" to the legal system. If it were stated to "complete" the legal system, we might understand case law as a source of law, but this is not the case.

However, *de facto* the case law of the Supreme Court is very important. It is said that the law reigns and case law governs, and it has even been argued on occasion that the case law of the Supreme Court, while not a source in the formal sense, is indeed a "material", "indirect", "secondary" or "improper" source, with an orientative and authoritative interpretative value, though not binding and without general effect but limited to the litigants in question. Case law does not bind lower courts, which depend only upon legislation. Neither does it bind itself, given that the Supreme Court can change case law, abandon a generally established opinion and adopt another (and another, and so on). Nevertheless, in the context of change of case law, the Constitutional Court – starting from the recognition of the principle of equality in the Spanish Constitution – has developed a doctrine which, for some, implies the instalment of said constitutional justice as an authentic precedent and source of law. This

164 See, M. J. FALCÓN Y TELLA, *Lecciones de Teoría del Derecho, op. cit.* pp. 93-94 from the edition of 2006.

relates to the requirement that a particular judicial organ cannot amend the meaning of its decisions without providing sufficient and reasonable justification for that amendment.

3.6. The "Sources-Argument" Theory

Another solution to the question of whether or not Continental case law is in fact a source of law is proposed by Leonor Moral Soriano in her work "The Judicial Precedent" (*El precedente judicial*), in which she speaks of "argument sources". According to this idea, we should not concern ourselves with considering whether case law is one of the "designated" formal sources of law in a legal system, but instead we should adopt a different concept of the source: the "argument source". This construction would consider all material that can, should or must be used in the resolution of legal disputes to have the character of a source of law. In the context of this concept, arguments used to argue or prove a case are considered sources of law.[165] In the instant book, we have already referred to analogy and equity as being types of legal arguments. In the present section, we will refer to other lines of argument which also support the consideration of Continental case law as a source of law (in the meaning given to the expression by Leonor Moral Soriano). These are the following:[166]

165 See, J. HABERMAS, *Faktizität und Geltung. Beiträge zur Diskurstheorie des Rechts und des demokratischen Rechtsstaats*, Frankfurt am Main, Suhrkamp, 1992. *Id*, *Justification and Application. Remarks on Discourse Ethic*, translation by C. CRONIN, Cambridge, Polity Press, 1993. *Id*, *Between Facts and Norms*, translation by W. REHG, Cambridge – Massachusetts, The MIT Press, 1996.

166 L. MORAL SORIANO, *El precedente judicial*, *op. cit.*, pp. 10, 17, 19-20 and 125-154. See also, on the subject, R. ALEXY, "Justification and Application of Norms", in *Ratio Juris*, 6, 1993, pp. 155-170. *Id*, *Teoría de la argumentación juridica*, translation into Spanish by M. ATIENZA and I. ESPEJO, Madrid, 1997. M. ATIENZA RODRÍGUEZ, *Las razones del Derecho. Teorías de la argumentación jurídica*, Madrid, Centro de Estudios Constitucionales, 1991. M. GASCÓN ABELLÁN, *La técnica del precedente y la argumentación racional*, Madrid, Tecnos, 1993. N. MACCORMICK, *Legal Reasoning and Legal Theory*, Oxford, Clarendon Press, 1978. *Id*, "Why Cases Have Rationes and What These Are", in L. GOLDSTEIN (ed.), *Precedent in Law*, Oxford, Clarendon Press, 1987, pp. 155-182. *Id*, *Interpreting Precedent: A Comparative Study*, R. S. SUMMERS (ed.), Darmouth, 1997. N. MACCORMICK – R. SUMMERS (eds.), *Interpreting Precedents. A Comparative Study*, Dartmouth, Ashgat, 1997. G. RODRÍGUEZ MOUROLLO, *Aplicación judicial*

- The *ab exemplo* argument, in accordance with which examples offer rational support for particular decisions.
- The "authority" argument, according to which the authority of previous decisions should be respected – even more so when those decisions were made by superior judicial bodies.
- The "principle of justice", which argues that it is appropriate to make similar decisions in similar cases, and therefore that dissention from precedent must be justified.

3.6.1. The *Ab Exemplo* Argument

According to this argument, the meaning given to a stated regulation or rule is the same as that previously attributed to the rule, purely by virtue of this prior attribution. Judicial precedent has its basic, essential foundations in this premise. Judgements offer examples, guidance, standards or opinions regarding interpretation of law, via *ratio decidendi*. That is to say, judicial decisions assist from the perspective of argument – of legal reasoning – and not because they are recognized as a formal source of law. In this manner – and, given the universality of logic, in contrast to formal sources, which may vary from one legal system to another – they provide a valid model for any legal system to follow.

3.6.2. The Authority Argument

Judicial decisions carry the authority accorded to the judge or tribunal from which they come. But in Continental systems, more than the power to bind, judges possess influence in terms of their decisions being followed by other judges. In these systems, there would not be a rigid requirement to follow precedent, given the principle of judicial independence and that, to hold significance, authority must be accepted and recognized. Furthermore, the authority argument does not exclude other arguments, such as that of applying rational logic when handing down judgements.

In terms of the hierarchical position of the judge creating the precedent and the judge who may follow that precedent, it is worth distinguishing between:

1. "Vertical" precedents, which consist of following decisions made by superior judicial bodies who are normally better prepared in terms of available resources – here, annulment by the Supreme Court stands

del Derecho y lógica de la argumentación jurídica, Madrid, Ed. Cuadernos Civitas, 1988.

out – and therefore guarantee the predictability and uniformity of judicial decisions, contributing to unity in the application of the law.

2. "Horizontal" precedents, which refer to a "homologous" judicial body which is not hierarchically inferior. Here, more than setting a "precedent" in the strict sense, previous decisions serve an illustrative purpose.
3. "Auto-precedents", which consist of a judge or court following its "own" decisions, more in accordance with the principle of universality which would require similar cases to be treated in a similar way than in recognition of any hierarchical obligation.

So, while vertical precedents are based on the principle of authority, horizontal precedents adhere to the *ab exemplo* argument and auto-precedents are linked to the principle of universality, or formal justice.

It is worth emphasizing that the concept of authority is not equivalent to that of power. Power refers to potential or real use of force to ensure orders are obeyed. Authority, on the other hand, implies a voluntary offering of obedience, as a result of the prestige or moral superiority of the person making the order.

Two practical, and distinct, models of reasoning need to be analysed: the *iuspositivista* of Joseph Raz, and the New Rhetoric of Chaïm Perelman. The latter model is distinctly deliberate and argumentative, being founded on the idea of "reasonability". The former is based on the exclusionary function of authority – the authority of a legal or moral norm excludes other reasons in which authority is absent.

According to Raz, judges have to follow two rules: one of "recognition", which indicates the norms they should apply, precedent being one of these; and the other of "discretion", to be applied in those cases where the solution according to the first rule is unclear. In this sense, as opposed to legislation, precedents are less obligatory for the judge, who can characterize them as "distinguishing" or "overruling". However, judges enjoying discretion in dubious cases does not mean they can be arbitrary in their decision-making. It is necessary to reconcile "following" of a precedent with judicial discretion.[167]

167 See, on the subject, J. RAZ, *La autoridad del Derecho. Ensayos sobre Derecho y Moral*, translation into Spanish by R. TAMAYO Y SALMORÁN, México, Universidad Nacional Autónoma de México, 1985. *Id*, *The Morality of Freedom*, Oxford, Clarendon Press, 1986. *Id*, "Authority and Justification", in J. RAZ, *Authority*, Oxford, Basil Blackwell, 1990. *Id*, *Razón práctica y*

Perelman, meanwhile, studies the "discursive arguments or techniques" which allow the "audience" to "adhere" to the thesis of an "orator", whenever the audience is convinced by that thesis. The "reasonableness" of the argument carries more weight in this process than whether the argument is logically rational in accordance with classical formal logic. Every option is possible, but the audience will only accept the most reasonable as a solution to practical conflict. If we move from this general theory of legal reasoning to judicial reasoning in particular, we see that the role of the orator falls to the "judge". But we see divergences between the forms of reasoning, which affect the very structure of the deliberations:[168]

- The judge "decides" on the law, while in the theoretical model the judge "knows" the law, and interprets it.
- The audience changes from being "universal" – in theoretical reasoning – to being "specific" – the parties, judges or superior courts, and the qualified public.
- The judge, meaning a person with "authority" to resolve, is the person who resolves legal controversy in the area of judicial reasoning. In contrast, in philosophical or theoretical reasoning, authority generally lies with the internal strength of the arguments themselves. While in philosophical reasoning the dialogue between orator and audience is favoured, judicial reasoning, as a type of legal reasoning, favours the fact of "deciding". Legal security places limits on the reasoning of the judge, these limits being temporal (dialogue cannot be indefinite, and must end with a binding decision), procedural (formal channels must be followed), and, above all, that derived from the fact that the judge is not in a position of equality, coordination and symmetry compared with the parties, but instead has authority *ex ante.*

The question arises whether judicial decisions are accepted because they are rational, or because the judge unilaterally imposes them. In short, the criteria for correction of judicial discourse will not exclusively be that of "reasonability" – "legal security" will also play a critical role. But authority – attributed in legal reasoning to legislators (in the development of

normas, translation into Spanish by J. RUÍZ MANERO, Madrid, Centro de Estudios Constitucionales, 1991.

168 See, CH. PERELMAN – L. OLBRECHTS-TYTECA, *Traité de l'argumentation. La nouvelle Rethorique,* Bruxelles, Université de Bruxelles, 1970.

rules), and judges (in the application of those rules) – is not absolute, but rather a question of degrees, being greater or smaller depending upon reasonableness. This suggests that the concept of authority is qualified by the strength of the arguments used. For the authority of the judge to be legitimately exercised, an argumentative procedure or technique must be utilised. Authority is conceived of by Perelman as one more consideration among all those the judge can use to ensure the compliance of the audience, meaning that it is impossible to independently evaluate acts and persons, *absque titulo* legitimacy and *absque modo* or *absque exercito* legitimacy. The value of precedent and case law will also depend on the merit and authority of the judge, of his persuasive force – although this raises a doubt, given that judges, as such, are in principle accorded the same legitimate authority to resolve legal disputes. This means that, *a priori*, judges have the same "competence" in discharging their judicial function. Despite this, one thing is "attributed" authority, and quite another is the authority "recognized" by the audience in relation to judges' exercise of their functions, this exercise submitted to a "posterior evaluation" regarding the reasonableness and appropriateness of their work as judges. The audience has the last word. Not all judges are equal: there are those who enjoy great prestige, just as there are those whose authority is negligible. Competence and recognition/respect are the criteria used to evaluate judges.[169]

3.6.3. The Principle of Formal Justice in Coordination with the Principle of Inertia

According to the principle of justice, the justification for following precedent is equality: identical cases should be treated identically.[170] Perelman states that, in order that justice be done, the principle of formal justice must be completed by the principle of "inertia", thanks to which it is possible to introduce changes in the treatment of parallel cases in the event that such changes are justified. Otherwise, there would be an inflexibility creating a major barrier to the evolution of law and to its adaptation to the "real" requirements of justice. We need decisions to be predictable,

169 L. MORAL SORIANO, *El precedente judicial, op. cit.*, pp. 25-73. A. PECZENIK – R. ALEXY, *Grundlagen der juristischen Argumentation*, New York, Springer Verlag, 1983. *Id*, "Sui Precedenti vincolanti", in *Ragion Pratica*, 6, 1996, pp. 35-43.

170 See, on the subject, E. ROCA TRIAS, "Jurisprudencia, precedentes y principio de igualdad", in *Revista Jurídica de Cataluña*, 4, 1986, pp. 7-40.

but we also need them to be correct and acceptable. Incorrect or unacceptable decisions must be rejected via "justified change", which consists of sustaining the uniform following of an interpretative opinion except where reasons justifying change or the abandonment of a precedent arise, in which case a new precedent must be created. This provides justification for a movement from past to future cases, explaining "new" decisions and changes in the line of case law.

The principle of formal justice refers to the "logical" or "external" aspect, to "universality". But it must be accompanied by a "moral" or "internal" aspect, one which aims for "consistency and coherence". The principle of formal justice must be both backward and forward looking. Precedent normally involves looking backward, and means that the judge must determine cases in an identical manner to that in which previous identical cases were determined. More recent is the idea of looking forward, which requires some certain coherence between the instant decision and future circumstances. Judges decide similar cases in a similar fashion to how those cases were determined in the past, and in a similar fashion to how those cases will be determined in the future.

3.6.4. Respect for Tradition

One of the fundamental elements of observance of precedent is respect for tradition, even though common philosophy may have rejected this idea. Hobbes, for example, considered that the past had no relevance and that whatever judges had decided in the past should carry no significance. From this argument, there has been a recent insistence on the necessity of a "rational" foundation for the use of precedents, avoiding the hindrances that the past and tradition may impose.

3.6.5. The Pragmatic Argument

According to the "pragmatic" argument, the justification for following precedent is found in the benefits thereby obtained: uniform application of laws, procedural economy, predictability of judicial decisions, legal security, and the prestige of judges and courts, among others.

The principle of justice and the pragmatic argument, as distinct from respect for tradition, are accepted from a philosophical perspective, given that they do not make reference to spatial-time considerations.

3.7. *The Models of Judge: Hercules, Jupiter and Hermes*

François Ost, Professor in the *Facultés Universitaires Saint-Louis* and Director of the *Académie Europëene de Théorie du Droit* in Brussels, has established a parallel between three models of judge: Hercules, Jupiter and Hermes. This metaphor is an interesting one to develop, providing as it does a demonstration of how, in each of the three conceptions, the judge has greater or lesser freedom of choice.

The Herculean system, taken from North American realist theories, particularly of Ronald Dworkin – who describes a judge that "takes rights seriously", an expression used as the title for one of Dworkin's most well-known works, which seeks to find a "correct answer" in "hard cases" – refers to a demigod judge, capable of going to exhaustive lengths to judge and ending up carrying the world on his extended arms, thereby providing a faithful reproduction of the image of a funnel – an inverted pyramid. Here, the only law is case law. As opposed to the generality of legislation, the singularity of the instant case prevails. A "dossier" replaces a Code. This "dossier" carries the entire range of specific, singular decisions and judgements of the court, as opposed to the generality and abstraction of legislation. The role of case law is absolutely fundamental in this model. The funnel evokes the prevalence of a justice inspired by the way we balance our daily, material, secular calculations. It is the theory used by the social or welfare State of the 20th Century. The Herculean model brings us back to earth. In contrast with the model of Jupiter – a man of legislation – the Herculean judge reveals himself to be a social engineer. Time here is conceived of as something discontinuous, created by sporadic – and, post-use, disposable – judicial intrusions. This is a pluralistic model.

The law of Jupiter, proffered from on high, as if from Mount Sinai, is contained in the tables of the law that are the modern Codes and Constitutions. The image here is one of a normative pyramid – *Stufenbau* – at the summit of which lies the sacred, the transcendental. The movement feeding the construction of the pyramid is always linear and unidirectional. The model of the pyramid represents the legal requirements of the liberal State of the 19th Century. Codified, general legislation is predominant in this model, reflective of an abstract conception of justice, as opposed to the idea of equitable case-specific justice. Jupiterian law fits an understanding of time oriented towards a "better" future; it fits the modern belief in the progress of History, via law, towards a possible and preferable paradigm. This is a monist model, as opposed to the pluralistic model found in the Herculean conception.

Postmodern law considers both the Herculean and the Jupiterian models to be superseded. As an alternative, it posits the characteristics of Hermes, the messenger of the Gods – the interpreter, the mediator, the spokesman. If the mountain or pyramid conveyed the majesty of Jupiter, and the pragmatic funnel that of Hercules, the image of Hermes would take the form of a network. Not so much one extreme – equity-based case law – nor the other – abstract legislation – and not even a combination of both, but instead a multitude of interrelated points. Information no longer fits into a "dossier" or a Code, but must be expressed in the form of a database. Hermes is neither transcendental in terms of legitimacy, nor immanent in terms of efficiency, but instead a combination of the two. The key characteristics of the model of Hermes would include: graduality and relativism (as opposed to dogmatism and skepticism); a circular nature (as opposed to a hierarchical structure); the abandoning of monophony in favour of polyphony without necessarily falling into the cacophony as a result – the "noise" referred to in information technology to denote the absence of meaning; the conception of law as something necessarily unfinished, always in suspense and always relaunching, like a complex game with multiple actors – the judge, the legislator, civil society, for example. As opposed to "hard" or "soft" law, the Hermes view conceives of law as flexible, porous, "liquid", fluid, interstitial and informal.

There is a link, here, to the theme of case law. In contrast with law associated with the idea of rigidity – law as hard rules – the judge instead intervenes and creates a "fluid", liquid law. We can recall the case law metaphor which compares it with the rule of lead, a flexible metal used for construction in Lesbos because it could be moulded to the intricacies of stone. Could not a comparable "liquid" rule exist if even certain metals, like mercury, display this characteristic? Is it genuinely a coincidence that the alchemists of the Middle Ages gave the name "mercury" – the Latin equivalent of the Greek "Hermes" – to this specific metal? Between order and disorder, between the letter and the spirit, the model of the judge Hermes is found, combining in variable proportions rules and chance, convention and invention, opening and closing, playing "games" with rules, such as football or chess and simply "playing" in a free and improvised form, like dressing up at carnivals or lovemaking.[171]

3.8. *Formalism and the Anti-formalist Revolt, with Particular Reference to Case Law*

With the transition from natural to positive law in philosophy, from Capitalism to Socialism in economic terms, and from the liberal State to the

171 See, F. OST, "Juge pacificateur, juge-arbitre, juge entraîneur", in *Fonction de juger et pouvoir judiciaire*, Bruxelles, Bruylant, 1983. *Id*, "Júpiter, Hércules y Hermes: Tres modelos de juez", in *Doxa*, 14, 1993, pp. 169-194.

socialist welfare State in politics, the end of the 19th Century saw the rise of the "clash of methods" in methodology – a revolution in the science of methods. This change manifests itself in legal thinking as a crisis of legal conceptualism, of the Jurisprudence of Concepts, and a transition from legal formalism – as much conceptually as in a legal or jurisprudential sense – to an "anti-formalist reaction". This involves the change from a modern science of positive law to the contemporary positivist science of law. Here we observe that the term "positive" no longer applies to the object of reflection (positive law), but instead is preached as a method in science of law (positivist science). It moves, then, from being united with substantive law to being linked to the name of science, and from "legal positivism" to "scientific positivism". The aim is to apply the positivist methodology of the social sciences in the legal arena.[172]

This anti-formalist movement can be observed from the legal perspective as legal anti-formalism, in a widening of the number of sources of law. This approach takes into account sources such as custom, general principles of law, and, depending on the legal system, even contracts, case law, equity or scientific doctrine, in addition to legislation. On the conceptual plane of anti-formalism, there is an evolution from the formalist conception of a legal system to the consideration of law as a specifically social phenomenon, which may produce gaps requiring integrative mechanisms due to the stagnation and outdated nature of the Codes in the face of the reality of social change. There is a movement from considering judicial activity to be a syllogistic and mechanical application of legislation towards emphasizing the interpretative freedom of the judge, which may even involve the creation of new law, thereby in a sense placing the judge on the same level as the legislator. Finally, the reaction against jurisprudential formalism has an effect in the arena of case law jurisprudence: in this area, we see case law moving from being an "object" of theoretical and analytical study towards constituting a method of study in itself: the "method" of cases.

The specific doctrinal adjustment of the anti-formalist movement is historically manifested in a series of trends: (1) in France, the French

172 See, on the subject, J. ITURMENDI MORALES, "Una aproximación a los problemas del método jurídico desde la Filosofía del Derecho", in *Estudios de Filosofía del Derecho y Ciencia Jurídica en Memoria y Homenaje al Catedrático D. Luis Legaz y Lacambra (1906-1980)*, t. I, Centro de Estudios Constitucionales, Facultad de Derecho, Universidad Complutense, edited by J. ITURMENDI MORALES and J. LIMA TORRADO, p. 577.

Scientific School of François Gèny and the French Sociological School of Leon Duguit give voice to legal anti-formalism. (2) In Germany, the "Jurisprudence of Interests" of the second Ihering expresses conceptual anti-formalism, finding a parallel in France and Germany with the Free School of Law represented by Hermann Kantorowicz and Eugen Ehrlich. (3) Finally, in the Anglosaxon context, the formalism of analytical jurisprudence is opposed by sociological jurisprudence, which in the strictest sense refers to the school of thought developed in the USA by the figures of Roscoe Pound, Benjamin N. Cardozo and Oliver Wendell Holmes. Next, we analyse each of these doctrinal trends, paying particular attention to the contributions each has made in the field of case law.

3.8.1. French Legal Anti-Formalism

A. The French Scientific School of François Gèny

Gèny,[173] in his work "Methodology of interpretation and sources of positive private law", describes free scientific investigation (alongside custom, authority and tradition) as a supplementary source of law to be employed wherever the resolution of a specific case betrays a gap in legislation. For Gény, the jurist's activity oscillates between two extremes: that which is given (*donné*), and that which is constructed *(construit)* by human will via interpretation.[174]

In turn, the process of construction requires that four types of information be borne in mind: 1) real, factual information, related to the constitution of things; 2) historical information, related to the experience of precedent; 3) rational information, meaning principles forming part of natural law; and 4) ideal information, describing the objective of achieving a desirable organization of legal relationships which, in contrast to the previous types, may be neither universal nor invariable. Case law would seem to be most appropriately framed in this last category, in terms of the method employed to obtain justice in a specific case – for that reason, be-

173 F. GÈNY, *Método de interpretación y fuentes en Derecho privado positivo*, 2nd. ed., Madrid, Reus, 1925. Preface by R. SALEILLES.

174 See, G. JÈZE, *Cours de Droit Public*, Paris, R. Pichon, 1935, pp. 3 ff.; L. DUGUIT, *Traité de Droit Constitutionel*, t. I, Paris, 1927, pp. 105 ff.; H. DE PAGE, *De la interpretation des lois. Contribution a la recherche d'une méthode positive et theories en presence*, Bruxelles, 1925; J. DABIN, *La technique de l'elaboration du Droit Positif, specialement en Droit privé*, Paris, Sirey, 1935, p. 27.

ing neither universal nor invariable – as opposed to natural justice, with its innate character of eternality and immutability.

B. *The French Sociological School of Leon Duguit*

Together with the above methodical sincretism, we find the conception of those other thinkers who, excluding all natural law considerations, turn to the sociological and experimental method, as opposed to metaphysics and in agreement with positivism. This is the French Sociological School.[175]

In contrast with the spiritualist character of the Scientific School, this new trend contains deterministic overtones. Along these lines, we find the idea of Durkheim of the existence of a collective conscience, resulting from the combination of individual consciences but becoming a sum greater than the total of its parts.[176] But this perspective is put forward, above all, by Leon Duguit, for whom law is "much less the work of the legislator than the spontaneous and constant product of facts", in accordance with a realist, sociological and deterministic understanding of History.[177]

From the above we can infer the easy positioning of case law in this sociological trend, linked more to reality than abstraction, and more to case-specific justice than to any abstract notion of justice.

175 See, G. TARDE, *Les transformations du Droit*, Paris, 1893, there is a translation into Spanish, *Las transformaciones del Derecho*, with preface and notes by A. POSADA, Madrid, La España Moderna, s. a. L. LEVY-BRUHL, *La morale et la Science des moeurs*, Paris, Librarie Felix Alcan, 1937, there is a translation into Spanish by R. URBANO, Madrid, J. Pueyo, 1929; and *Sociologie du Droit*, Paris, Presses Universitaires de France, 1981, there is a translation into Spanish by MYRIAM DE WINIZKY, 4th. ed., Buenos Aires, Eudeba, 1976. G. GURVITCH, *L'idee du Droit Social...*, Paris, Sirey, 1932, preface by L. LE FUR.

176 É. DURKHEIM, *Les régles de la méthode sociologique*, Paris, 1950, p. 127; there is a translation into Spanish by L. E. ECHEVARRÍA RIVERA, 4th. ed., Madrid, Morata, 1984 ; and *La division du travail social*, Paris, 1960, there is a translation into Spanish by C. G. POSADA, introduction by L. R. ZÚÑIGA, Madrid, Akal, 1982.

177 L. DUGUIT, *Les transformations du Droit privé depuis le Code Napoleon*, Paris, 1912, pp. 3 ff. ; there is a translation into Spanish by C. G. POSADA, Madrid, Francisco Beltrán, s. a.

3.8.2. German Conceptual Anti-Formalism

A. *The Jurisprudence of Interests of Ihering and Philipp Heck*

In Germany, conceptual anti-formalism finds its voice in the legal sciences via Jurisprudence of Interests, as opposed to the previous and formalist Jurisprudence of Concepts.[178] Rudolf Von Ihering, in what we may refer to as his second stage, best personifies this school. Ihering stresses that the total mass of law no longer presents itself as a system of principles, but instead as a collection of legal bodies. Those bodies enjoy a legal existence similar to that of living beings in that they are born, relate to each other, occasionally conflict, go through metamorphoses and, eventually, die.[179] This lends the legal phenomenon a dynamic dimension which tends towards an end – that of legal protection of practical interests. In this sense, a subjective right may be conceived of as "a legally protected interest". The interest here would be the nerve, or the nucleus, and the right simply its protective shell.

Ihering had initially argued that the production of these legal bodies was characteristic of "superior jurisprudence", arrived at via a tripartite process of "analysis" by way of which law is separated into its basic "concepts"; "logical concentration" of dispersed elements, giving rise to "principles" and finally, as a consequence, the legal construction of "institutions" within a system. Opposed to this idea of superior jurisprudence as argued by the "first" Ihering, we find the "second" Ihering's later argument: one which speaks of "low jurisprudence", which exhausts its activity in mere interpretation and no longer works with concepts and institutions but with legal norms and principles, thereby avoiding detachment from reality.[180]

We can properly describe the interpretative method of the second Ihering as teleological. His understanding of science of law as based on results can be referred to as *Wirklichkeitsjurisprudenz*. The key to a philosophical system for the second phase Ihering is not simply its intellectual

178 A. DE COSSIO Y CORRAL, "Jurisprudencia conceptual y jurisprudencia de intereses", in *Revista General de Legislación y Jurisprudencia*, CLXXIV, II, 1943, pp. 462-477.

179 R. VON IHERING, "Unsere Aufgabe", in *Jahrbüchern für die Dogmatik*, 1857, pp. 3-14.

180 R. VON IHERING, *Geist des römischen Rechts*, II, Leipzig, 1898, pp. 312-389; there is a translation into Spanish by F. VELA, 2nd ed., Madrid, Revista de Occidente, 1962.

merit, but its practical function. Authentic law, in this sense, is not that which is formulated in abstract terms by general rules, but rather what is actually applied in singular decisions and rules. Authentic law is not abstract justice, divorced from reality, but jurisprudence, meaning justice in the specific case. Law, then, is not an end in itself, but a means to an end – that end being Society. The interpreter, according to Ihering in his work *The Struggle for Law*, is charged with finding compromises between individual and societal interests.

Ihering was seeking to give expression to the method of the Roman jurists, distancing himself from the Jurisprudence of Concepts – *Begriffsjurisprudenz*.[181] The difference between these two channels would be that "in jurisprudence of concepts, in contrast to what occurred in Rome, legal logic does not exist for the benefit of life but for the benefit of legal logic… it then appeared that jurisprudence of concepts, to the extent that it followed the Roman model, followed the same path that marked that model", but this appearance does not correspond to reality. "The Roman jurists thought in a consistent manner, but abandoned this consistency where practical concerns required that they do so. Though abiding by legal logic, they never lost sight of the realities of life. In contrast, the modern jurisprudence of concepts does not consider these realities but instead continues undaunted along its path, even when doing so means that conceptual jurisprudence occasionally reaches results which are totally incompatible with the aim of the application of law, destroying itself in its own impossibility."[182]

However, Jurisprudence of Interests, represented by Philipp Heck[183] in addition to Ihering in his second phase, is not a general philosophy of law, but simply a meditation regarding the essence of the judicial function. As opposed to the Free School of Law, to which we will later refer, it is not incumbent on the judge to freely create a new legal order but merely to work within the valid legal system to bring to bear the ideals on

181 See, J. ITURMENDI MORALES, "Acerca de Rudolf von Ihering (1818-1892) y el sistema de los juristas romanos", in *Anuario de la Facultad de Derecho, Universidad de Extremadura*, 11, 1993, pp. 416-479, esp. pp. 430-434.

182 R. VON IHERING, *Scherz und Ernst in der Jurisprudenz. Eine Weihnachtsgabe für das juristischem Publikum*, Leipzig, Breitkopf und Härtel, 1rst. ed., p. 363, cited by J. ITURMENDI MORALES, "Acerca de Rudolf von Ihering…", *cit.*, p. 428.

183 See, P. HECK, *Begriffsbildung und Interessenjurisprudenz*, Tübingen, J. C. B. Mohr, 1932.

which it is founded. Jurisprudence of Interests does not deny the need for the jurist to formulate classificatory concepts, but it does affirm that the function of those concepts should not go beyond the purposes of exposition and ordering. In no manner should those concepts become sources to generate new norms as occurred in the Jurisprudence of Concepts, which via the method of "construction" and interpretation of concepts first derived a conception of existing norms and then deduced new rules related to those norms, thereby making those concepts independent and autonomous entities, existing in themselves with a consistency analogous to that of the natural bodies. To the contrary, as its name suggests, Jurisprudence of Interests gives precedence to conflicts of interests, arguing that identical conflicts must be resolved in an identical manner. In contrast to conceptual jurisprudence, here we see the use of a method of comparative evaluation of interests.[184]

We can differentiate Jurisprudence of Interests from the German Free School of Law in two aspects: firstly, its conception of normative interpretation, and secondly, its method of development of legal science. The first aspect holds the greater interest for us in relation to case law. As opposed to the freedom of judicial action permitted by Free Jurisprudence, as we have seen, Jurisprudence of Interests imposes a limit on the will of the judge in the necessary balancing and evaluation of the interests at stake: this evaluation must reflect the values attributed to the interests by legislation. For this reason, interpretation in this secondary sense must be focused on correcting the defects in the expression of legislation, this constituting a limited form of interpretation. It could from this perspective be deduced that case law, in the sense that it is not limited to a literal interpretation which declares the letter of the law but does not investigate its spirit and is to a certain point innovative in relation to legislation, would fit more easily into the Free School of Jurisprudence than into the Jurisprudence of Interests. Despite this, case law could also be located in the latter, but always with the restriction of having to balance and evaluate those interests already present in the legislation.

Jurisprudence of Interests is related in Germany to the modern antirationalists, for whom the element of emotion takes precedence. The observations of Maier and Schreier are along these lines. According to these writers, the act of will, which propels us towards determined ends that may often conflict with our own interests, prevails over the conscious

184 L. RECASÉNS SICHES, *Nueva filosofía de la interpretación del Derecho*, México, Porrúa, 1980, pp. 57-67.

acts of the same. Along the same lines, Rumelin[185] praises the sentiment and conscience of law, the emotional element that, in practice, the judge expresses. The emotive and irrational character of the Jurisprudence of Interests explains its great political success in the service of National Socialism, functioning as a working tool for the jurist and not a mere methodological chimera.

B. *The Free School of Law of Hermann Kantorowicz and Eugen Ehrlich*

It is undoubtedly in the Free School of Law where case law has a major role, in the sense that the School recognizes the great freedom of the judge in terms of resolving disputes.

Eugen Ehrlich carries out a sociological offensive, taking the perspective that life is incomparably richer than the legal schema which attempt to capture it.[186] Ehrlich can be included within the German pro-"free law" movement. This school of thought starts with Hermann Kantorowicz in his work *The Struggle over Legal Science*, and is followed by Ernst Fuchs, among others. It has a precedent in the judgements of the French judge Magnaud, known as "the good judge" because he worked from the principle that legislation must be humanely interpreted, the judge being guided in said task by human solidarity, even if this might mean moving away from the letter of the law. He was concerned more with a practical form of judging than with developing any interpretative theory. In this sense, it can be asserted that the "good judge" Magnaud, despite possessing accurate practical intuition, nonetheless failed to develop the reasoning which would justify his decisions.

For his part, Kantorowicz is opposed to the unique character of legislation as a source of law, proposing to revive natural law, being non-State law, in its manifestation of free law, as positive law of a certain society.[187] Here, the key would be selecting from the possible premises those leading to just conclusions, this choice being a problem not of rationality but of will. It can therefore be asserted that the interpretative conception of Kantorowicz possesses an anti-logical and strong-willed character.

185 M. RUMELIN, *Rechtsgefühl und Rechtsbewustein*, Tübingen, Mohr, 1925, p. 27; *Id*, *Die Billigkeit im Recht*, Tübingen, Mohr, 1921, pp. 39-40.

186 L. RECASÉNS SICHES, *Nueva filosofía de la interpretación del Derecho, op. cit.*, pp. 48-52.

187 See, H. KANTOROWICZ, *La definición del Derecho*, Madrid, Revista de Occidente, 1964, translation by J. M. DE LA VEGA.

The movement in favour of free law is in opposition to the Jurisprudence of Concepts. According to the free law movement, the courts must turn to good faith, good custom, equity and prudent judicial resolutions in their interpretations. The work of judging requires attachment to legislation where its text is clear and the decision would not violate free law. When the text of the legislation is unclear, or the solution implausible, the judge must resolve the case as in his judgement the State would have done had it considered that point. If the judge is unable to form a view as to what the State would do, he must take inspiration from free law. Finally, the judge must apply his own discretion in resolving hopelessly complicated cases.[188]

The idea here is one of living law, meaning that which genuinely prevails in life rather than that which is established according to precepts. And what is case law if not justice brought to life, if not the adaptation of the cold, distant justice that comes about if the law is remotely applied to the specific circumstances that are encountered daily by the courts?

3.8.3. Jurisprudential Anti-formalism: The North American Sociological Jurisprudence of Oliver Wendell Holmes, Roscoe Pound and Benjamin Cardozo; North American Realism

For a complete overview of anti-formalism, we must consider the reaction beyond the European continent to the formalist English work by John Austin, "Analytical Jurisprudence".[189] North American "Sociological Jurisprudence" involved taking the step from casuistic case law in its objective sense to a methodical casuism, or method of cases, in the study of law.

Oliver Wendell Holmes inspired this school of thought. The result of his experience as a judge in the Supreme Court of the United States was an idea that the "real life" of law had not consisted of logic, but rather "practical experience". According to this conviction, the process of identification of law involves considering arguments that make "good sense", within which reasoning case law would belong, together with the argu-

188 L. RECASÉNS SICHES, *Nueva filosofia de la interpretación del Derecho, op. cit.*, pp. 52-57.

189 See, on the subject, C. A. GARBER, "La interpretación en el sociologismo jurídico norteamericano", in *Anuario de Filosofía Jurídica y Social*, 9, 1989, pp. 71-139. J. AUSTIN, *Sobre la utilidad del estudio de la jurisprudencia.* Translation into English by F. GONZÁLEZ VICÉN, Madrid, Centro de Estudios Constitucionales, 1981.

ments of traditional logic – which are above all defended because they create judicial security. The problem according to this perspective is not so much the correction of judicial syllogism but the specific premises from which the opinion starts, for which purpose it is necessary to bear in mind the vital and historical evaluations and arguments.

For his part, Benjamin N. Cardozo outlines four methods in the mental process of passing judgement: 1) logical deduction or progression; 2) history; 3) that which is relevant to custom and current social convictions; 4) inspiration by justice and social welfare, which, in addition to being the fourth method, would be the criterion for deciding the form of action to take in each case.

Roscoe Pound, another representative of this school of thought, sought to free himself from the dominant, dogmatic 19th Century trends of logical-deductive exegesis and the romantic historicism of the School of Savigny.[190]

North American Legal Realism rose to prominence in the United States as a criticism of the Analytical School of Austin and his conception of law as commands by sovereign powers. For North American Legal Realism, doctrinal law is that which the judicial body resolves in doubtful cases – prophecies of what judges will do in the future. Representatives of the movement include Underhill Moore, Herman Oliphant,[191] Walter W. Cook, Charles E. Clark and, above all, Karl N. Llewellyn and Jerome Frank.[192] All these representatives draw a distinction between what the judge says in his judgements and what he actually does – the two not always coinciding. It is necessary to differentiate "paper rules", which include as the basis of court decisions legislation and general norms as much as judgements and individual norms, from "real norms" – declared or otherwise – in accordance with which the judges actually determine

190 See, on the subject, R. POUND, "Common Law and Legislation", in *Harvard Law Review*, 21, 6, 1908, pp. 383-407. *Id*, "The Future of the Common Law", in *University of Cincinnati Law Review*, 7, 4, 1933, pp. 1-18. *Id*, "The Development of American Law and its Deviation from English Law", in *The Law Quarterly Review*, 67, January 1951. *Id*, *El espíritu del "Common Law"*, Barcelona, Bosch, 1954. *Id*, *Jurisprudence*, vols. I, II, III, St. Paul – Minn., West Publishing Co., 1959.

191 See, H. OLIPHANT, "A Return to Stare Decisis", in *American Bar Association Journal*, 14, 2, 1928, pp. 71-77.

192 See, J. FRANK, *Law and the Modern Mind*, New York, Brentano's Publ., 1930. *Id*, *Courts on Trial. Myth and Reality in American Justice*, Princeton – New Jersey, Princeton University Press, 1949.

cases. With respect to the latter, appreciation and classification of the facts of the case tend to carry more important than the legal arguments posited. In the process of classification of the facts, a series of filters will have an effect on the judge – factors and prejudices which influence the perspective of the judge regarding those facts. Here, the personality of the judge will prove decisive in shaping the decision, exposing as syllogistic the mechanical conception of the judicial function.[193]

3.8.4. Other Anti-formalist Trends

Following Recaséns Siches in his *New Philosophy of the Interpretation of Law*,[194] the trends outlined below, among others, might also be cited as anti-formalist.

First, we encounter the "experimental logic" of John Dewey, which is rooted in consideration of consequences rather than originating from precedent as in the case of deductive logic. In experimental logic, general legal rules and principles must be considered as a working hypothesis to be constantly verified from the perspective of the effects of applying them in specific cases. In opposition to the entrenched immutability of precedent, Dewey argues that rules have to be flexible and variable in order to be adaptable to future circumstances.

Second, Recaséns Siches refers to the revolution advocated by Joaquín Dualde in his 1933 work *A Revolution in the Logic of Law (Concept of Interpretation of Private Law)*, consisting of taking into account the subconscious elements which, together with the conscious, shape individual and collective psychology. For Dualde, the motives of the legislator are not always shaped by reflection, but often obey impulse and sentiment. The interpretative method applied must therefore be instinctive, intuitive, along Bergsonian lines. One must understand and live law. Here is the crux of the method, consisting in experimenting with ideas and bringing them into the real world from whence they escaped, in the same way as an actor brings to life a theatrical work created by an author without limiting himself to a merely reproductive role. In this process of bringing life to law, jurisprudence would have much to say, in the sense that the aim is not to limit oneself to rendering a weak interpretation

193 L. RECASÉNS SICHES, *Nueva filosofía de la interpretación del Derecho, op. cit.*, pp. 67-82 and 92-112. *Id, Tratado General de Filosofía del Derecho*, 8th ed., México, Porrúa, 1983.

194 L. RECASÉNS SICHES, *Nueva filosofía de la interpretación del Derecho, op. cit.*, pp. 82-92, 112-185 and 277-292.

of legislation, not to simply execute, but rather, via interpretation in the strong sense, to construct and contribute something which did not initially form part of the content of the norm in question.

The constructions of Carlos Cossio in his "egological conception" of law are also of an anti-formalist nature. In this conception, Cossio argues that the conscience of the judge must be taken into account in the interpretative process wherever that conscience produces what Cossio calls "experience of contradiction".[195] The theory of Juan David García Bacca also shows that in the field of law, pure logical is inapplicable, and in fact *logoid* elements and structures are applied – these being derived from "practical or human logic".

Further, the anti-deductive and anti-syllogistic criticism of Michel Villey[196] is anti-formalist, in the classic Aristotelian, Roman and Aquinas style, but adapted to the requirements of the 20th Century.

Fourth, it is fitting to cite the claim made by Theodor Viehweg from the "aporetic" (in the words of Nicolai Hartmann) perspective, which sees the topics and dialectic of Aristotle, Cicero and the Roman jurisconsults not as systematic or deductive thought, but as "thought regarding problems".

Along the same lines we find the "theory of argumentation" of Chaïm Perelman, who, reasoning from this perspective, does not seek absolute evidence but rather the most acceptable, plausible or fairest solution to the practical problems that may be encountered – in summary, the most equitable solution.

In Belgium, the School of Paul Foriers, Henri Buch and A. Bayart criticizes an unequivocal separation of questions of fact and questions of law. Additionally, and in a similar sense to the theories of Viehweg or Perelman, we find the line of thought of Julius Stone, who re-develops the rhetoric of Classical Antiquity, adapting it to current circumstances.

195 See, on the subject, J. C. CUETO RUA, "El método jurídico en la teoría egológica", in *Anuario de Filosofía Jurídica y Social*, 9, 1989, pp. 141-153.

196 See, on the subject, R. VIGO, "La interpretación jurídica en Michel Villey", in *Anuario de Filosofía Jurídica y Social*, 9, 1989, pp. 171-194; J. A. MARTÍNEZ MUÑOZ, "El Derecho natural en Michel Villey", in *Revista de la Facultad de Derecho de la Universidad Complutense de Madrid*, 78, 1990-1991, pp. 173-203; M. VILLEY, "Iusnaturalisme. Essay de definitio", in *Revue Interdisciplinaire d'Etudes Juridiques*, 1986, pp. 25-32; also in *Revista de la Facultad de Derecho de la Universidad Complutense de Madrid*, 77, 1990-1991, pp. 341-347, translation into Spanish by J. M. SERRANO RUIZ-CALDERÓN.

Recaséns continues his study referring to the "prudential" line of argument of Tomar Ballweg and to the material logic of Karl Engisch. The German professor argues that one cannot argue the theoretical truth or falsehood of a legal rule – one can only comment on its correctness or otherwise from a practical perspective. This is because, in legal reality, there are certain limits within specified margins of approximate probability, but never absolute certainty and precision. For that reason, according to Engisch, the logic to be applied must be of a material ilk, and never formal logic of a mathematical character.

Newer anti-syllogistic criticisms have come from Joachim Hruschka, professor at the University of Munich, from the intuitive logic of Lotear Philipps, and from the Norwegian jurist Vilhelm Aubert.

Edward Levi, for his part, reminds us that law is never sufficiently clear and acquires its real meaning only upon application to a specific dispute or controversy. As Kelsen would say, the legislator offers a kind of blank cheque to the jurisdictional body, and that cheque only assumes a real value in relation to specific situations.

Along similar lines, Thomas Cowan differentiates science, which seeks to know the truth, from law, which aims to justly resolve human conflict. The applicable method varies in accordance with these different objectives. The scientist generalizes. On the other hand, the jurist specifies, even if they may develop various generalizations in order to do so. Nonetheless, equality in law does not equate to uniformity in science. True legal equality consists in recognizing that no two cases are truly the same.

According to Francesco Carnelutti, the judge is more important than the legislator since it is the judge who is faced with the living person. A legal system can be constituted without legislation, but not without judges. It would, says Carnelutti, be preferable to have bad legislation with good judges than to have bad judges with good legislation.

After this panoramic view given by Recaséns Siches of the anti-formalist movement, the author advances his own theory of intepretation: the "logos of the human or the reasonable". It concerns the logos of the act, what Ortega called "vital or historical reasons" – the circumstances, the specific instance. This is a material logic, of content, as opposed to formal, *a priori* logic, which is mathematical in nature. The key aspect is the singularities of the specific case, rather than the general, universal or immutable. It is a dialectical, aporetic, uncertain, deliberative and argumentative logos, based on dialogue, debate and conflict of arguments. It is not the systematic, Cartesian logos of rationalist evidence, 19th Century Codes, conceived of as *ratio scripta*. This theory is about deliberating, weighing up, evaluating and balancing, but without pretensions of precision, exactness or exclusivity. This reasoning inspires the virtues of prudence, good and common sense, consistency, characterization, good judgement, discretion, equanimity, balance, circumspection, precaution, equity and foresight when interpreting. All these qualities are summarized in the "logos of the reasonable". In contrast to the obvious and the proven, the field is opened to deliberation – nobody deliberates regarding things which could not be any other way. And the fact is that there exist forms of reasoning which are not mathematical in nature. Reason and logic include, together with the "rational", the "reasonable". The aim is to ensure the means used to achieve the ends are adequate – which is to say, legitimate (an axiological issue) and effective (an issue of experience). As opposed to the neutral character of traditional logic, reasonable logic starts from the premise of rough judgements just as from experience and "vital" grounds, as much individual as from collective historical grounds. Here, too, case law has a role to play.

In this way, the lawyer and the judge are equipped with a technique allowing them to work without having to use dress up fair decisions that are in fact made in accordance with the "human logos" as if they were the result of a construction borne of traditional logic. Reasonable logic does not advocate departure from a legal order, but rather a better interpretation of that order in the context of the instant case. It is an affirmation of equity, rather than a negation of justice.

Applying the "logos of the reasonable" to interpretation, it can be asserted that the judge is not bound in advance to any particular interpretative method, and neither should the judge give hierarchical preference to certain procedures over others. Instead, the judge should select *a posteriori*, in each case, the procedure that results in the interpretation that best serves justice. The correct method would be that which, in the specific case, leads to a conclusion that is considered satisfactory.

The pure logic of syllogistic inference is limited to explaining cause-effect links and relationships, and logical conclusions. In contrast, the "logos of the reasonable" seeks to "know", rather than simply to identify – and, furthermore, to check and evaluate conclusions. Faced with the bounds of necessity of the natural world, legal sciences are governed by conventional imputation and free of legal consequences in specific cases, as much on the normative as the judicial plane. For that reason, a global perception requires a certain intellectual intuition, a mentality capable of entirely covering the heterogenous components that comprise human relations.[197]

4. Changes in Case Law, Especially by the Supreme Court

This section is applicable to the case law of the Spanish Supreme Court. Constitutional case law requires, as we have seen, the equal treatment of equal cases except in the event good reasons permit different treatment.

4.1. Can Case Law Be Changed?

It is possible to change case law as it does not constitute a source of law, and is not therefore obligatory or binding in nature – not even for the court which made the original decision – except for the caveats and exceptions in relation to case law emanating either from the Supreme Court in relation to inferior tribunals for the purpose of unification of case law, or from the Constitutional Court when it resolves an issue of constitutionality. It is "possible" to change case law because the Supreme Court is not bound by previous opinions it has held – Supreme Court Judgements of 19 July 1965 and 25 April 1972. The Court is free at all times to choose the most appropriate interpretation of legal norms. The case law of the court is not static, but must instead be dynamic.

4.2. Is it Advisable to Change Case Law?

Changes in case law, particularly that of the Supreme Court, is not only possible – it is even, often, advisable. It is "advisable" because previous case law may be mistaken, given that to err is human – *humanum est errare* – and wisdom, therefore, consists in rectifying and correcting errors. The issue is that even though it may be initially correct, case law can over time be superseded by changes in society, or new opinions coming to prominence. When advisable, "in view of the social reality of the time in which a norm is to be applied", case law needs to be changeable and not static. As affirmed by the Supreme Court Judgement of 1 February 1958, case law must be respected for as long as it does not need to be changed

197 See, L. RECASÉNS SICHES, "Equity and Logic of the Reasonable", in R. A. NEWMAN (ed.), *Equity in the World's Legal Systems, op. cit.*, pp. 411-425.

– but it must be modified if advisable (Supreme Court Judgement 3 April 1945).[198]

4.3. *If there Is a Change of Case Law, Which Prevails?*

Change of case law presents a problem. If there is more than one line of case law regarding a particular issue, which should be followed – which should be considered "the" case law? On certain occasions, the Supreme Court has sustained that the "most modern" should prevail, yet the truth is that, as the Supreme Court is not bound by its own precedents, it retains the freedom to follow the most modern line of case law – in parallel with the maxim that later law repeals earlier law – or to return to the "old" line of precedent, or even to adopt a distinct third line of precedent, as has in fact happened on occasion.

4.3.1. The Oldest Case Law

One doctrinal stance argues that where multiple lines of precedent exist, the oldest line should prevail. This view is based on granting tradition a significant role – on a respect for the old. The suggestion here appears to be that simply by dint of being older and having been sustained over the course of time, case law improves in quality like a fine wine – or, like titled nobles, becomes of refined stock. However, this attitude appears to ignore that respecting case law on the grounds of age is an argument with little rationality. The institution of capital punishment, for example, enjoyed an undeniable and deep-rooted tradition over a long period of time, until in the 18th Century, a rational argument was employed which questioned the foundations upon which the institution was established. The mere historical existence of the Inquisition or of papal bulls – to provide two examples of obsolete institutions – would not justify their continuing in force today. Antiquity is like "youth", a merit the value of which is diminished by time itself.

198 See, on the subject, B. GESCHE MULLER, *Jurisprudencia dinámica (La desvalorización monetaria y otros problemas en el Derecho)*, Santiago de Chile, Editorial Jurídica de Chile, 1971. P. MENCHEN HERREROS, "Jurisprudencia : unidad y evolución del Derecho", paper presented to the *Jornadas sobre El Poder Judicial*, held by the Dirección General de lo Contencioso del Estado, III, Madrid, Instituto de Estudios Fiscales, 1983, pp. 1951-1981. I. DE CASSO, Lecture on "El Derecho y su dinámica", in *Revista General de Derecho*, 1950, pp. 62 ff. V. SILVA MELERO, "Jurisprudencia y evolución", in *Revista General de Legislación y Jurisprudencia*, LXIX, 237, October 1974.

4.3.2. The Most Recent Case Law

Another doctrinal opinion is in direct contrast to that described above – a perspective according to which, in the event of multiple lines of precedent, the most recent line should be given priority. This argument has been advanced by various writers. The stance is based, perhaps, on the idea of parallelism with what is occurring in relation to legislation, in the aphorism *lex posterior derogat priori* – later law repeals earlier law. It relates to the situation where, in contrast to respect due to age, the quality of newness is a point in favour of the line of precedent – the argument is that more recent resolutions should always be preferred because "the new is better than the old".

But this line of argument ignores that, if the reader will excuse the repetition, "progress is not always progressive" – we do not always necessarily evolve from less to more with the passage of time. There are often movements of regression, return, zig-zag, or loops. Something similar takes place when a language is being learnt, when at some point the learner feels that they are not advancing – or, even, that they are regressing. Despite this, zig-zags are nothing if not small. In the mid-term and longer term, advances are indeed made.

4.3.3. A Third, Distinct Line of Case Law

It is clear that change is sometimes necessary – "something needs to change so everything can stay the same", as the Count of Lampedusa said in *El Gatopardo*. It is not always possible to remain stagnant in the past, in the field of case law just as on a personal level. For this reason, it is fitting to ask whether it would not be possible to find a third doctrinal stance, one which argues that in choosing between modern and older lines of precedent in a particular area, and if we are not bound by anything with obligatory character, we can take a middle route and find a third, distinct line of case law when circumstances dictate. Technically, nothing advises against this route, given that the case law of the Supreme Court – at least in a formal sense – is not a source of law, and therefore not binding. On the other hand, an excessive, mushrooming proliferation of lines of precedent may not be convenient. But with the appropriate judgement and prudence, this possibility should not be discounted.

5. Main Rules on the Sources of Law and Case Law in the Spanish Legal System

5.1. The Pre-1978 Situation

5.1.1. The Civil Code

The regulation of case law in the Spanish legal system was set out in a series of legal texts, among which the Preliminary Title of the Civil Code stood out, particularly prior to 1978. This Title was reformed by Decree on 31 May 1974. We should remember that this Title possesses a quasi-constitutional force, if not in formal terms – since it is not found in the text of the Constitution, but rather in the Civil Code – then certainly in material terms, due to the great significance of the issues regulated therein.[199]

A. Pre-reform of the Preliminary Title of 31 May 1974, article 6

Article 6 of the Preliminary Title of the Civil Code, prior to the reform of 31 May 1974, stated:

> *A Court which refuses to judge on grounds of silence, obscurity or insufficiency of statute shall incur liability.*

199 See, on the subject, P. BELTRÁN DE HEREDIA Y ONIS, *La función judicial y el Código Civil a través de un siglo, Centenario del Código Civil (1889-1989)*, I, Madrid, Ed. Centro de Estudios Ramón Areces, 1990. F. DE CASTRO Y BRAVO, *Derecho civil de España*, Introduction by L. DIEZ-PICAZO, Madrid, Civitas, 1984. *Id*, "Fuentes de Derecho e interpretación jurídica", in *Anuario de Derecho Civil*, XI, I, January-March 1958. *Id*, "El recurso en interés de ley y el valor de la jurisprudencia", in *Anuario de Derecho Civil*, XXIII, III, July-September 1970. Comment on the book by CREMADES, *El recurso de casación en interés de la ley. Estudio de su regulación en los artículos 185 y ss. de la Ley Procesal Laboral*, preface by M. ALONSO OLEA, Sevilla, Instituto Gª Oviedo, 1969. F. CLEMENTE DE DIEGO, "La función jurisdiccional de los jueces y la aplicación del Derecho en general", in *Revista de Derecho Privado*, 3, December 1913. *Id*, "El artículo 6º del Código Civil español", in *Revista de Derecho Privado*, I, 1, October 1913. *Id*, *La jurisprudencia como fuente del Derecho*, Madrid, Ed. Revista de Derecho Privado, 1925. L. MARTÍNEZ-CALCERRADA Y GÓMEZ, *Derecho judicial y Código Civil (función interpretadora, correctora o integradora), Centenario del Código Civil (1889-1989), II*, Madrid, Ed. Centro de Estudios Ramón Areces, 1990.

When there is no statute directly applicable to the point at issue, the Court shall apply the custom of the place and, in its absence, general legal principles.

Article 6 established the rule of legislation, reduced the role of custom, and destroyed that of case law. In relation to case law, in the parliamentary debates which preceded the current Civil Code in Spain between 1850 and 1888, we can distinguish two sectors: 1) that of "substantive" positive law, against considering case law to be a source of law. 2) That of "procedural" positive law, inclined to grant case law an element of effectiveness.[200]

B. Post-reform of the Preliminary Title of 31 May 1974, article 1.6

Following the reform of the Preliminary Title, article 1.1 identified sources of law as "statutes, customs and general legal principles". Article 1.6 established:[201]

200 See, on the subject, D. DE BUEN LOZANO, *Introducción al estudio del Derecho civil*, Madrid, Ed. Revista de Derecho Privado, 1932; There is a 2nd. ed., with a Preliminary Note by N. DE BUEN, México, Porrúa, 1977. *Id*, "Las normas jurídicas y la función judicial (alrededor de los artículos 5 y 6 C.C.)", in *Revista General de Legislación y Jurisprudencia*, 129, 1916; 130, 1917-I; 131, 1917-II. A. D'ORS, "Para una interpretación realista del artículo 6 del C.C. español", in *Studi in Onore di Emilio Betti*, 1, Milano, Giuffrè, 1962. FERNÁNDEZ DEL CORRAL, "La jurisprudencia en el Título preliminar del C.C.", in *Boletín de Información* 15 December 1972.

201 See, A. CRISTOBAL MONTES, "La costumbre, la jurisprudencia y la equidad en el nuevo Título preliminar del C.C. español", in *Revista General de Legislación y Jurisprudencia*, LXXV, 243, 1977. V. FAIRÉN GUILLÉN, "Notas sobre el valor de la jurisprudencia", in *Revista Crítica de Derecho Inmobiliario*, 509, July-August 1975. *Id*, "Ponencia sobre la jurisprudencia en el nuevo Título preliminar del C.C", in *Jornadas de Derecho Civil* (Zaragoza-Valladolid, 1975). L. DIEZ PICAZO (*et al.*), "Comentario al artículo 1.6", en *Comentarios a las reformas del C.C. (El nuevo Título Preliminar del Código y la Ley de 2 de mayo de 1975)*, I, Madrid, Tecnos, 1977. *Id*, "Comentario al artículo 1.6", in *Comentario al C.C.*, I, directed by C. PAZ AREZ, R. BERCOWITZ, L. DIEZ PICAZO and P. SALVADOR, Madrid, Ministerio de Justicia, 1991. A. DE LA OLIVA SANTOS, "La jurisprudencia en el nuevo Título Preliminar del Código Civil", in *Anuario de Derecho Civil*, XXVII, II, Madrid, Instituto Nacional de Estudios Jurídicos, April-June, MCMLXXV, pp. 331-517. M. FERNÁNDEZ MARTÍN-GRANIZO, "La jurisprudencia en el Código Civil después de la Reforma de 1974", in *Anuario de Derecho Ci-*

Case law shall complement the legal system by means of the doctrine repeatedly upheld by the Supreme Court in its interpretation and application of statutes, customs and general legal principles.

Article 1.7 added:

Judges and Courts shall have the inexcusable duty to resolve in any event the issues brought before them, abiding by the system of sources set forth herein.

Despite the preparatory drafts for the development of the Law of Bases (*Ley de Bases*) of 17 March 1973 stating that case law was situated among the sources of our legal order, this doctrinal stance did not manage to find its way into the definitive text of the law. Article 1.6 of the Civil Code, as quoted above, appears to establish an intermediate, equitable position, somewhere between the "yes" and "no" counterpoints concerning case law being a source of law.[202]

vil, XXIX, II, Madrid, Instituto Nacional de Estudios Jurídicos, April-June 1976, pp. 281-641. *Id, Código Civil. Doctrina y jurisprudencia, I, artículos 1 a 332,* in cooperation with J. L. ALBACAR LÓPEZ, Madrid, Trivium, 1991. C. QUINTANA REDONDO, "Las fuentes del Derecho en el Nuevo Título Preliminar del Código Civil", in *Libro Homenaje a Ramón Mª Roca Sastre,* I, Madrid, Universidad Complutense de Madrid, 1976, pp. 657-672. J. RODRÍGUEZ DEL BARCO, "La jurisprudencia como fuente jurídica en el nuevo Título Preliminar del C. C., aprobado por Decreto 1836/1974, de 31 de mayo", in *Revista de Derecho Privado,* LIX, 1975. E. RUIZ VADILLO, "El nuevo Título Preliminar del Código Civil (Comentarios a los capítulos I, II y III)", in *Libro Homenaje a Ramón Mª Roca Sastre,* I, Madrid, Universidad Complutense de Madrid, 1976, pp. 781-823. *Id,* "Algunas ideas sobre el valor y significación de las fuentes del Derecho en el nuevo Título Preliminar del C. C.", in *Anuario de Derecho Civil,* XXX, I, 1977. C. DE LA VEGA BENAYAS, *Introducción al Derecho judicial,* Madrid, Montecorvo, 1970. *Id,* "La doctrina de las fuentes del Derecho en el Nuevo Título Preliminar del Código Civil (arts. 1º y 2º)", in *Libro Homenaje a Ramón Mª Roca Sastre,* I, Madrid, Universidad Complutense de Madrid, 1976, pp. 673-752. E. ZULETA PUCEIRO, "Jurisprudencia y fuentes del Derecho", in *Estudios sobre el Título Preliminar del C. C., Parte General, vol. I,* Academia Matritense del Notariado, Edersa, 1977.

202 See, on the subject, A. DE LA OLIVA SANTOS, "La jurisprudencia en la Ley de Bases para un nuevo Título Preliminar del Código Civil", in *Revista de Derecho Procesal Iberoamericana,* IV, October-December 1973. *Id,* "La ju-

a. The Systematic Argument or *Sedes Materiae*

The fact that one finds case law included in the First Chapter of the Preliminary Title, and within the very article dealing with sources of law, has led some writers to argue from a systematic or *sedes materiae* perspective – according to which the position of a provision in a legal text has relevance in terms of its real significance – that case law must be considered to be a source of law within the Spanish legal system. The systematic position given to case law in the Civil Code means it can be thought of as a *cuasi inmediata* source, and in a certain sense "extra-positive" in terms of creation of law.

b. The Literal Argument and the Exhaustive List of article 1.1 of the Civil Code

From a literal interpretation of the tenor of Article 1.1 regarding the sources of law, one understands that case law of the Supreme Court cannot be, *stricto sensu,* a formal source, since the Article provides an expressly exhaustive list of those formal sources. It contains a *numerus clausus* list: the sources of law are statute, custom, *and* general principles of law. If, in place of the copulative conjunction "and", the disjunctive "or", "among others", or "etc" had been used, the list would be simply exemplificative, *numerus apertus.* This is not the case. In the light of Article 1.1, the majority of doctrines therefore consider that case law of the Supreme Court is not a source of law – at least, not one that is equivalent to statute, custom and general legal principles. Decisions do not establish the rule; rather, it is brought about via the sources stated in the Article.

c. Case Law "Complements" but does not "Complete" the Legal System

Another argument against case law of the Supreme Court being a source of law is the use by Article 1.6 of the Preliminary Title of the Civil Code, after the reform of 31 May 1974, of the term "complement" rather than "complete" in referring to the role of that case law in the legal system.[203]

risprudencia en el nuevo Título Preliminar del C. C.", in *Anuario de Derecho Civil,* XXVIII, 2, 1975.

203 See, R. LÓPEZ VILAS, *La jurisprudencia y su actual eficacia normativa, Centenario del Código Civil (1889-1989)*, II, Madrid, Centro de Estudios Ramón Areces, 1990. *Id, La jurisprudencia y su función complementaria del ordenamiento jurídico,* Madrid, Civitas, 2002.

The expression "complement" is little short of unintelligible – and, in any case, is not illuminative. The term is ambiguous, equivocal and causes doubt. A complement – from the Latin *complere* (meaning "to fill") – is something added to something else in order to make that second thing perfect, or complete. The key question here, then, lies in clarifying whether the words "complement" and "complete" are equivalent or can be differentiated. The reality is that the answer to this question would appear to lie with the latter perspective, that of differentiation. The General Commission of Codification would not have avoided so strictly the use of the word "complete", clear and emphatic, and preferred the ambiguity of "complement", had it not wished to make clear that the legal system is complete without case law, which is "adhered or incorporated as an additional element, rather than being fully integrated in the substance [of the legal system]." Given that individuals – at least, some of them – do not always voluntarily respect legislation – at least, not all of it – it is necessary that the work of legislation be "complemented" by a subsequent layer of the State, the judiciary, in order that the legislation be effective.

d. The Expression "Certain Legal Transcendence" in Reference to Case Law in the Preamble of the 1974 Reform of the Preliminary Title of the Civil Code

Another great "open question" posed by the 1974 reform of the Preliminary Title of the Civil Code is what explanation should be given for the expression "certain normative transcendence", which appears in the Statement of Motives of said reform, in the following paragraph:

> *In terms of case law, while not included as a source of law, it is recognized as having a mission to complement the legal system. In effect, the task of interpreting and applying rules in contact with the realities of life and conflicts of interests gives rise to the formulation by the Supreme Court of opinions, which, if not entailing the production of rules in a full and proper sense, contain singularly authorized developments, which with their reiteration are worthy of acquiring a certain normative transcendence.* (Author's underlining)

The fact that this expression is found within the Statement of Motives must lead us to question the value of the Statements of Motives and the Preambles. It is fitting to accord them a moral authority as an expression of their *ratio legis*. But, as stated by the Supreme Court in its judgement of 14 October 1965, and previously on 25 February 1943: "statute cannot be distorted by what is said in the Statement of Motives". In any case, it appears wholly problematic and even paradoxical to emphatically reject case law as a source of law while at the same time attributing to it a "certain normative transcendence", given that it cannot be and not be simultaneously.

e. The Express Recognition of "Analogy" Post-reform of the Preliminary Title of the Civil Code

The transcendence of the case law function also emanates from the express recognition of analogy, which, although employed by the Supreme Court, was not explicitly recognized within the Civil Code as a method of application-interpretation-integration of the legal system until the 1974 reform of the Preliminary Title. Although analogy may not be a source of law – as we have already seen – it is, especially as *analogia iuris*, a method of creating "general principles of law".[204]

As a conclusion, it is worth affirming that the case law of the Supreme Court is not a source in the Civil Code, neither before nor after the reform of the Preliminary Title, and that although its systematic position in the same article and chapter as the sources of law brings it close to those sources, its assigned function is that of "complementing" the legal system.[205]

5.1.2. The Rules of Civil Procedure; the Reform of 2000

If the Civil Code is almost silent in relation to case law, the Law of Civil Trial (*Ley de Enjuiciamiento Civil*), which established high court appeals "for infringement of statute or legal doctrine", is different. It gave writers reason to argue that this "legal doctrine", or case law, was a source of law along with statute, thereby giving rise to a perception that there is a contradiction or disparity between the Civil Code and the Law of Civil Trial.

The following doctrinal stances have been adopted with respect to this issue: 1) some authors argued that the Civil Code repealed the articles of the Law of Civil Trial which allowed high court appeals for infringement of legal doctrine, as the Code was subsequent to the Law of Civil Trial. 2) Others maintained that "legal doctrine" as mentioned in the Law of Civil Trial was in substance the same as the general principles of law established as sources of law in the Civil Code. If case law could not

204 See, M. J. FALCÓN Y TELLA, *El argumento analógico en el Derecho*, Preface by J. ITURMENDI MORALES, Madrid, Civitas, 1991.

205 F. M. CALVO VIDAL, *La jurisprudencia ¿Fuente del Derecho?*, *op. cit.*, pp. 289-299.

become a source of law by the front door, it would enter through the back. 3) Finally, some thought that there was in fact no contradiction between the two texts, given that "legal doctrine" did not have the character of a source of law, and was merely the phrasing used to allow the admission of appeal to the high court.[206]

Today, following the reform of the Law of Civil Trial in 2000, we talk of "case law doctrine". As stated by Juan Montero Aroca and José Flors Matíes, "in the drafting of article 477.1 of the Law of Civil Trial, regarding the only grounds for appeal to the high court, there is no mention of infringement of case law as a potential ground for appeal, this constituting an apparent reduction of its content, which only encompasses in an express manner the infringement of the norms of the legal system. This is really so when the decision appealed is one of the types contemplated in the cases foreseen in sub-clauses 1 and 2 of clause 2 of article 477, but in the cases referred to in number 3, with relation to clause 3 of the same article (on which the sources of appeal seeking annulment are based), the importance – and even primacy – of case law in the shaping of appeal to the high court is made clear. This is not strictly as a ground for appeal, but it is recognized as a requirement for the origins of the same, to the extent that, in those cases, the infringement of the rule is not sufficient in itself to constitute grounds for appeal but also requires the decision to contradict case law precedent regarding the issue at hand, or the need exists to unify or establish lines of precedent.

... Case law has not diminished in importance in the new Law of Civil Trial, but its significance has in fact increased, given that appeal to the high court has, in great measure, the objective of forming and unifying case law.

For that reason, the civil procedural legislator has not "forgotten" case law, but rather has given it their true consideration: it is not a source of law and, hence, cannot be a direct ground, but does constitute an integral basis for an appeal for annulment."[207]

5.2. *The Post-1978 Situation*

Following the coming into force of the Spanish Constitution in 1978, there was a profound change in Spain, not merely at a political level but

206 *Ibid.*, pp. 249-252.

207 J. MONTERO AROCA – J. FLORS MATÍES, *El recurso de casación civil. Casación e infracción procesal*, Valencia, Tirant lo Blanch, 2009, pp. 411-413.

also legally. This would have repercussions in terms of the value that case law possesses in the Spanish legal system.[208]

5.2.1. Spanish Constitution of 1978 and its Main New Contributions on the Matter

The provisions of Article 117 of the Spanish Constitution also lead one to the conclusion that case law is not a source of law. This article states:

> *Justice emanates from the people and is administered on behalf of the King by judges and magistrates, members of the judiciary, who shall be independent, have fixed tenure, be accountable and subject only to the rule of law* (Article 117.1 Spanish Constitution, author's underlining).[209]
>
> *The exercise of judicial authority in any kind of action, both in judging and having judgements executed, is vested exclusively in the judgements and courts as established by the law, in accordance with the rules of jurisdiction and procedure established therein* (Article 117.3 Spanish Constitution).
>
> *Judges and courts shall not exercise any powers other than those indicated in the foregoing sub-article and those which are expressly allocated to them by law as a guarantee of any right* (Article 117.4 Spanish Constitution).

Article 9.3 of the Constitution leads us to reach the same conclusion, proclaiming the "principle of legality" which excludes the possibility of freely creating law.[210]

208 See, on the subject, A. PREDIERI, "El sistema de fuentes del Derecho", in *La Constitución española de 1978, Estudio sistemático*, directed by PREDIERI and GARCÍA DE ENTERRÍA, Madrid, 1984, pp. 159-260. O. BACHOF, *Jueces y Constitución*, Madrid, Civitas, 1985. F. BALAGUER CALLEJÓN, *Fuentes del ordenamiento constitucional*, I and II, Madrid, Tecnos, 1991, 1992. M. GORDILLO GARCÍA, "La jurisprudencia en la Constitución", in *Jornadas de la Dirección General de lo Contencioso sobre "La Constitución española y las fuentes del Derecho"*, II, Madrid, Ed. Instituto de Estudios Fiscales, 1979, pp. 1181-1190. D. GRIMM, "La Constitución como fuente del Derecho", in BARATTA, GRIMM, RUBIO LLORENTE *et al.*, *Las fuentes del Derecho, Anuario de la Facultad de Derecho*, Barcelona, Estudi General de Lleida, 1983.

209 See, J. MONTERO AROCA, *Independencia y responsabilidad del juez*, in Cuadernos Civitas, Madrid, Civitas, 1990.

210 See, E. GARCÍA DE ENTERRÍA, "Principio de legalidad, estado material de Derecho y facultades interpretativas y constructivas de la jurisprudencia en la Constitución", in *Revista Española de Derecho Constitucional*, 10,

Opposed to this opinion is another doctrinal perspective – expressed by Professor Lalaguna, for example – which argues that case law is a source, albeit not formal and direct but at least indirect and complementary to statute, although always subordinate to it in the sense that one cannot or must not behave *contra legem*, but instead *secundum legem* or *praeter legem*.[211] Others, like Santos Briz, talk of case law as a "real" or "institutional" source of law, in the form of "elementary authority".[212]

It is essential that judgements have "reasons" and be "published". In the Spanish legal system, giving reasons for judicial resolutions is required by Article 120.3 of the Constitution:

> *Judgements shall always have grounds, and those grounds shall be stated in a public hearing.*

The obligation to provide grounds for judgements is also connected to the subjective right to judicial protection guaranteed by Article 24 of the Constitution, as a "control" on judicial activity. In this manner, if a judge or court does not give reasons for a judgement, or judges erroneously – in an irrational form – said decision may, via the exercise of the corresponding right of appeal, be declared null and without effect – Supreme Court Judgement of 22 October 1995.

1984, pp. 11-61. F. GARRIDO FALLA (dir.), *Comentarios a la Constitución española de 1978*, 2nd. ed., Madrid, Civitas, 1985. *Id*, "Función jurisdiccional y poder judicial", in *Estudios jurídicos en honor a José Gabaldón López*, Madrid, Trivium, 1990. J. PRIEUR, "Jurisprudence et principe de séparation des pouvoirs", in *Archives de Philosophie du Droit*, 30, *La jurisprudence*, Paris, Sirey, 1985, pp. 117-130. M. PULIDO QUECEDO, *La Constitución española con la jurisprudencia del Tribunal Constitucional*, Pamplona, 1996.

211 See, E. LALAGUNA DOMÍNGUEZ, "Valor de la jurisprudencia en la elaboración de la Ciencia del Derecho", in *Revista Crítica de Derecho Inmobiliario*, 468, September-October 1968, pp. 1217-1238. *Id*, *Jurisprudencia y fuentes del Derecho*, Pamplona, Aranzadi, 1969. *Id*, "Jurisprudencia", in *Nueva Enciclopedia Jurídica Seix*, Barcelona, 1971.

212 See, J. SANTOS BRIZ, "El Tribunal Supremo como órgano jurisdiccional superior. Valor de la jurisprudencia", in *Revista de Derecho Público*, 84-85, July-December 1981. *Id*, "La aplicación de las normas jurídicas en el nuevo Título Preliminar del Código Civil", in *Libro Homenaje a Ramón Mª Roca Sastre*, I, Madrid, Universidad Complutense de Madrid, 1976, pp. 753-779.

5.2.2. The Organic Law regarding the Judiciary

What is the situation regarding the matter of sources, especially in relation to case law, following the reform of the Organic Law of Judicial Power 6/1985, of 1 July? Has the controversial Article 5, in its sub-articles 1 and 4, varied the existing situation? Does the principle of separation of powers remain intact?[213]

Article 5 of the Organic Law states:

> *The Constitution is the supreme rule of the legal system, binding all judges and courts, who shall interpret and apply statute and regulations in accordance with the constitutional rules and principles and conforming to the interpretation of the same adopted in judgements of the Constitutional Court in all processes.*

To start, it can be asserted that the Organic Law of Judicial Power continues to respect the principle of separation of powers as a basic pillar of the rule of law. However, there are writers who go further, claiming that Article 5.1 of this statute transforms case law into a formal source of law together with statute, custom and general principles of law. The article cited would, according to this argument, not only establish that interpretation of statute must be undertaken in a manner conforming to constitutional rules and principles, but also create a binding requirement to follow constitutional case law.

In relation to sub-article 4 of the same Article 5, it is also established that:

> *In every case where, according to statute, there is a right to appeal, infringement of constitutional rules is sufficient to allow the exercise of that right. In this case, the Supreme Court shall always be the authority entitled to determine the appeal, whatever the issue, the applicable law and the jurisdictional order.*

In this sub-article, the right to appeal for infringement of the Constitution is guaranteed. This does not imply an absolute change in the regime of appeal. All that it seeks to demonstrate is that infringement of the Constitution is a type of "infringement of the rules of the legal system". Infringement of the constitution is included as a type of "infringement

213 E. VÁZQUEZ BOTE, "El sistema de fuentes y la Ley Orgánica del Poder Judicial", in *Revista de Derecho Inmobiliario*, 575, July-August 1986.

of state or of the rules of the legal system". It must therefore be related to a constitutional rule directly applicable to the case at hand, this circumstance appearing most likely to occur in relation to the protection of rights susceptible to appeal when development of those circumstances by statute is lacking. What, then, does Article 5.4 mean? It cannot be the substitution of appeal for legal protection, but rather, in contrast, that a decision regarding right to appeal will be susceptible to an appeal for legal protection.[214]

6. Case Law in Other Continental Legal Systems

6.1. German Law

Judgements in the German legal system must contain the following elements:

- *Kopf*, or heading, in which the parties to the dispute, their legal representatives, the court, the names of the judges and the date of the judgement are all stated.
- *Urteilsformel*, or description of the law in dispute in the instant case.
- *Tatbestand*, or suppositions of fact, where the claim, proven facts, and legal foundation of the claim are detailed.
- *Entscheidungsgründe*, where the foundations of law on which the judgement is based are assembled.

Reasoning follows a rational method – logical-deductive – but at the same time, some judicial bodies such as the BVerfG and the Federal Courts adopt a more argumentative, discursive style.

Official newspapers exist in order to publish judgements. However, the more extensively used source is that of unofficial reports, and also that of academic journals – like the *Neue Juristische Wochenschrift*, or *Juristenzeitung*. There are even publications in ordinary newspapers.

214 P. PÉREZ TREMPS, "Constitución, Ley Orgánica del Poder Judicial y jueces ordinarios", in *Documentación Jurídica*, 45 /46, 1985, pp. 33-34; L. DIEZ-PICAZO, "Tribunal Constitucional y Poder Judicial", in "Constitucionalidad, Derecho Comunitario Europeo y jurisdicción ordinaria", in Various Authors, *División de Poderes e interpretación (hacia una teoría de la praxis constitucional)*, edited by LÓPEZ PINA, Madrid, Tecnos, 1987, pp. 86-87; F. M. CALVO VIDAL, *La jurisprudencia ¿Fuente del Derecho?, op. cit.*, pp. 217-221.

German law only contains one case which clarifies the "binding" nature of judgements: paragraph 31.II BVerfGG, in relation to the decisions of the BVerfG. In this paragraph, *Gesetzskraft* – force of law – is given to judgements of the BVerfG which relate to the constitutionality or otherwise of legal rules. On the other hand, paragraph 31.I BVerfGG establishes that all decisions of the Constitutional Court have binding value – *Bindungswirkung* – for constitutional bodies, as much for the Federal State as the "Länder". "Force of law" and "binding value" must be distinguished. The first implies *erga omnes* effects. Force of law only affects the "sense" of the judgement, which is to say its *ratio decidendi*, and not the line of argument itself.[215]

215 L. MORAL SORIANO, *El precedente judicial, op. cit.*, pp. 191-219. See, also, R. ALEXY – R. DREIER, "Precedent in the Federal Republic of Germany", in N. MACCORMICK – R. SUMMERS (eds.), *Interpreting Precedents. A Comparative Study*, Darmouth, Aldershot, 1997. R. BOCANEGRA SIERRA, "Cosa juzgada, vinculación, fuerza de ley en las decisiones del Tribunal Constitucional alemán", in *Revista Española de Derecho Constitucional*, 1.1, January-April 1981, pp. 235-274. O. BÜLLOW, *Gesetz und Richterant*, 1885, Lecture in Tubingae. F. BYDLINSKI, "Hautpositionen zum Richterrecht", in *Juristen Zeitung*, 40, 1985, pp. 149-155. See, also, K. GÜNTHER, *Der Sinn für Angemessenheit. Anwendungsdiskurse in Moral und Recht*, Frankfurt am Main, Suhrkamp, 1988. CH. GUSY, "Richterrecht und Grundgesetz", in *Die öffentliche Verwaltung*, 45, 1992, pp. 461-470. W. J. HABSCHEID, "Sobre la creación jurisprudencial del Derecho en el Derecho alemán", in *Boletín Mexicano de Derecho Comparado*, VIII, 24, México, Instituto de Investigaciones Jurídicas, UNAM, September-December 1975. M. KRIELE, "Das Präjudiz im kontinental-europäischen und anglo-amerikanischen Rechskreis", in *La sentenza in Europa, metodo, tecnica e stile*, Padova, CEDAM, 1988.
K. LARENZ, "Über die Bindungswirkung von Präjudizien", in H. W. FASCHING – W. KRÁLIK, *Festschrift für H. Schima*, Wiew, 1969. P. KOTHE, "Vorlage, Richterrecht und Anspruch auf den gesetlichen Richter", in *Die öffentliche Verwaltung*, 41, 1988, pp. 284-290. W. LÜKE, "Die Bedeutung von Präjudizien im deutsche Zivilprocess", in K. KROESCHELL (ed.), *Recht und Verfahren*, Heidelberg, Müller Juristischer Verlag, 1993. C. MISCHKE, "The Inseparability of Powers: Judge-Made Law in the German Legal System", in *Publiekreg /Public Law*, 7, 1992, pp. 253-263. H. L. PILNY, *Präjudizienrecht im angloamerikanischen und deutschen Recht*, Baden-Baden, Nomos Verlag, 1993. M. REINHARDT, *Consistente Jurisdiktion: Grundlegung einer verfassungrechtlichen Theorie der rechtsfestaltenden Rechtsprechung*, Tübingen, Mohr Siebeck, 1997. H. SENDLER, "Überlegungen zum Richterrecht und richterlicher Rechtsforbildung", in *Deutsches Verwaltungsblatt*, 103, 1988, pp. 828-839. H. J. SEASONGOOD, "Jurisdiction", in

6.2. *The Swiss Civil Code and the Legislator Judge*[216]

From case law in other contexts,[217] the system of the Swiss Civil Code stands out, in which the power of judges to create law is such that they may be compared to legislators.

R. J. JANOSIK (ed.), *Encyclopedia of the American Judicial System,* II, New York, Charles Scribner's Sons, 1987, pp. 825-841. R. WAGNER-DÖBLER – L. PHILIPPS, "Präjudizien in der Rechtsprechung: statische Untersuchungen anhad der Zitierpraxis deutscher Gerichte", in *Rechtstheorie,* 23, 1992, pp. 228-241. R. WANK, "Richterliche Rechtsforbildung und Verfassungsrecht", in *Zeitschrift für Unternehmens und Gesselschaft,* 3, 1988, pp. 314-380. E. SCHLÜCHTER, *Mittlefunktion der Präjudizien,* Berlin, Gruyter, 1986.

216 See, M. COSTANZA, "I poteri creatori del giudice Svizzero", in *La giurisprudenza forense e dottrinale como fonte di diritto,* Milano, Giuffrè, 1985.

217 On case law in Latin-America, see, BUSTAMANTE Y MONTORO, "La jurisprudencia en la jerarquía de las fuentes del Derecho positivo cubano", in *Revista de Derecho Privado,* 1934. L. CABRERA, *La jurisprudencia, en la Suprema Corte de Justicia y el pensamiento jurídico,* México, Suprema Corte de Justicia de la Nación, 1985. E. GUERRERO LARA – E. GUADARRAMA, *La interpretación constitucional de la Suprema Corte de Justicia (1917-1982),* I, México, Instituto de Investigaciones Jurídicas, UNAM, 1984. A. MUÑOZ DELGADO, *Algunas consideraciones acerca de la Jurisprudencia de la Suprema Corte de Justicia de la Nación y de los Tribunales Colegiados de Circuito,* Thesis, México, Facultad de Derecho, UNAM, 1976. J. G. VALLARTA PLATA, "El poder judicial y el sistema de la Declaración de inconstitucionalidad en Latinoamérica", in *Función del Poder Judicial en los Sistemas Constitucionales Latinoamericanos,* México, Instituto de Investigaciones Jurídicas, UNAM, 1977. R. VILAR BADÍA, "La sentencia judicial, proceso creador del Derecho", in *Revista de Derecho Procesal Iberoamericano,* 2 and 3, 1977. H. G. ZERTUCHE GARCÍA, *La jurisprudencia en el sistema jurídico mexicano,* México, Porrúa, 1990.

Bibliography

—AARNIO, AULIS, "On the Truth and Validity of Interpretative Statements in Legal Dogmatics", in AARNIO, AULIS — ALEXY, ROBERT — PECZENIK, ALEXANDER, "The Foundation of Legal Reasoning", in *Rechtstheorie*, 12, 1981, pp. 423—448.

—"On the Sources of Law", in *Rechtstheorie*, 15, 1984, pp. 393—401.

—ABRAHAM, HENRY J., *The Judicial Process*, New York—Oxford, Oxford University Press, 1986.

—ADAME GODDARD, JORGE, "Jurisprudencia", in *Diccionario Jurídico Mexicano*, V, México, Instituto de Investigaciones Jurídicas, UNAM, 1984, p. 289.

—ADAMS, G. BURTON, "The Origin of English Equity", in *Columbia Law Review*, 16, 1916, pp. 87—98.

—ADAMS, JOHN, *The Doctrine of Equity*, 8th ed., Philadelphia, Johnson, 1890.

—AFTALIÓN, ENRIQUE R. — VILANOVA, JOSÉ, "La jurisprudencia como fuente del Derecho", in *Revista La Ley*, Buenos Aires, 81.

—AGUIAR DE LUQUE, LUIS, "El Tribunal Constitucional y la función legislativa: el control del procedimiento legislativo y de la inconstitucionalidad por omisión", in *Revista de Derecho Político*, Madrid, Universidad Nacional de Educación a Distancia, 24, summer 1987, pp. 9—30.

—AGÚNDEZ FERNÁNDEZ, ANTONIO, "La jurisprudencia: ciencia, técnica y arte del Derecho", in *El Poder Judicial*, I, Madrid, 1983, pp. 353—379.

—ALBALADEJO GARCÍA, MANUEL, "La jurisprudencia", in *Revista de Derecho Privado*, 54, 1970.

—*Curso de Derecho Civil español, I, Introducción y Parte General*, 3rd ed., Barcelona, Bosch, 1983.

—*Derecho civil, I, Introducción y Parte General, vol. I, Introducción y Derecho de la Persona*, 12nd ed., Zaragoza, 1991.

—ALCALÁ ZAMORA Y CASTILLO, NICETO, "Ensayo de diferenciación entre la jurisprudencia y los «usos forenses»", in *Boletín de la Universidad de Santiago*, 1933.

—*Jueces. Jurisdicción, Jurisprudencia. (Estudios de Derecho procesal)*, Madrid, 1934, pp. 303—326.

— "Derecho consuetudinario y función judicial", in *Estudios Jurídicos*, 1934.

—ALCALÁ ZAMORA Y TORRES, NICETO, *La jurisprudencia y la vida del Derecho.* Discurso leído en el acto de recepción. Contestación de Rafael de Ureña y Smenjaud el día 22 de febrero de 1920, Madrid, Real Academia de Ciencias Morales y Políticas, 1920.

—ALEXANDER, L., "Precedent", in D. PATTERSON, *A Companion to Philosophy of Law and Legal Theory*, Oxford, Blackwell, 1996.

—ALEXY, ROBERT, "Reschtsregeln und Rechtsprinzipien", in *A.R.S.P.*, Beiheft NF, 25, 1985, pp. 25 ff.

—"Justification and Application of Norms", in *Ratio Juris*, 6, 1993, pp. 155—170.

—*Teoría de la argumentación jurídica*, translation into Spanish by MANUEL ATIENZA and I. ESPEJO, Madrid, 1997.

—ALEXY, ROBERT — DREIER, RALF, "Precedent in the Federal Republic of Germany", in NEIL MACCORMICK — ROBERT SUMMERS (eds.), *Interpreting Precedents. A Comparative Study*, Darmouth, Aldershot, 1997.

—ALMAGRO NOSETE, JOSÉ, *Justicia Constitucional (Comentarios a la Ley Orgánica del Tribunal Constitucional)*, 2nd ed., in cooperation with P. SAAVEDRA GALLO, Valencia, 1989.

— ALMEDA Y ROIG, J., "La costumbre como fuente de Derecho", in *Revista Jurídica de Cataluña*, 1908.

—ALONSO GARCÍA, ENRIQUE, "Los efectos formales de la declaración de inconstitucionalidad en el sistema constitucional norteamericano", in *Revista Española de Derecho Constitucional*, 6, 1982, pp. 209—257.

—*La interpretación de la Constitución*, Madrid, 1984.

—"El control por el Tribunal Constitucional del sistema español de fuentes del Derecho a través del artículo 24 de la Constitución", in *Revista Española de Derecho Constitucional*, 24, 1988, pp. 191—211.

—ALONSO GARCÍA, RICARDO, "El Tribunal Constitucional y la eficacia temporal de sus sentencias anulatorias", in *Revista de Administración Pública*, 119, May—August 1989, pp. 255—268.

—ÁLVAREZ CONDE, ENRIQUE, "La posición constitucional del Poder Judicial", in *Jornadas sobre el Poder Judicial, de la Dirección General de lo Contencioso*, IEF, I, Madrid, 1983.

—ÁLVAREZ DORREGO, MATÍAS, *La Corte Penal Internacional: hacia la inclusión en el Estatuto de Roma del crimen de terrorismo*, Buenos Aires, Fabián J. de Plácido, 2004.

—ÁLVAREZ SUÁREZ, URSICINO, *La jurisprudencia romana en la hora presente*, discurso leído el día 2 de mayo de 1966, en su recepción pública, y constestación de Leonardo Prieto—Castro y Ferrandiz, Madrid, Real Academia de Jurisprudencia y Legislación, 1966.

—ÁLVAREZ VIGARAY, RAFAEL, "Las mutuas influencias entre la legislación y la jurisprudencia", in el *Libro Homenaje a Ramón María Roca Sastre*, I, Madrid, Junta de Decanos de los Colegios Notariales, 1976, pp. 825—841.

—ALLEN, CARLETON KEMP, SIR (1887—1966*), Law in the Making*, 2nd ed. revised, Oxford, Clarendon Press, 1930.

—"Case Law: an Unwarrantable Intervention", in *The Law Quarterly Review*, 51, 1935, pp. 333—346.

—*Las fuentes del Derecho inglés*, Preface by ANTONIO ORTIZ GARCÍA, Madrid, Instituto de Estudios Políticos, 1969.

—ANDRADA HERRERO, NARCISO, *La equidad como elemento catalizador entre la norma jurídica y la justicia,* Thesis directed by JOSÉ ITURMENDI MORALES, Madrid, Editorial de la Universidad Complutense de Madrid, 1988.

—ANDREWS, N. H., "Reporting Case Law: Unreported Cases, the Definition of a Ratio and the Criteria for Reporting Decisions", in *Legal Studies,* 5, 1, 1985, pp. 205—235.

—ANGLADA VILARDEBO, JUAN, "La jurisprudencia ¿fuente del Derecho?", in *Estudios de Derecho Civil en Homenaje al Profesor Castán Tobeñas,* IV, Pamplona, Ediciones Universidad de Navarra, 1969, pp. 71—85.

—ANTONIOLLI DEFLORIAN, LUISA, "Il ruolo del precedente giudiziale nel common law inglese", in VINCENTI, UMBERTO (a cura di), in cooperation with GIANNI SANTUCCI, *Il valore dei precedenti giudiziali nella tradizione europea,* Padova, CEDAM, 1998, pp. 167—235.

— ANTONOPOULOS, *La jurisprudence des organes de la Convention eurpéenne des droits de l'homme,* Leyden, 1967.

—ANZON, ADELA, *Il valore del precedente nel giudizio sulle leggi,* Milano, Giuffrè, 1995.

—"Algunas consideraciones sobre la justicia y el poder judicial", in *Revista Jurídica de Cataluña,* 4, 1983.

—"Algunas consideraciones sobre el Tribunal Constitucional", in *Revista Jurídica de Castilla—La Mancha,* 1, 1987, pp. 27—53.

—ARAGÓN REYES, MANUEL, "Dos cuestiones interesantes en nuestra jurisdicción constitucional: control de las leyes anteriores y de la jurisprudencia", in *Jornadas de la Dirección General de lo Contencioso del Estado sobre el Tribunal Constitucional,* I, Madrid, Instituto de Estudios Fiscales, 1981, pp. 555—574.

—Under "Tribunal Constitucional", in *Enciclopedia Jurídica Básica,* vol. IV, Madrid, Civitas, 1995.

—ARCHIVES DE PHILOSOPHIE DU DROIT, *La jurisprudence,* XXX, Paris, Sirey, 1985.

—AROZAMENA SIERRA, JERÓNIMO, "Valor de la jurisprudencia constitucional", in *La Constitución española y las fuentes del Derecho,* I, Madrid, 1979, pp. 253—279.

—ARROYO ZAPATERO, LUIS, "Jurisprudencia constitucional en materia penal", in *Cuadernos de Política Criminal,* 17, 1982, pp. 385—405.

—ASHBURNER, WALTER, *Principles of Equity,* London, 1902, 2nd ed., by Browne Butterworth, London, 1933. (1rst ed. 1902).

—ATIENZA RODRÍGUEZ, MANUEL, *Las razones del Derecho. Teorías de la argumentación jurídica,* Madrid, Centro de Estudios Constitucionales, 1991.

—ATIYAH, PATRICK S. — SUMMERS, ROBERT S., *Form and Substance in Anglo—American Law,* Oxford, Clarendon Press, 1987.

—AUBENQUE, PIERRE, *La prudence chez Aristote,* Paris, 1963.

—AUSTIN, JOHN, *Sobre la utilidad del estudio de la jurisprudencia.* Translation into Spanish and Preface by FELIPE GONZÁLEZ VICÉN, Madrid, Centro de Estudios Constitucionales, 1981.

— AVILA, JUAN JOSÉ, "Principios jurídicos y positivismo jurídico de Carrió", in *La Ley,* 141, Buenos Aires, 1971.

—AZUELA GUITRÓN, MARIANO, "Importancia, límites y riesgos de la jurisprudencia", in *La Interpretación Constitucional de la Suprema Corte de Justicia de la Nación en Materia de Impuestos 1917—1985,* México, Instituto de Investigaciones Jurídicas, UNAM, Tribunal Fiscal de la Federación, 1986.

— BACON, FRANCIS, "Sur la legislation et la jurisprudence", in *Archives de Philosophie du Droit,* 30, "La jurisprudence", 1985, pp. 351—362.

—BACHI, MARIO, "I poteri del giudice in un sistema di codice, di 'judge made law' e di equità", in *Rivista Internazionale di Filosofia del Diritto,* 1952.

—BACHOF, OTTO, *Jueces y Constitución,* Madrid, Civitas, 1985.

—BAKER, JOHN H. (ed.), *Judicial Records, Law Reports, and the Growth of Case Law,* Berlin, Duncker & Humblot, 1989.

—"Records and the Origins of Case—Law in England", in JOHN H. BAKER (ed.), *Judicial Records, Law Reports and the Growth of Case Law,* Berlin, Duncker & Humblot, 1989, pp. 15—46.

—BALAGUER CALLEJÓN, F., *Fuentes del ordenamiento constitucional,* I and II, Madrid, Tecnos, 1991, 1992.

— BALLADORE PALLIERI, GIORGIO, *I principi generali del Diritto riconosciuti dalle nazioni civili nell'art. 38 dello statuto della Corte Permanente di Giustizia Internazionale,* Memorie del'Istituto Giuridico, Torino, 1931.

—BALLOW, HENRY, *A Treatise of Equity,* Dublin, S. Cotter, 1756.

—BALOSSINI, CAJO ENRICO, *Consuetudini, usi, pratiche, regole del costume,* Milano, Giuffrè, 1958.

—"L'accertamento del diritto consuetudinario compito del giurista e del sociologo", in *La prassi amministrativa,* Milano, Giuffrè, 1963.

—*La categoria del 'diritto dei privati' nei rapporti commerciali 'internazionali',* Milano, Giuffrè, 1968.

—BARATTA, ALESSANDRO, "Le fonti del diritto ed il diritto giurisprudenziale", in *Materiali per una Storia della Cultura Giuridica,* XX, 1, 1980, pp. 189—211.

—"La jurisprudencia y la ciencia jurídica como fuente del Derecho", in Various Authors (BARATTA, GRIMA, RUBIO LLORENTE *et al.*), *Las fuentes del Derecho, Anuario de la Facultad de Derecho, Estudi General de Lleida,* Barcelona, 1983.

—BARBERO, DOMENICO, *Sistema del Derecho Privado, I —Introducción, Parte preliminar, Parte general—,* translation into Spanish by S. SENTÍS MELENDO, Buenos Aires, Ediciones Jurídicas Europa—América, 1967.

—BARNEY, CHARLES NEAL, *Equity and its Remedies,* Boston, Jackson, 1915.

—BELAID, S., *Essai sur le Pouvoir Createur et Normatif du Juge,* preface by MICHEL VILLEY, Paris, Librairie Generale de Droit et de Jurisprudence, Bibliotheque de Philosophie du Droit, directed by CH. EISENMANN, HENRI BATTIFOL and MICHEL VILLEY, vol. XVII, 1974.

—BELL, GARY F., *What do we Mean by Equity?,* 1993.

—BELLONI PERESSUTTI, GIAMPAOLO, "Metodo e strategie nell'utilizzazione di precedenti giudiziali : riflessioni di un avvocato civilista", in VINCENTI, UM-

BERTO (a cura di), in cooperation with GIANNI SANTUCCI, *Il valore dei precedenti giudiziali nella tradizione europea,* Padova, CEDAM, 1998, pp. 147—163.

—BELTRÁN DE HEREDIA Y ONIS, P., *La función judicial y el Código Civil a través de un siglo, Centenario del Código Civil (1889—1989),* I, Madrid, Ed. Centro de Estudios Ramón Areces, 1990.

—BENION, F. A. R., *Statute Law,* London, Oyez Pub., 1980.

—BIBENT, MICHEL, *L'informatique appliquée à la jurisprudence. Une méthode de traitment de la documentation juridique,* preface by PIERRE CATALA, Paris, Librairies Techniques, 1976.

—BILLSON, W.W., *Equity in its Relations to Common Law,* Boston, Boston Book Co., 1917.

—BISPHAM, GEORGE TUCKER, *The Principles of Equity,* 9th ed., New York, Banks Law Publ. Co., 1915. 11rst ed., New York, Baker, 1931.

—BLACK, IAIN J. — TWEED, ELISABETH, *Equity in a Nutshell,* London, Sweet & Maxwell, 1951.

—BLACK, VIRGINIA, "Legal Equity ad its Misuse", in *Vera Lex,* 11, 1, 1991, pp. 8—10.

—BLACKSTONE, WILLIAM, *Commentaries of the Laws of England (A Facsimile of the First Edition of 1765—1769, I, 1765),* Chicago—London, University of Chicago Press, 1979.

—BLECHER, M.D., "Equitable Delimitation of Continental Shelf", in *American Journal of International Law,* 73, 1979, pp. 60 ff.

—BLUM, YEHUDA Z., "The Role of Equity in International Law", in A. MORDECHAI RABELLO (ed.), *Aequitas and Equity...,* op. cit., pp. 229—239.

—BLYTH, EDWARD EGBERT, *An Analysis of Snells Principles of Equity: with Notes Thereon,* London, 14th ed., Stevens & Haynes, 1929. (6th ed. 1898).

—BOBBIO, NORBERTO, *La consuetudine come fatto normativo,* Padova, Cedam, 1942.

—"Principi Generali del Diritto", in *Novissimo Digesto Italiano,* XXI, 1—2, 1966, pp. 3—32.

—BOCANEGRA SIERRA, RAÚL, "Cosa juzgada, vinculación, fuerza de ley en las decisiones del Tribunal Constitucional alemán", in *Revista Española de Derecho Constitucional,* 1.1, January—April 1981, pp. 235—274.

—*El valor de las sentencias del Tribunal Constitucional,* Madrid, Instituto de Estudios de Administración Local, 1982.

—"Sobre el alcance objetivo de las sentencias del Tribunal Constitucional", in *Estudios sobre la Constitución. Homenaje al profesor Eduardo García de Enterría, vol. I, El ordenamiento jurídico,* 1991, pp. 509—536.

—BODENHEIMER, EDGAR, *Jurisprudence. The Philosophy and Method of Law,* Cambridge —Massachusetts—, Harvard University Press, 2nd ed. 1974.

—BODENHEIMER, EDGAR — OAKLEY, JOHN BILYEU — LOVE, JEAN C., *An Introduction to the Anglo—American Legal System,* St. Paul —Minnesota—, West Publ. Co., 1988.

—BOEHMER, GUSTAV, *El Derecho a través de la jurisprudencia. Su aplicación y creación,* translation and notes of Spanish law by JOSÉ PUIG BRUTAU — from the German original *Praxis der Richterlichen Rechtsschöpfung*, Tubingen, J. C. B. Mohr (Paul Siebeck), 1952—, Barcelona, Bosch, 1959.

—BOLANGER, JULIEN, "Notations sur le pouvoir createur de la jurisprudence civile", in *Revue Trimestrielle de Droit Civil*, LIX, Sirey, 1961.

—BONFANTE, PIETRO, *Historia del Derecho romano*, I, translation into Spanish by SANTACRUZ TEJEIRO, Madrid, Editorial Revista de Derecho Privado, 1944.

—BONNECASE, J., *Elementos de Derecho Civil, I (Nociones preliminares, persona, familia y bienes)*, translation into Spanish by CAJICA, México, 1945.

—BORDA, GUILLERMO A., "Reglas prácticas para la interpretación de la ley civil", in *Revista General de Legislación y Jurisprudencia*, 190, 1951, pp. 507 ff.

— BORJA, ERNESTO EDUARDO, "La naturaleza de los principios generales del Derecho", in *Revista del Colegio de Abogados de la Plata*, 1962.

—BRADNEY, A. — FISCHER, V — MASSON, J — NEAL, A. — NEWELL, D, *How to Study Law*, London, Sweet and Maxwell, 1986.

—BRADY, "Equity without the Equity Lawyers", in *Acta Juridica*, Cape Town, 1978, pp. 125—134.

—BRATZ, DAVID C., "Stare Decisis in Lower Courts: Predicting the Demise of the Supreme Court Precedent", in *Washingon Law Review*, 60, 1, 1984, pp. 87—100.

—BRENNER, SAUL — SPAETH, HAROLD J., *Stare Indecisis: the Alteration of Precedent on the Supreme Court, 1946—1992*, New York, University of Cambridge, Cambridge University Press, 1995.

—BRONAUGH, RICHARD, "Persuasive Precedent", in L. GOLDSTEIN (ed.), *Precedent in Law*, Oxford, Clarendon Press, 1987, pp. 217—247.

—BROWN, BRENDAN F., "Equity in the Law of the United States of America", in R. A. NEWMAN, *Equity in the World's Legal Systems. A Comparative Study*, from the Congress of the Hastings College of Law of the University of California in Bellagio, August 1972, dedicated to RENÉ CASSIN, Brussels, Établissements Émile Bruylant, 1973, pp. 205—223.

—BROWNSON, JAMES IRWIN, *Equity in Pennsylvania from the Historical Point of View*, Washington, Washington Bar Association, 1914.

—BUCKLAND, WILLIAM WARWICK — MACHAIR, ARNOLD D., *Derecho romano y common law: una comparación en esbozo*, translation from English by IGNACIO CREMADES UGARTE, Madrid, Editorial Centro de Estudios Ramón Areces, S. A., 1994.

—BUEN LOZANO, DEMÓFILO DE, "Las normas jurídicas y la función judicial (alrededor de los artículos 5 y 6 C.C.)", in *Revista General de Legislación y Jurisprudencia*, 129, 1916; 130, 1917—I; 131, 1917—II.

—*Introducción al estudio del Derecho civil*, Madrid, Ed. Revista de Derecho Privado, 1932; there is a second edition with preface by NÉSTOR DE BUEN, México, Porrúa, 1977.

—BULYGIN, EUGENIO, "Sentencia judicial y creación de Derecho", in *La ley*, Buenos Aires, CXXIV, 1967. There is an Italian translation, "Sentenza giudiziaria e creazione del Diritto", in *Rivista Internazionale di Filosofia del Diritto*, 1967, pp. 164—180.

—BÜLLOW, O, *Gesetz und Richterant*, 1885, Speech in Tubingae, Leipzig.

—BURROWS, J. F., "The Interrelation Between Common Law and Statute Law", in *Otago Law Review*, 3, 4, 1976, pp. 583—600.

—BUSTAMANTE Y MONTORO, "La jurisprudencia en la jerarquía de las fuentes del Derecho positivo cubano", in *Revista de Derecho Privado*, 1934.

—*Introducción a la Ciencia del Derecho (Concepto y Fuentes del Derecho)*, I, 3rd ed., La Habana, 1945.

—BYDLINSKI, FRANZ, "Hautpositionen zum Richterrecht", in *Juristen Zeitung*, 40, 1985, pp. 149—155.

—CABANILLAS GALLAS, PÍO, "Consideraciones sobre los principios generales del Derecho". Discurso leído en la Real Academia de Jurisprudencia y Legislación el 2 de mayo de 1977, Madrid, Real Academia de Jurisprudencia y Legislación, 1977.

—CABRERA, LUCIO, *La jurisprudencia, en la Suprema Corte de Justicia y el pensamiento jurídico*, México, Suprema Corte de Justicia y de la Nación, 1985.

—CADOPPI, ALBERTO, "Introduzione allo studio del valore del precedente giudiziale nel diritto penale italiano", in VINCENTI, UMBERTO (a cura di), in cooperation with GIANNI SANTUCCI, *Il valore dei precedenti giudiziali nella tradizione europea*, Padova, CEDAM, 1998, pp. 106—147.

—*Il valore del precedente nel Diritto penale: uno studio sulla dimensione in action della legalità*, Torino, G. Giappichelli, 1999.

—CALABRESI, GUIDO, *A Common Law for the Age of Statutes*, Cambridge —Massachusetts—, London —England—, Harvard University Press, 1982.

—CALAMANDREI, PIERO, "La funzione della giurisprudenza nel tempo presente", in *Rivista Trimestralle di Diritto e Procedura Civile*, 1955, pp. 252—272.

—CALVO VIDAL, FÉLIX M., *La jurisprudencia ¿fuente del Derecho?*, Valladolid, Lex Nova, 1992.

—CANTOS, VICENTE, "¿Función automática o función creadora?", in *Revista Crítica de Derecho Inmobiliario*, 1917, September 1934.

—CAPPELLETTI, MAURO, "Reflessioni sulla creatività della giurisprudenza nel tempo presente", in *Rivista Trimestrale di Diritto e Procedura Civile*, 1982, pp. 774—792.

—*Giudici legislatori?*, Milano, Giuffrè, 1984.

—"¿Renegar de Montesquieu? La expansión y la legitimidad de la justicia constitucional", translation into Spanish by P. DE LUIS DURÁN, in *Revista Española de Derecho Constitucional*, 17, 1986, pp. 9—45.

—CARDOZO, BENJAMIN, *La naturaleza de la función judicial*, Buenos Aires, Ed. Arayú, 1955. English version, *The Nature of the Judicial Process*, New Haven and London, Yale University Press, 1949.

—CARON, PIER GIOVANNI, *"Aequitas" romana, "misericordia" patristica, ed "epicheia" aristotelica nella dottrina dell "aequitas" canonica (Dalle origini al Rinascimento)*, Milano, Giuffrè, 1971. Review by FRANCESCO D'AGOSTINO, in *Rivista Internazionale di Filosofia del Diritto*, 48, 1972, pp. 123—124.

—CARPENTER, CHARLES E., "Court Decisions and the Common Law", in *Columbia Law Review*, 17, 7, 1917, pp. 593—607.

—CARRETERO PÉREZ, ADOLFO, "El Tribunal Constitucional, el Tribunal Supremo y los Tribunales Superiores de las Comunidades Autónomas", in *El Tribunal*

Constitucional, I, Dirección General de lo Contencioso del Estado, Instituto de Estudios Fiscales, 1981, pp. 603—627.

—CARRETERO PÉREZ, ADOLFO — LÓPEZ VILAS, R., "Las menciones a jueces y tribunales en el Código Civil", in *El Centenario del Código Civil en el Tribunal Supremo. Ciclo de Conferencias organizado por la Presidencia del T. S.*, Madrid, 6 and 7 June, 1989, Madrid, Ministerio de Justicia, 1989.

—CARRIO, GENARO RUBÉN, *Principios jurídicos y positivismo jurídico,* Buenos Aires, Abeledo—Perrot, 1970.

—"Judge Made Law under a Civil Code", in *Louisiana Law Review,* 41, 1981, pp. 990 ff.

—"Sobre la administración de justicia y el derecho de la jurisdicción", in *Anuario de Derechos Humanos,* 5, 1988—89, pp. 41—53.

—CARTHY, ANTHONY, "L'impact de Dworkin sur la Philosophie du Droit Anglo—americaine", in *Droit et societé,* 2, January 1986, pp. 7—14.

—CARTY, HAZEL, "Precedent and the Court of Appeal: Lord Denning's Views Explored", in *Legal Studies,* 1, 1, 1981, pp. 68—76.

—CASSO, IGNACIO DE, Lecture on "El Derecho y su dinámica", in *Revista General de Derecho,* 1950.

—CASTÁN TOBEÑAS, JOSÉ, *La formulación judicial del Derecho (jurisprudencia y arbitrio de equidad),* 2nd ed., Madrid, Reus, 1934.

—*Teoría de la aplicación e investigación del Derecho (Metodología y técnica operativa en el Derecho privado positivo,* Madrid, Reus, 1947.

—*Derecho civil, común y foral,* I, 1, 12nd ed. revised by DE LOS MOZOS, Madrid, Reus, 1982.

—CATLETT, FRED W., "The Development of the Doctrine of Stare Decisis and the Extent to Which it Should Be Applied", in *Washington Law Review,* 21, 1946, pp. 159—170.

—CHAFEE, ZECHARIAH, *Some Problems of Equity,* 1950.

—*Cases and Materials on Equity,* Brooklyn, Foundation, 1958, 5ª ed., 1967.

—CHECCHINI, C., "Storia della giurisprudenza e interpretazione della legge", in *Archivio Giuridico Filippo Serafín,* XC, 1923, pp. 167 ff.

—CLAVERO, BARTOLOMÉ, *Los derechos y los jueces,* Madrid, Cuadernos Civitas, 1988.

—COBDEN, A. L., "El juez y la regla de Derecho", in *Revista de Derecho Privado,* December, 1989.

—COCA PAYERAS, MIGUEL, *La doctrina legal. (Estudio de su naturaleza y contenido, así como de la incidencia ejercida sobre ella por la doctrina jurisprudencial del Tribunal Supremo),* Barcelona, Bosch, 1980.

—COIPEL, M., "Les reactions de la doctrine à la cuestion de droit par les juges en droit civil", in *Travaux de l'Association Henri Capitant, Les reactions de la doctrine à la creation du droit par les juges (Journeès italiemmes, XXXI),* Paris, 1980.

—COLESANTI, VITTORIO ; "Giurisprudenza", in *Novissimo Digesto Italiano,* VII, Torino, 1961, pp. 1101—1106.

—COLIN, A. — CAPITANT, N., *Curso elemental de Derecho Civil, I (Introducción, estado civil, domicilio y ausencia)*,with notes by D. DE BUEN, Madrid, Reus, 1922.

—COMOTTI, GIUSEPPE, "Il valore del precedente giudiziale nella tradizione canonica", in VINCENTI, UMBERTO (a cura di), in cooperation with GIANNI SANTUCCI, *Il valore dei precedenti giudiziali nella tradizione europea*, Padova, CEDAM, 1998, pp. 81—106.

—CONSEJO GENERAL DEL PODER JUDICIAL, *La posición constitucional del Tribunal Supremo*, in Discurso de Apertura de los Tribunales, Madrid, Consejo General del Poder Judicial, 1995.

—CONSTANTINOFF, J., "Two Creations of Praetorium Jurisprudence under French Law", in *Tulane Law Review*, XXIV.

—*CONTROL CONSTITUCIONAL DE LAS JURISDICCIONES: EL TRIBUNAL CONSTITUCIONAL FRENTE A LOS PROCESOS*, Miraflores, Perú, Gaceta Jurídica, 2006.

—COOK, KAREN S. — MESSICK, DAVID M., "The Powers of Courts of Equity", New York, *Columbia Law Review*, vol. XV, 1915.

—"Equitable Defenses", in *Yale Law Journal*, XXXII.

—*Cases and Materials on Equity*, 3rd ed., Ed. Warren A. Seavey (American Casebook Series), St. Paul, Minnesota West Publishing, 1940.

—COOK, WALTER WHEELER, "The Place of Equity in our Legal System", in *American Bar Association Report*, vol. XXXVII, 1912, pp. 997—1009.

—COOPER, H. H. A., "Ratio Decidendi", in *The New Law Journal*, 118, 1968, pp. 1180—1181.

—COSSIO Y CORRAL, ALFONSO DE, "Jurisprudencia conceptual y jurisprudencia de intereses", in *Revista General de Legislación y Jurisprudencia*, CLXXIV, II, 1943, pp. 462—477.

—"La concepción anglosajona del Derecho", in *Revista de Derecho Privado*, XXXI, April 1947.

—COSTA, "Requisitos de la costumbre jurídica según los autores", in *Revista General de Legislación y Jurisprudencia*, 1881.

—*El problema de la ignorancia del Derecho y sus relaciones con el "status" individual, el referéndum y la costumbre*, Discurso de recepción a la Academia de Ciencias Morales y Políticas, Madrid, Academia de Ciencias Morales y Políticas, 1901.

—COSTANZA, M., "I poteri creatori del giudice Svizzero", in *La giurisprudenza forense e dottrinale come fonte di diritto*, Milano, Giuffrè, 1985.

—COWAN, THOMAS A., "Legislative Equity in Pennsylvania", in *University of Pittsburgh Law Review*, 4, 1, 1937.

—CRISAFULLI, VEZIO, "A proposito dei principi generali di diritto e di una loro enunciazione legislativa", in *Jus*, I, 1940, pp. 193—214.

—"I principi costituzionali dell'interpretazione ed applicazione delle leggi", in *Scritti in Onore di Santi Romano*, vol. I, Padova, Cedam, 1940, pp. 663—703.

—"Per la determinazione del concetto dei principi generali del diritto", in *Rivista Internazionale di Filosofia del Diritto*, 1941, I, II, pp. 41—63; III, pp. 157—181; and IV—V, pp. 230—264.

—"Variazione sul tema delle fonti con particolare riguardo alla consuetudine", in *Scritti in memoria di Antonino*, Milano, Giuffrè, vol. III, 1967, pp. 253—278.

—CRISCUOLI, GIOVANNI, "La sentenze della giustizia inglese: i precedenti 'vincolanti' e i precedenti 'persuasive'", in *Economia e Credito*, 3, 1976, pp. 1—32.

—CRISTOBAL MONTES, ÁNGEL, "La costumbre, la jurisprudencia y la equidad en el nuevo Título Preliminar del C.C. español", in *Revista General de Legislación y Jurisprudencia*, LXXV, 243, 1977.

—CROSS, SIR RUPERT, "Stare Decisis in Contemporary England", in *The Law Quarterly Review*, 82, 1966, pp. 203—214.

—"The Ratio Decidendi and a Plurality of Speeches in the House of Lords", in *The Law Quarterly Review*, 93, 1977, pp. 378—385.

—"The House of Lords and the Rules of Precedent", in P. M. S. HACKER — J. RAZ (eds.), *Law, Morality and Society*, Oxford, Clarendon Press, 1988, pp. 145—160.

—*Precedent in English Law*, Oxford, Clarendon Press, 1961; J.W. HARRIS (editor), Oxford, Clarendon Press, 4th ed., 1991.

—CUETO, JOSÉ A. DEL, Discurso leído en la solemne apertura de los Tribunales el 2 de septiembre de 1918, Tribunal Supremo, Habana, Librería e Imprenta "La Moderna Poesía", 1918.

—CUETO RUA, JULIO C., "El método jurídico en la teoría egológica", in *Anuario de Filosofía Jurídica y Social*, 9, 1989.

—CURRIER, THOMAS S., "Time and Change in Judge—Made Law: Prospective Overruling", in *Virginia Law Review*, 51, 2, 1965, pp. 201—272.

—CURZON, LESLIE BASIL, *Equity*, London, Macdonald & Evans, 1967, (2nd ed. 1974. 3rd ed. 1979).

—*Jurisprudence*, Plymouth, Macdonald & Evans, 1979.

—DABIN, JEAN, *La technique de l'élaboration du Droit Positif, specialement en Droit privé*, Paris, Sirey, 1935.

—D'AMATO, ANTHONY, *Jurisprudence. A Descriptive and Normative Analysis of Law*, Netherlands, Martinus Nijhoff Publishers, 1984.

—DAVID, RENÉ, *Les grands systèmes du droit contemporains*, 4th ed, Paris, Dalloz, 1971. 7th ed., 1978.

—DAVIES, JACK, "A Response to Statutory Obsolescence : the Nonprimacy of Statutes Act", in *Vermont Law Review*, 4, 2, 1979, pp. 203—231.

—DE ASIS ROIG, RAFAEL, *Jueces y normas. La decisión judicial desde el ordenamiento*, Madrid, 1995.

—DE CASTRO Y BRAVO, FEDERICO, *La idea de equidad y su relación con otras ideas, morales y jurídicas, afines. Discurso leído en la solemne apertura de los tribunales celebrada el 15 de septiembre de 1950*, Madrid, Instituto Editorial Reus, 1950. In *Revista General de Legislación y Jurisprudencia*, 1950, 2nd semester.

—"Fuentes de Derecho e interpretación jurídica", in *Anuario de Derecho Civil*, XI, I, January/March 1958.

—"El recurso en interés de ley y el valor de la jurisprudencia", in *Anuario de Derecho Civil*, XXIII, III, July—September 1970. Comment on the book by CREMADES, *El recurso de casación en interés de la ley. Estudio de su regulación en los artículos 185 y ss. de la Ley Procesal Laboral*, preface by MANUEL ALONSO OLEA, Sevilla, Instituto Gª Oviedo, 1969.

—*Derecho civil de España*, from the editions of 1949 and 1952 by the Instituto de Estudios Políticos, Introduction by LUIS DIEZ—PICAZO, Madrid, Civitas, 1984.

—DE DIEGO, FELIPE CLEMENTE, "La función jurisdiccional de los jueces y la aplicación del Derecho en general", in *Revista de Derecho Privado*, 3, December 1913.

—"El artículo 6° del Código Civil español", in *Revista de Derecho Privado*, I, 1, October 1913.

—*La jurisprudencia como fuente del Derecho*, Madrid, Ed. Revista de Derecho Privado, 1925.

—DE FIGUEREIDO TEIXEIRA, SALVIO, "Consideraciones y reflexiones sobre el Derecho norteamericano", in *Revista de la Facultad de Derecho de México*, XXIX, 13, México, UNAM, Dirección General de Publicaciones, May—August 1978.

—DE FUNIAK, *Handbook of Modern Equity*, Boston—Toronto, 1956.

—DE LA OLIVA SANTOS, ANDRÉS, "La jurisprudencia en la Ley de Bases para un nuevo Título Preliminar del Código Civil", Sample from the *Revista de Derecho Procesal Iberoamericana*, IV, October—December 1973.

—"La jurisprudencia en el nuevo Título Preliminar del Código Civil", in *Anuario de Derecho Civil*, XXVII, Volume II, Madrid, Instituto Nacional de Estudios Jurídicos, April—June, MCMLXXV, pp. 331—517.

—"El Tribunal Constitucional como última instancia jurisdiccional", in *Revista de Derecho Procesal Iberoamericana*, 2—3, Madrid, 1987.

—"Tribunal Constitucional y jurisdicción ordinaria: causas, ámbitos y alivios de una tensión", in Id — IGNACIO DIEZ—PICAZO GIMÉNEZ, *Tribunal Constitucional, jueces ordinarios y derechos fundamentales*, I, Madrid, 1996, pp. 19 ff.

—DE LA VEGA BENAYAS, CARLOS, *Introducción al Derecho judicial*, Madrid, Montecorvo, 1970.

— "La doctrina de las fuentes del Derecho en el Nuevo Título Preliminar del Código Civil (arts. 1° y 2°)", in *Libro Homenaje a Ramón Mª Roca Sastre*, vol. I, Madrid, Universidad Complutense de Madrid, 1976, pp. 673—752.

— DE LUCA, "Aequitas canonica ed equity inglese alla luce del pensiero di C. Saint—Germain", in *Eph.* i.c., 1947.

—DEL VECCHIO, GIORGIO, *Los principios generales del Derecho*, Barcelona, Bosch, 1978. (Italian original version "Sui principi generali del diritto", in *Archivio Giuridico*, 1921, LXXXV), 2nd ed. Translation into Spanish by J. OSORIO MORALES and preface by DE DIEGO. There is a 3rd ed. of 1971.

—DENNING, LORD, *From Precedent to Precedent*, Oxford, Clarendon Press, 1959.

—DE OTTO PARDO, IGNACIO, "La posición del TC a partir de la doctrina de la interpretación constitucional", in *El Tribunal Constitucional*, Madrid, III, 1981, pp. 1939—1945.

—*Derecho constitucional. Sistema de fuentes*, Barcelona, Ariel, 1987. 2nd ed., 1988.

—*Estudios sobre el Poder Judicial*, Madrid, Secretaría General Técnica del Ministerio de Justicia, 1989.

—DE PAGE, HENRI, *De la interpretation des lois. Contribution a la recherche d'une méthode positive et theories en presence*, Bruxelles, 1925.

—DE SILVA Y NAVA, CARLOS, "La jurisprudencia", in *Curso de Actualización del Amparo,* México, División de Estudios Superiores de la Facultad de Derecho, UNAM, 1973.

—DEVLIN, LORD, "Judges and Lawmakers", in *Modern Law Review,* 39,1, 1976, pp. 1—16.

—DIAS, R. W. D., *Jurisprudence,* London, Butterworths, 5th ed., 1985.

—DÍAZ REVORIO, FRANCISCO JAVIER, "Interpretación constitucional de la ley y sentencias interpretativas", in *Repertorio Aranzadi del Tribunal Constitucional,* 2, April 2000, pp. 15—40.

—DIEZ PICAZO Y PONCE DE LEÓN, LUIS, "Fuentes de Derecho. Valor de la jurisprudencia", in *Anuario de Derecho Civil,* XI, Anotación a la sentencia del T.S. de 1 de febrero de 1958.

—"Reflexiones sobre la jurisprudencia del Tribunal Supremo", in *Revista de Derecho Privado,* 1964, pp. 925—936.

—*Estudios sobre la jurisprudencia civil,* Madrid, Tecnos, 1979.

—"Constitución y fuentes del Derecho", in *La Constitución española y las fuentes del Derecho,* I, Madrid, 1979, pp. 653—665.

—"La jurisprudencia", in vol. I, *El poder judicial,* Jornadas de la Dirección General de lo Contencioso del Estado, Madrid, Centro de Estudios Fiscales, 1983, pp. 267—284.

—"La doctrina de las fuentes del Derecho", in *Libro Homenaje a Jaime Guasp,* Granada, 1984, pp. 187—202.

—"Constitución, ley y juez", in *Revista Española de Derecho Constitucional,* 15, September—December, 1985.

—"Tribunal Constitucional y Poder Judicial", in "Constitucionalidad. Derecho comunitario europeo y jurisdicción ordinaria", in Various Authors, *División de poderes e interpretación (hacia una teoría de la praxis constitucional),* edition by LÓPEZ PINA, Madrid, Tecnos, 1987.

—DIEZ PICAZO, LUIS — GULLÓN BALLESTEROS, ANTONIO, *Sistema de Derecho civil, vol. I, "Introducción. Derecho de la persona. Autonomía privada. Persona jurídica",* Madrid, Tecnos, 1990.

—DIEZ PICAZO, LUIS (et al.), "Comentario al artículo 1.6", in *Comentarios a las reformas del C.C. (El nuevo Título Preliminar del Código y la Ley de 2 de mayo de 1975),* I, Madrid, Tecnos, 1977.

—"Comentario al artículo 1.6", in *Comentario al C.C.,* I, directed by CÁNDIDO PAZ AREA, RODRIGO BERCOWITZ, LUIS DIEZ PICAZO and PABLO SALVADOR, Madrid, Ministerio de Justicia, 1991.

—DOLEZALEK, GERO, "I precedente giudiziali nello ius commune", in VINCENTI, UMBERTO (a cura di), in cooperation with GIANNI SANTUCCI, *Il valore dei precedenti giudiziali nella tradizione europea,* Padova, CEDAM, 1998, pp. 55—81.

—DOMINGUEZ DE ANDRADES, "Sentido e valor da jurisprudença", "O raçao da sapiença" 30—X—53. University of Coimbra. 1973.

—DOMÍNGUEZ MARTÍN, SALVADOR, "Visión constitucional de la jurisprudencia", in *Boletín del Ministerio de Justicia,* 1.155, 1979, pp. 5—14.

—"Análisis crítico sobre la juridicidad del Tribunal Constitucional español", in *El Tribunal Constitucional*, Madrid, 1981, pp. 737—795.

—DOMÍNGUEZ RODRIGO, LUIS MARÍA, *Significado normativo de la jurisprudencia: ¿Ciencia del Derecho o decisión judicial?*, I and II, Madrid, Centro de Publicaciones General Técnico, Ministerio de Justicia, 1984.

—D'ORS, ALVARO, "De la prudentia iuris a la jurisprudencia del Tribunal Supremo", in *Información Jurídica*, 55, 1947, pp. 63—82.

— "Para una interpretación realista del artículo 6 del C.C. español", in *Studi in Onore di Emilio Betti*, 1, Milano, Giuffrè, 1962.

—DOUGLAS, WILLIAM O., "Stare Decisis", in WALTER F. MURPHY — C. HERMAN PRITCHETT (eds.), *Courts, Judges and Politics*, New York, Random House, 3rd ed., 1979, pp. 521—526.

—DRION, J., *Stare Decisis. Het gezag van precedenten*, Den Haag, Martinus Nijhoff Publishers, 1950.

—DUGUIT, LEON, *Les transformations du Droit privé depuis le Code Napoleon*, Paris, 1912, Spanish translation by CARLOS G. POSADA, Madrid, Francisco Beltrán, s. a.

—*Traité de Droit Constitutionel*, t. I, Paris, 1927.

—DUPEYROUX, OLIVIER, "La jurisprudence, source abusive de droit", in *Mélanges offerts à Jacques Maury*, II, Paris, 1960, pp. 349—377.

—DURKHEIM, ÉMILE, *Les régles de la méthode sociologique*, Paris, 1950; Spanish tranlation by L. E. ECHEVARRÍA RIVERA, 4th ed., Madrid, Morata, 1984.

—*La division du travail social*, Paris, 1960, there is a translation into Spanish by CARLOS G. POSADA, preface by LUIS R. ZÚÑIGA, Madrid, Akal, 1982.

—DUVERGER, MAURICE, *Instituciones políticas y Derecho constitucional*, 6th ed., Barcelona, Ariel, Caracas, México, 1980.

—DWORKIN, GERALD, "Stare Decisis in the House of Lords", in *The Modern Law Review*, 255, 1962, pp. 163—178.

—DWORKIN, RONALD, *Los derechos en serio*, translation into Spanish by MARTA GUASTAVINO, preface by A. CALSAMIGLIA, Barcelona, Ariel, 1984.

—*A Matter of Principle*, Cambridge —Massachusetts—, Harvard University Press, 1985.

—*Law's Empire*, Cambridge —Massachusetts—, Harvard University Press, 1986.

—ECHEVARRIA (de), LAMBERTO, "Riflessioni sulla funzione della giurisprudenza", in *Studi in memoria di Mario Condorelli*, vol. III, Milano, Giuffrè, 1988, pp. 147—160.

—EDDEY, KEITH J., *The English Legal System*, London, Sweet and Maxwell, 1987.

—EHRLICH, EUGEN, *Escritos sobre sociología y jurisprudencia*, translation into Spanish by JUAN ANTONIO GÓMEZ GARCÍA, GREGORIO ROBLES MORCHÓN and J. L. MUÑOZ DE BAENA, Madrid, Marcial Pons, Ediciones Jurídicas y Sociales, S.A., 2005.

—EHRMANN, HENRY W., "Civil Law Systems", in ROBERT J. JANOSIK (ed.), *Encyclopedia of American Judicial Systems*, III, New York, Charles Scribner's Sons, 1987, pp. 490—499.

—ELDERS, J. L. M., "Dans quelle mesure la jurisprudence et la doctrine sont—elles des sources de Droit?", in *Nederlandse Vereniging voor Rechtsvergelijkin*, vol. 14, Deventer, Kluwer, 1974.

—ELIZALDE Y AYMERICH, PEDRO DE, "El Tribunal Constitucional y la jurisprudencia", in *Jornadas de la Dirección General de lo Contencioso del Estado sobre el Tribunal Constitucional*, I, Madrid, Ed. Instituto de Estudios Fiscales, 1981, pp. 859—899.

—ENRÍQUEZ SALIDO, MARÍA CARMO, *Pautas para el análisis del léxico de la jurisprudencia del Tribunal Supremo*, Madrid, Civitas, 2005.

—ENTRENA KLETT, CARLOS MARÍA, *La equidad y el arte de juzgar*, Pamplona, Aranzadi, 1979. 2nd ed., 1990.

—ESCRICHE, JOAQUÍN, "Jurisprudencia", in *Diccionario Razonado de Legislación y Jurisprudencia*, III, México, Manuel Porrúa, S.A., 1979.

—ESMEIN, P A. ?, "La jurisprudence et la loi", in *Revue Trimestrielle de Droit Civil*, January—March, 1952, I, pp. 17—23.

—ESSER, JOSEF, *Principio y norma en la elaboración jurisprudencial del Derecho Privado*, Barcelona, Bosch, 1961. Translation into Spanish form the first German edition (1956): *Grundsatz und Norm in der Richterlichen Fortbildung des Privatrechts*, by EDUARDO VALENTÍ FIOL. There is a 3rd ed. 1974.

—EVANS HUGHES, CHARLES, *La Suprema Corte de los Estados Unidos*, 2nd ed., México, Fondo de Cultura Económica, 1971.

—EVANS, JIM, "Change in the Doctrine of Precedent During the Nineteenth Century", in L. GOLDSTEIN (ed.), *Precedent in Law*, Oxford, Clarendon Press, 1987, pp. 35—72.

—EVERSHED, SIR RAYMOND, *Aspects of English Equity*, Jerusalem, Magnes Press, The Hebrew University, 1954.

—EVERTON, ANN H., *What is Equity About?*, London, Butterworths, 1970.

—"Equitable Interests and Equities — In Search of a Pattern", in *Conv.* 40, 1976.

—EZQUIAGA GANUZAS, FRANCISCO JAVIER, "Los juicios de valor en la decisión judicial", in *Anuario de Filosofía del Derecho*, 1984, pp. 33—59.

—*La argumentación en la justicia constitucional española*, Bilbao, Instituto Vasco de Administración Pública, 1987.

—"Diez años de fallos constitucionales (sentencias interpretativas y poder normativo del Tribunal Constitucional)", in *Revista Vasca de Administración Pública*, 31, pp. 117—141.

—FAIRÉN GUILLÉN, VICTOR, "Notas sobre el valor de la jurisprudencia", in *Revista Crítica de Derecho Inmobiliario*, 509, July—August 1975.

—"Ponencia sobre la jurisprudencia en el nuevo Título preliminar del C.c.", in *Jornadas de Derecho Civil* (Zaragoza—Valladolid, held in Zaragoza, 23 to 26 April 1975).

—FALCÓN Y TELLA, FERNANDO, *Tridimensionalismo y Derecho*, Madrid, Servicio de Publicaciones de la Facultad de Derecho de la Universidad Complutense de Madrid, 2004. Review by JUAN ANTONIO MARTÍNEZ MUÑOZ, in *Foro. Revista de Ciencias jurídicas y Sociales*, Facultad de Derecho, Universidad Complutense de Madrid, 0, 2004, pp. 317—320.

—“Valeurs, norms et faits dans le Droit”, in *Revue Interdisciplinaire d’Études Juridiques,* 53, December 2004, pp. 123—139.

— *Nuevos retos de los derechos humanos,* Preface by CARLA FARALLI, Madrid, Difusión Jurídica y Temas de Actualidad, 2006. There is a note in *Economist & Jurist,* 104, Año XIV, October 2006, pp. 34 and 126. Reviews by: — MARÍA DE LOS ANGELES NOGALES NAHARRO, in *Anuario de Derechos Humanos, Nueva Época,* Instituto de Derechos Humanos, Facultad de Derecho, Universidad Complutense de Madrid, 25 Aniversario, 7, 1, 2005, pp. 499—508. — MARÍA EUGENIA PÉREZ MONTERO, in *Foro, Revista de Ciencias Jurídicas y Sociales,* 1, 2006, pp. 499—510. — JOSÉ MARÍA CARABANTE MUNTADA, in *Persona y Derecho,* 2009. There is a translation into English: *Challenges for Human Rights,* translation by HOWARD SHNEIDER, revised by the author, Boston—Leiden, Martinus Nijhoff Publishers, 2007. And a French translation, *Nouveaux défis des droits de l’homme,* translation by NICOLE BREGAIN, revised by DANIELE RENS and the author, Genève, Editions Diversités, 2007.

—FALCÓN Y TELLA, MARÍA JOSÉ, *El argumento analógico en el Derecho.* Thesis, directed by JOSÉ ITURMENDI MORALES, Madrid, Editorial de la Universidad Complutense de Madrid, 1989.

—“Papel de la ‘ratio’ en la argumentación jurídica. Ensayo de una nueva configuración teórica del argumento ‘a contrario’”, in *Revista de la Facultad de Derecho de la Universidad Complutense de Madrid,* 75, 1989—1990, pp. 259—283.

— *El argumento analógico en el Derecho,* Preface by JOSÉ ITURMENDI MORALES, Madrid, Civitas, 1991. Selected and reviewed by ARMANDO S. ANDRUET, in *Reseñas Jurídicas Selectas. Revista Foro de Córdoba — Argentina —,* 25, 1995, pp. 267—281.

— *Concepto y fundamento de la validez del Derecho,* Preface by FRANÇOIS OST, Madrid, Civitas, 1994. Review by JOAQUÍN R. TOUBES MUÑIZ, in *Dereito. Revista Xurídica da Universidade de Santiago de Compostela,* 3/1, 1994, pp. 309—313.

— *Conceito e fundamento da validade do Direito.* Translation by STEFANI BORBA DE ROSE TRUNFO, Brasil, Livraria do Advogado, 1rst ed., 1998. 2nd ed., 2000.

— *The Validity of Law: Concept and Foundation.* Translation into English by PETER MUCKLEY, Brasil, Livraria do Advogado, 2000.

— *Lecciones de Teoría del Derecho,* Madrid, Servicio de Publicaciones de la Facultad de Derecho de la Universidad Complutense de Madrid. 1rst ed., October 2001. 2nd ed., November 2003. 3rd ed., September 2006. 4th ed. revised, September 2009.

— *Equidad, Derecho y Justicia.* Preface by JUAN IGARTUA SALAVERRÍA, Madrid, Editorial Universitaria Ramón Areces, 2005. Review in: —*Foro. Revista de Ciencias Jurídicas y Sociales. Nueva Época,* Facultad de Derecho, Universidad Complutense de Madrid, 1, 2005, pp. 375—376. —*Otrosí. Publicación informativa del Colegio de Abogados de Madrid,* January 2006, p. 72. Reviews by: — TERESA GARCÍA—BERRIO HERNÁNDEZ, in *Foro. Revista de Ciencias Jurídicas y Sociales. Nueva Época,* Facultad de Derecho, Universidad Complutense de Madrid, 2, 2005, pp. 468—472. — JOSÉ MARÍA CARABANTE MUNTADA, in *Revista de Estudios Políticos.* Nueva época, 133, July/September 2006, pp. 263—265. — ISABEL RUIZ—GALLARDÓN, in *Anuario de Derechos Humanos, Nueva Época, 25 Aniversario,* Instituto de Derechos Humanos, Facultad de Derecho,

Universidad Complutense de Madrid, 7, 2006, pp. 478—489. — JOSÉ MARÍA CARABANTE MUNTADA, in *Persona y Derecho,* 55, 2006, pp. 518—521. Translation into English by Dr. PETER MUCKLEY, *Equity and Law,* Boston—Leiden, Martinus Nijhoff, 2008.

—FALCÓN Y TELLA, RAMÓN, *Introducción al Derecho Financiero y Tributario de las Comunidades Europeas,* Madrid, Civitas, 1988.

—FERNÁNDEZ DEL CORRAL, "La jurisprudencia en el Título preliminar del C.C.", in *Boletín de Información,* 15 September 1972.

—FERNÁNDEZ MARTÍN—GRANIZO, MARIANO, "La jurisprudencia en el Código Civil después de la Reforma de 1974", in *Anuario de Derecho Civil,* XXIX, II, Madrid, Instituto Nacional de Estudios Jurídicos, April—June, 1976, pp. 281—641.

—*Código Civil. Doctrina y jurisprudencia, I, artículos 1 a 332,* in cooperation with JOSÉ LUIS ALBACAR LÓPEZ, Madrid, Trivium, 1991.

—FERNÁNDEZ SEGADO, FRANCISCO, *La jurisdicción constitucional en España,* Madrid, 1984.

—FERRAJOLI, LUIGI (1940—), *Derecho y razón. Teoría del garantismo penal,* 3rd ed., Madrid, 1998.

—FERRARA, FRANCESCO, "Potere del legislatore o funzione del giudice", in *Rivista di Diritto Civile,* anno II, 1911.

—FINN, P. D., (ed.), *Essays in Equity,* Sydney, Law Book Company, 1985.

—FISCHER, R., "El perfeccionamiento del Derecho por la jurisprudencia", translation into Spanish by MANUEL NOVALVOS, in *Revista de Derecho Procesal—Iberoamericano,* 2—3, 1980.

—FISHER, S. G., "The Administration of Equity through Common Law Forms", in *Law Quarterly Review,* vol. I, 1885, pp. 445—465. New edition in Association of American Law Schools: *Selected Essays in Anglo—American Legal History,* 3 vols, Boston, 1907—1909.

—FIX ZAMUDIO, HÉCTOR, "Breves reflexiones acerca del origen y de la evolución de la jurisprudencia obligatoria de los Tribunales Federales", in *Lecturas Jurídicas,* 41, Chihuahua, México, Universidad Autónoma de Chihuahua, December, 1969, pp. 87—105.

—FONSECA, ROGER W. (*et al.*), "The Legitimacy of Civil Law Reasoning in the Common Law: Justice Harlan's Contribution", in *The Yale Law Jornal,* 82, 2, 1972, pp. 258—285.

—FORNACCIARI—TERRÉ, DOMINIQUE, "La jurisprudence chez Hegel", in *Archives de Philosophie du Droit,* 30, La jurisprudence, Paris, Sirey, 1985, pp. 73—82.

—FRANCESCHELLI: under "Consuetudine" and "Desuetudine", in *Nuovo Digesto Italiano,* Torino, UTET.

—FRANK, JEROME, *Law and the Modern Mind,* New York, Brentano's Publ., 1930.

—*Courts on Trial. Myth and Reality in American Justice,* Princeton —New Jersey—, Princeton University Press, 1949.

—FRANKFURTER, FELIX, "Some Reflections and the Reading of Statutes", in *Columbia Law Review,* 47, 4, 1947, pp. 527—546.

—FRIEDLAND, MARTIN L., “Prospective and Retrospective Judicial Lawmaking”, in *University of Toronto Law Review*, 24, 1974, pp. 170—190.

—FRIEDMANN, W., “A Re—Examination of the Relations between English, American and Continental Jurisprudence”, in *The Canadian Bar Review*, 20, 3, 1942, pp. 175—211.

—FROEHLICH, HANS THEODOR, *Observations on the History of Judicial Precedent, Especially During the Middle Ages*, 1931.

—FUEYO LANERI, FERNANDO, *Interpretación y juez*, Santiago de Chile, Universidad de Chile y Centro de Estudios “Ratio Iuris”, 1976.

—GALGANO, FRANCESCO, “Giurisdizione e giurisprudencia in materia civile”, in *Contratto e impresa*, 1, 1985, pp. 29—48.

—GALLARDO RUEDA, ARTURO, Under “equidad”, in *Nueva Enciclopedia Jurídica*, F. Seix Editor, VIII, pp. 631—634.

—GAMBARO, ANTONIO, “Les reactions de la doctrine à la creation du droit par les juges en droit civil”, *Journées Italiennes. Travaux de l'Association Henri Capitant*, XXXI, 1980.

—GARAPON, ANTOINE, “Peine fixe v. individualisation: analyse d'un clivage culturel”, in *Justices. Revue Générale de Droit Processuel. Justice et Équité*, 9, January/March 1998.

—GARBER, CARLOS A., “La interpretación en el sociologismo jurídico norteamericano”, in *Anuario de Filosofía Jurídica y Social*, 9, 1989.

—GARCÍA BERRIO HERNÁNDEZ, TERESA, *Las lagunas de la ley. Hacia un Derecho flexible*, Madrid, Servicio de Publicaciones de la Facultad de Derecho de la Universidad Complutense de Madrid, 2006.

—GARCÍA DE ENTERRÍA, EDUARDO, “La posición jurídica del Tribunal Constitucional en el sistema español: posibilidades y perspectivas”, in *El Tribunal Constitucional*, I, Madrid, 1981, pp. 21—129; and in *Revista Española de Derecho Constitucional*, Centro de Estudios Constitucionales, 1.1, January—April 1981, pp. 35—131.

—*Reflexiones sobre la ley y los principios generales del Derecho*, Madrid, Civitas, 1rst ed., 1984.

—“Principio de legalidad, estado material de Derecho y facultades interpretativas y constructivas de la jurisprudencia en la Constitución”, in *Revista Española de Derecho Constitucional*, 10, 1984, pp. 11—61.

—*La Constitución como norma jurídica y el Tribunal Constitucional*, 3rd ed., Madrid, Civitas, 1985.

—“Un paso importante para el desarrollo en nuestra justicia constitucional: la doctrina prospectiva en la declaración de ineficacia de las leyes inconstitucionales”, in *Revista de Derecho Administrativo*, 61, 1989, pp. 5—17.

—GARCÍA DE ENTERRÍA, E. - LINDE, E. - ORTEGA SÁNCHEZ MORÓN, L. I., *El sistema europeo de protección de los derechos humanos*, Madrid, Civitas, 1979.

—GARCÍA GARRIDO, MANUEL J., *Casuismo y jurisprudencia romana: responsa*, 2nd ed., 1rst imp., Ediciones Académicas, S.A., 2006.

—GARCÍA MAYNEZ, EDUARDO, *Filosofía del Derecho*, 3rd ed., México, Porrúa, S.A., 1980.

—*Introducción al estudio del Derecho*, 33rd ed., México, Porrúa S.A., 1982.

—GARCÍA ORMAECHEA, RAFAEL, "Notaciones sobre jurisprudencia", in *Revista General de Legislación y Jurisprudencia*, CLXIII, II, Madrid, 1933, pp. 306—329.

—GARCÍA-PABLOS, ANTONIO, "Relevancia de los cambios de criterio de la doctrina jurisprudencial y los Plenos no Jurisdiccionales del Tribunal Supremo", in *Cuadernos de Derecho Judicial*, VII, 2006, Nuevas posiciones de la dogmática jurídica penal. Consejo General del Poder Judicial. Escuela Judicial, pp. 183-213.

—GARCÍA PELAYO, MANUEL, "El 'status' del Tribunal Constitucional", in *Revista Española de Derecho Constitucional*, Centro de Estudios Constitucionales, 1.1, January—April 1981, pp. 11—34.

— GARCIA VALDECASAS, "Los principios generales del Derecho en el nuevo Título Preliminar del Código Civil", in *Anuario de Derecho Civil*, XXVIII, II, 1975.

—GARDNER, GEORGE E., *A Review on Laws and Equity for Law Students: a Handbook for Law Students*, New York, Baker, Voorhis, 1895.

—GARDNER, JOHN CLANACHAN, *Judicial Precedents in Scots Law*, with an Introduction by Lord MACMILLAN, Edinburgh, W. Green & Son, Limited, 1936.

—GARGAGLIONE, ELVIRA L., "Los jueces crean derecho como profecía", in *Notas de Filosofía del Derecho*, 5, 1969.

—GARRIDO FALLA, FERNANDO, *Comentarios a la Constitución española de 1978*, directed by..., 2nd ed., Madrid, Civitas, 1985.

— "Función jurisdiccional y poder judicial", in *Estudios jurídicos en honor a José Gabaldón López*, Madrid, Trivium, 1990.

—GARSIA, M., *Equity in a Nutshell*, 3rd ed., London, Sweet and Maxwell, 1941.

—GASCÓN ABELLÁN, MARINA, *La técnica del precedente y la argumentación racional*, Madrid, Tecnos, 1993.

—GAZZONI, FRANCESCO, *Equità e autonomia privata*, Milano, Giuffrè, 1970.

—GÈNY, FRANÇOIS, *Método de interpretación y fuentes en Derecho privado positivo*, 2nd ed., Madrid, Reus, 1925. Preface R. SALEILLES. There is a second edition of the book, in French, Paris, Librairie Générale de Droit et de Jurisprudence, 1954.

—GERARD, PHILIPPE, *Droit, égalité, ideologie. Contribution a l'étude critique des principes generaux*, Bruxelles, Publications des Facultés Universitaires Saint—Louis, 1981.

—GESCHE MULLER, BERNARDO, *Jurisprudencia dinámica (La desvalorización monetaria y otros problemas en el Derecho)*, Santiago de Chile, Editorial Jurídica de Chile, 1971.

—GIBERT Y SÁNCHEZ DE LA VEGA, RAFAEL, *Historia general del Derecho español*, Granada, 1968.

—GIL CREMADES, JUAN JOSÉ, "Jurisprudencia", in *Gran Enciclopedia Rialp*, XIII, Madrid, Ediciones RIALP, S.A., 1973.

—GILISSEN, JOHN, *Introduction historique au droit. Esquisse d'une histoire universelle du droit. Les sources du droit depuis le XIIIe siècle. Eléments d'histoire du droit privé*, Bruxelles, Bruylant, 1979.

—GIZBERT—STUDNICKI, F., "How Many Theories of Truth are Needed in Jurisprudence?", in MacCORMICK, N. — PANOU, S. — LOMBARDI VALLAURI,

L., *Conditions of Validity and Cognition in Modern Legal Thought,* Wiesbaden, Franz Steiner, 1985, pp. 153—161.

—GOLDSMITH, GEORGE, *The Doctrine and Practica of Equity: or a Concise Outline of Proceedings in the High Court of Chancery,* 5th ed., London, 1867.

—GOLDSTEIN, L. (ed.), *Precedent in Law,* Oxford, Clarendon Paperbacks, 1987.

—GÓMEZ DE LA SERNA—MONTALBÁN, P., *Tratado académico forense de procedimientos judiciales,* II, Madrid, Calleja, 1848.

—GONZÁLEZ, JERÓNIMO, "Jurisprudencia constructiva", in *Revista Crítica de Derecho Inmobiliario,* Madrid, 1935.

—GOODHART, ARTHUR L., *Precedent in English and Continental Law; an Inaugural Lecture Delivered Before the University of Oxford,* London, Stevens and Sons, 1934. Also in *The Law Quarterly Review,* 50, 1934, pp. 40—65.

—*Essays in Jurisprudence and the Common Law,* Cambridge, Cambridge University Press, 1937.

—"The Ratio Decidendi of a Case", in *The Modern Law Review,* 22, 2, 1959, pp. 117—124.

—GORDILLO CAÑAS, ANTONIO, "Ley, principios generales y Constitución: Apuntes para una relectura, desde la Constitución, de la teoría de las fuentes del Derecho", in *Anuario de Derecho Civil,* XLI, II, April—June, 1988.

—GORDILLO GARCÍA, MANUEL, "La jurisprudencia en la Constitución", in *Jornadas de la Dirección General de lo Contencioso sobre "La Constitución española y las fuentes del Derecho",* II, Madrid, Ed. Instituto dc Estudios Fiscales, 1979, pp. 1181—1190.

—GORLA, Gino, "Giurisprudenza", in *Enciclopedia del Diritto,* XIX, Milano, Giuffrè, 1970.

—Under "Precedente Giudiziario", in *Enciclopedia Giuridica Treccani,* XXIII, Roma, 1990.

—GRANDE, E., "Principio de legalità e diritto giurisprudenziale: un'antinomia", in *Sistema penale in transizione e ruolo del diritto giurisprudenziale,* Padova, 1997, pp. 129—146.

—GRAY, JOHN CHIPMAN, *The Nature and Sources of Law,* New York, The Macmillan Company, 1927.

—GREGORZYK, CHRISTOPHE, "Jurisprudence: phènomene judiciaire, science ou méthode", in *Archives de Philosophie du Droit, XXX, "La jurisprudence",* Paris, Sirey, 1985, pp. 35—52 ; translation into Spanish by MARÍA CASADO, in *Revista General de Legislación y Jurisprudencia,* XCIII, 3, September 1986.

—GRIMM, D., "La Constitución como fuente del Derecho", in Various Authors — BARATTA, GRIMM, RUBIO LLORENTE (*et al.*)—, *Las fuentes del Derecho, Anuario de la Facultad de Derecho,* Barcelona, Estudi General de Lleida, 1983.

—GUERRA AGUILERA, JOSÉ CARLOS, "Apuntes sobre la jurisprudencia méxicana", in *Revista Michoacana de Derecho Penal,* 19, México, Michoacán, Facultad de Derecho y Ciencias Sociales de la Universidad Michoacana de San Nicolás de Hidalgo, 1986.

—GUERRERO LARA, EZEQUIEL, "Jurisprudencia judicial", in *Diccionario Jurídico Mexicano,* V, México, Instituto de Investigaciones Jurídicas, UNAM, 1984.

—GUERRERO LARA, EZEQUIEL — GUADARRAMA, ENRIQUE, *La interpretación constitucional de la Suprema Corte de Justicia (1917—1982)*, I, México, Instituto de Investigaciones Jurídicas, UNAM, 1984.

—GÜNTHER, KLAUS, *Der Sinn für Angemessenheit. Anwendungsdiskurse in Moral und Recht*, Frankfurt am Main, Suhrkamp, 1988.

—GURVITCH, GEORGES, *L'idee du Droit Social...*, Paris, Sirey, 1932, preface by LOUIS LE FUR.

—GUSY, CHRISTOPH, "Richterrecht und Grundgesetz", in *Die öffentliche Verwaltung*, 45, 1992, pp. 461—470.

—HABERMAS, JÜRGEN, *Faktizität und Geltung. Beiträge zur Diskurstheorie des Rechts und des demokratischen Rechtsstaats*, Frankfurt am Main, Suhrkamp, 1992.

—*Justification and Application. Remarks on Discourse Ethic*, translation by CRONIN, Cambridge, Polity Press, 1993.

—*Between Facts and Norms*, translation by W. REHG, Cambridge —Massachusetts—, The MIT Press, 1996.

—HABSCHEID, WALTER J., "Sobre la creación jurisprudencial del Derecho en el Derecho alemán", in *Boletín Mexicano de Derecho Comparado*, VIII, 24, México, Instituto de Investigaciones Jurídicas, UNAM, September—December 1975.

—HALE, MATTHEW, *The History of Common Law*, London, W. Strahan—M. Woodfall, 4th ed, 1779.

—HALL, KERMIT L. — WIECEK, WILLIAM M. — FINKELMAN, PAUL, *American Legal History. Cases and Materials*, New York—Oxford, Oxford University Press, 1991.

—HALPERIN, J. L., *Orígenes de la noción moderna de jurisprudencia. Una obra jurídica del Tribunal de Casación bajo la Revolución Francesa*, paper delivered at the "II Seminario de Historia del Derecho Privado", on "Derecho Privado y revolución burguesa", Gerona, 25—27 May 1988. Coordinated by Carlos Petit, Madrid, Marcial Pons, Ediciones Jurídicas, S.A., 1990.

—HANBURY, HAROLD GREVILLE, "The Field of Modern Equity", in *Law Quarterly Review*, 45, 1920, pp. 12 ff. Also in *Essays on Equity*, pp. 23—54.

—*Essays in Equity*, Oxford, Clarendon Press, 1934.

—"The Place of Equity in a Curriculum of Jurisprudence", in *Essays on Equity, op. cit.*, pp. 55—68.

—HANBURY, HAROLD GREVILLE — MAUDSLEY, RONALD HARLING, *Modern Equity*, 13rd ed. by JILL E. MARTIN, London, Stevens and Sons, 1989, 6th ed. (1952).

— HANSFORD, THOMAS G. — SPRIGGS, JAMES F., *The Politics of Precedent on the U.S. Supreme Court*, Princeton, Princeton University Press, 2006.

—HARDISTY, JAMES, "Reflections on Stare Decisis", in *Indiana Law Review*, 55, 1, 1979, pp. 41—69.

—HARDY, KENNETH A., "Equity in Court Dispositions", in *Evaluating Performance of Criminal Justice Agencies*, Beverly Hills, 1983, pp. 183—210.

—HART, H. L. A. (HERBERT LIONEL ADOLPHUS), *The Concept of Law*, Oxford, Clarendon Press, 1967.

— HAYNES: *Outlines of Equity*, Cambridge, Macmillan, 1858.

—HECK, PHILIPP, *Begriffsbildung und Interessenjurisprudenz*, Tübingen, J. C. B. Mohr, 1932.

—Lecture delivered in Tubingen —Germany— in 1912, and published in Spanish as: *El problema de la creación del Derecho*, with preface by JOSÉ PUIG BRUTAU, Barcelona, Ariel, 1961.

—HERNÁNDEZ GIL, ANTONIO, Lecture of reception as academic of Tomás Ogallar y Ayllón, who talked on *Creación judicial del Derecho*, Madrid, Real Academia de Jurisprudencia y Legislación, 3 March 1975. Both lectures were published by that Academia, Madrid, 1975.

—HERNÁNDEZ IGLESIAS, F., *El Derecho consuetudinario y la codificación*, Madrid, 1903.

—HERRERO—TEJEDOR, FERNANDO, "El Tribunal Constitucional y el sistema de fuentes", in *Repertorio Aranzadi del Tribunal Constitucional*, 1, March 2000, pp. 17—34.

—HERZOG, JACQUES BERNARD, *Le droit jurisprudentiel et le Tribunel Suprême en Espagne, Essai sur les conditions de creation du droit par la jurisdiction de cassation*, Touluse, Impr. F. Boisseau,1942.

—HOLDSWORTH, WILLIAM, "Case Law", in *The Law Quarterly Review*, 40, 1934, pp. 180—195.

—*Some Makers of English Law*, Cambridge, Cambridge University Press, 1938.

—*A History of English Law*, 17 vols., London, Methuen & Co., 7th ed. 1956.

—HOLLAND, KENNETH M., "The Courts in the United States", in JEROLD L. WALTMAN — KENNET M. HOLLAND, *The Political Role of Law Courts in Modern Democracies*, New York, St. Martin's Press.

—HORSFIELD, PETER M., *Equity in a Nutshell*, London, Sweet and Maxwell, 1960.

—HOWELLS, CENYD, *Equity in a Nutshell*, London, Sweet and Maxwell, 1966.

—IGARTUA SALAVERRÍA, JUAN, "Sobre 'principios' y 'positivismo legalista'", in *Revista Vasca de Administración Pública*, 14, 1986, pp. 23—41.

—"Unica solución correcta y principios jurídicos indeterminados", in *Reason in Law, Proceedings of the Conference held in Bologna 12—15 dic. 1984*, Milano, Giuffrè, 1988, II, pp. 321—332.

—*Márgenes y límites en la aplicación del Derecho*, Donostia, Librería Carmelo, Facultad de Derecho, 1992.

—*Teoría analítica del Derecho (La interpretación de la ley)*, Oñati, Instituto Vasco de Administración Pública, 1994.

—*Discrecionalidad técnica, motivación y control jurisdiccional*, Madrid, Civitas, 1998.

—*La motivación de las sentencias, imperativo constitucional*, Madrid, 2003.

—*El Comité de Derechos Humanos, la casación penal española y el control del razonamiento probatorio*, Madrid, Thomson—Civitas, 2004.

—IGLESIAS, M.: "¿Cabe el «usus fori contra legem»?", in *Información Jurídica*, November, 1950.

—IHERING, RUDOLF VON, "Unsere Aufgabe", in the *Jahrbüchern für die Dogmatik*, 1857.

— *Geist des römischen Rechts*, II, Leipzig, 1898, there is a translation into Spanish by FERNANDO VELA, 2nd ed., Madrid, Revista de Occidente, 1962.

— *Scherz und Ernst in der Jurisprudenz. Eine Weihnachtsgabe für das juristischem Publikum*, Leipzig, Breitkopf und Härtel, 1rst ed.

—INGMAN, TERENCE, *The English Legal Process*, London, Blackstone Press, 2nd ed. 1987.

—ITURMENDI MORALES, JOSÉ, "Una Aproximación a los problemas del método jurídico desde la Filosofía del Derecho", in *Estudios de Filosofía del Derecho y Ciencia Jurídica en memoria y homenaje al Catedrático D. Luis Legaz y Lacambra (1906—1980)*, I, Madrid, Centro de Estudios Constitucionales, Facultad de Derecho de la Universidad Complutense, ed. prepared by professors JOSÉ ITURMENDI MORALES and JESÚS LIMA TORRADO, 1983, pp. 571—608.

—"Acerca de Rudolf von Ihering (1818—1892) y el sistema de los juristas romanos", in *Anuario de la Facultad de Derecho. Universidad de Extremadura*, XI, 1993 (published in 1995), pp. 415—479.

— "La dimensión complutense de Juan Iglesias Santos. Alumno, Profesor Auxiliar, Doctor, Catedrático, Decano en Ejercicio, Decano Honorario y Maestro Complutense de Derecho", in *Seminarios Complutenses de Derecho Romano, Revista Complutense de Derecho Romano y Tradición Romanística*, XIII, 2001, Facultad de Derecho, Fundación Seminario de Derecho Romano "Ursicino Álvarez", pp. 263—447.

—ITURRALDE SESMA, VICTORIA, *El precedente en el Common Law*, Madrid, Civitas, 1995.

—IVES, E. W. (ERIC WILLIAM, 1931—), *The Common Lawyers of the Pre—Reformation*, England, Cambridge, Cambridge University Press, 1983.

—JACKSON, R. M. (RICHARD MEREDITH, 1903—1986), *The Machinery of Justice in England*, Cambridge, Cambridge University Press, 7th ed., 1977.

—JAUCH, LUCIANO, "Il precedente giudiziale nel diritto del lavoro", in VINCENTI, UMBERTO (a cura di), in cooperation with GIANNI SANTUCCI, *Il valore dei precedenti giudiziali nella tradizione europea*, Padova, CEDAM, 1998, pp. 163—167.

—JESTAZ, PHILIPPE, "La jurisprudente, ombre portée du contentieux", in *Recueil Dalloz—Sirey*, 24, 22 June 1989.

—JÈZE, GASTON, *Cours de Droit Public*, Paris, R. Pichon, 1935.

—JOLOWICZ, JOHN—ANTHONY, "La jurisprudence en droit anglais, aperçu sur la regle du précédent", in *Archives de Philosophie du Droit*, 30, *La jurisprudence*, Paris, Sirey, 1985, pp. 105—116.

—KALINOWSKI, GEORGES, "La interpretation du droit : ses règles juridiques et logiques", in *Archives de Philosophie du Droit*, 30, *La jurisprudence*, Paris, Sirey, 1985, pp. 171—180.

—KANTOROWICZ, HERMANN, *La definición del Derecho*, Madrid, Revista de Occidente, 1964, translation from English by J. M. DE LA VEGA.

—KEEFE, DONALD F. — MERRILL, ALLAN H., "The Attitude of Lower Courts to Changing Precedents", in *The Yale Law Journal*, 50, 8, 1941, pp. 1448—1459.

—KEETON, GEORGE WILLIAMS, *An Introduction to Equity*, 5th ed., London, Pitnam, 1961, (1rst ed. 1938; 2nd ed. 1948; 4th ed. 1956).

—*Equity*, Milton, Professional Books, 1976, 2nd ed., "The Study of Equity Today", *Jubilee Lectures of the Faculty of Law University of Sheffield*, pp. 59—81.

—KELSEN, HANS, *Teoría General del Derecho y del Estado,* 2nd. ed., México, UNAM, 1979.

—*Dio e Stato. La giurisprudenza come scienza dello spiritto.* Translation and Introduction by AGOSTINO CARRINO, Napoli — Roma, Edizione Scientifiche Italiane, 1988.

—*Teoría pura del Derecho,* translation into Spanish by ROBERTO J. VERNENGO, México, 1993.

—KERCHOVE, MICHEL VAN DE, "Jurisprudence et rationalité juridique", in *Archives de Philosophie du Droit,* 30, *La jurisprudence,* Paris, Sirey, 1985, pp. 207—242.

—KIRALFY, A. K. R., *The English Legal System,* London, Sweet & Maxwell Ltd., 2nd ed., 1956. 7th ed., London, Sweet and Maxwell, 1984.

—KIRCHMANN, J. H. (JULIUS HERMANN VON), *La jurisprudencia no es ciencia,* translation into Spanish and Introduction by A. TRUYOL SERRA, Madrid, 1949.

—KNIFFIN, MARGARET N., "Overruling Supreme Court Precedents: Anticipatory Action by United States Courts of Appeals", in *Fordham Law Review,* 51, 1, 1982, pp. 53—89.

—KOCOUREK, ALBERT, "Sources of Law in the United States of North America and their Relation to Each Other", in *American Bar Association Journal,* 18, 10, 1932, pp. 676—682.

—KOCOUREK, ALBERT — KOVEN, HAROLD, "Renovation of the Common Law through Stare Decisis", in *Illionois Law Review,* 29, 8, 1935, pp. 971—999.

—KOTHE, P., "Vorlage, Richterrecht und Anspruch auf den gesetlichen Richter", in *Die öffentliche Verwaltung,* 41, 1988, pp. 284—290.

—KOTTENHAGEN, *Van precedent tot precedent,* Arnhem, Gouda Quint, 1986.

—KRIELE, MARTIN, "Das Präjudiz im kontinental—europäischen und anglo—amerikanischen Rechskreis", in *La sentenza in Europa, metodo, tecnica e stile,* Padova, CEDAM, 1988.

—KRONMAN, ANTHONY T., "Precedent and Tradition", in *The Yale Law Journal,* 99, 1990, pp. 1029—1068.

—LACRUZ BERDEJO, JOSÉ LUIS (*et al.*), *Elementos de Derecho Civil, T.I, Parte General,* Madrid, Dykinson, 1998.

—LALAGUNA DOMÍNGUEZ, ENRIQUE, "Valor de la jurisprudencia en la elaboración de la Ciencia del Derecho", in *Revista Crítica de Derecho Inmobiliario,* September—October, 468, 1968, pp. 1217—1238.

— *Jurisprudencia y fuentes del Derecho,* Pamplona, Aranzadi, 1969.

—"Jurisprudencia", in *Nueva Enciclopedia Jurídica Seix,* Barcelona, 1971.

—LARENZ, KARL, "Über die Bindungswirkung von Präjudizien", in H. WALTER FASCHING — W. KRÁLIK, *Festschrift für H. Schima,* Wien, 1969.

—LASSO GAITE, JUAN FRANCISCO, "Aportación a la Historia del T. S.", in *Revista General de Legislación y Jurisprudencia,* LIX, 227, 1969.

—LAUREN, PAUL GORDON, "Nuevos retos para los derechos humanos. El futuro a la luz del pasado", II Jornadas Internacionales "Nuevos retos de los derechos humanos", Instituto de Derechos Humanos, November 2003, Facultad de Derecho, Universidad Complutense de Madrid. Translation into Spanish, "New Challenges for Human Rights: The Future in Light of the Past", by FERNANDO FALCÓN Y TELLA, *Anuario de Derechos Humanos, Nueva Época,* Instituto de Derechos Humanos, Facultad de Derecho, Universidad Complutense de Madrid, 5, 2004, pp. 369—386.

—LEADER, SHELDON, "Le juge, la politique et la neutralité. A propos des travaux de Dworkin", in *Droit et Societé,* 2, January 1986, pp. 23—41.

—LEE, DEREK, *The Power of Parliamentary Houses to Send for Persons, Papers & Records: A Sourcebook on the Law and Precedent of Parliamentary Subpoena Powers for Canadian and Other Houses,* University of Toronto Press, 1999.

—LEGAZ Y LACAMBRA, LUIS, *Introducción a la Ciencia del Derecho,* Barcelona, Bosch, 1943.

—LEÓN HURTADO, AVELINO, "Valor de la jurisprudencia", in *Revista de Derecho y Jurisprudencia,* 56, First Part, Santiago de Chile.

—LEVY—BRUHL, LUCIEN, *La morale et la Science des moeurs,* Paris, Librairie Felix Alcan, 1937; there is a translation into Spanish by RAFAEL URBANO, Madrid, J. Pueyo, 1929.

—*Sociologie du Droit,* Paris, Presses Universitaires de France, 1981; there is a translation into Spanish by MYRIAM DE WINIZKY, 4th. ed., Buenos Aires, Eudeba, 1976.

—LIEBMAN, ENRICO TULLIO, "Giurisprudenza", in *Nuovo Digesto Italiano,* VI, Torino, 1938, pp. 411—414.

—LOIS ESTÉVEZ, J., "La costumbre ante los principios fundamentales de la política del Derecho", in *Revista General de Derecho,* Valencia, April/May 1948.

—LOMBARDI VALLAURI, LUIGI, *Saggio sul diritto giurisprudenziale,* Milano, Giuffrè, 1967.

—Under "Giurisprudenza", in *Enciclopedia Giuridica Trecanni,* XV, Roma, 1989.

—LÓPEZ GUERRA, LUIS, "El Tribunal Constitucional y el principio 'stare decisis'", in Various Authors, *El Tribunal Constitucional,* II, Madrid, Instituto de Estudios Fiscales, 1981, pp.1437—1550.

—"Jurisdicción ordinaria y jurisdicción constitucional", in *La aplicación jurisdiccional de la Constitución,* edited by G. RUIZ—RICO RUIZ, Valencia, 1997, pp. 27—59.

—LÓPEZ MENUDO, FRANCISCO, "El principio de irretroactividad de las normas en la jurisprudencia constitucional", in *Estudios sobre la C.E. Homenaje a García de Enterría,* Madrid, 1991, pp. 455—508.

—LÓPEZ PINA, ANTONIO (*et al.*), Edition and Preface of *División de poderes e interpretación (Hacia una teoría de la praxis constitucional),* Madrid, Tecnos, 1987.

—LÓPEZ VILAS, RAMÓN, *La jurisprudencia y su actual eficacia normativa, Centenario del Código Civil (1889—1989),* II, Madrid, Centro de Estudios Ramón Areces, 1990.

—*La jurisprudencia y su función complementaria del ordenamiento jurídico,* Madrid, Civitas, 2002.

—LOUZAO, E., "La jurisprudencia. Su fuerza obligatoria", in *Revista de Derecho Privado,* 78, March 1920, pp. 74—77.

—LOWENSTEIN, KARL, *Teoría de la Constitución,* 2nd. ed., Barcelona, Ariel, 1983.

—LUCAS VERDÚ, PABLO, "Política y justicia constitucionales. Consideraciones sobre la naturaleza y funciones del Tribunal Constitucional", in Various Authors, *Tribunal Constitucional,* II, Madrid, Instituto de Estudios Fiscales, 1981, pp. 151 ff.

—LÜCKE, H. K., "The Common Law: Judge Impartiality and Judge Made Law", in *The Law Quarterly Review,* 98, 1982, pp. 92—93.

—LÜKE, W., "Die Bedeutung von Präjudizien im deutsche Zivilprocess", in K. KROESCHELL (ed.), *Recht und Verfahren,* Heidelberg, Müller Juristischer Verlag, 1993.

—LYONS, DAVID, "Formal Justice, Moral Commitment and Judicial Precedent", in *The Journal of Philosophy,* 10, 1984, pp. 380—387.

—"Formal Justice and Precedent", in *Vanderbilt Law Review,* 38, 1985, pp. 495—512.

—LLEWELLYN, KARL N., *The Common Law Tradition,* Boston—Toronto, Little, Brown and Company, 1960.

—*The Case Law System in America,* edited and with introduction by PAUL GEWIRTZ, translation by MICHAEL ANSALDI, Chicago (etc.), University of Chicago Press, 1989.

—LLORENTE HURTADO, F., "Poder judicial y justicia constitucional", in Various Authors, *El poder judicial,* II, Dirección General de lo Contencioso del Estado, Madrid, Ed. Instituto de Estudios Fiscales, 1983.

—LLOYD OF HAMSTEAD, DENNIS, *Introduction to Jurisprudence,* London, Stevens & Sons, 4th ed., 1979.

—MACADAM, ALASTAIR I. — PYKE, JOHN, *Judicial Reasoning and the Doctrine of Precedent in Australia,* Sydney, Butterworths, 1998.

—MACCORMICK, NEIL, *Legal Reasoning and Legal Theory,* Oxford, Clarendon Press, 1978.

—"Why Cases Have Rations and What These Are", in L. GOLDSTEIN (ed.), *Precedent in Law,* Oxford, Clarendon Press, 1987, pp. 155—182.

—MACCORMICK, NEIL —SUMMERS, ROBERT (eds.), *Interpreting Precedents. A Comparative Study,* Dartmouth, Ashgat, 1997.

—MAGALONI KERPEL, ANA LAURA, *El precedente constitucional en el sistema judicial norteamericano,* McGraw—Hill / Interamericana de España, S. A., 2001.

—MAITLAND, FREDERIC WILLIAMS (1850—1906*), Las formas de acción en el common law,* translation by IGNACIO CREMADES UGARTE, Madrid, Marcial Pons, Ediciones Jurídicas y Sociales, S. A., 2005.

—MALAURIE, PHILIPPE, "La jurisprudence combattue par la loi", in *Mélanges offerts à René Savatier,* Paris, 1965, pp. 603—620.

—MANCHESTER, COLIN — SALTER, DAVID, *Exploring the Law: The Dynamics of Precedent and Statutory Interpretation,* Sweet & Maxwell, 2006.

—MANJARREZ ALONSO, J. IGNACIO, *Concepto y función de la jurisprudencia,* México, 1950.

—MARÍN, J. A., *Naturaleza jurídica del Tribunal Constitucional,* Barcelona, 1998.

—MARÍN CASTÁN, MARÍA LUISA, "Consideraciones sobre el Derecho inglés como prototipo de sistema de *common law* y sus diferencias respecto de los sistemas romano—germánicos", in *Revista General de Legislación y Jurisprudencia,* 2, 1984, pp. 139—179.

—*Significado y alcance de la equity inglesa.* Thesis directed by JOSÉ ITURMENDI MORALES, Madrid, Editorial de la Universidad Complutense de Madrid, 1985.

—"Razón y Ciencia en la Equity Inglesa del Siglo XVI. Algunas Consideraciones sobre la Obra de C. Saint Germain 'Doctor and Student'", in *Reason in Law*, II, Milano, 1988, pp. 63—74.

—MARTÍN MAZUELOS, F. J., "Principios del Derecho inglés", in *Documentación Jurídica*, 17, January—March, 1978.

—MARTÍNEZ—CALCERRADA Y GÓMEZ, LUIS, *Derecho judicial y Código Civil (función interpretadora, correctora o integradora), Centenario del Código Civil (1889—1989), II*, Madrid, Ed. Centro de Estudios Ramón Areces, 1990.

—MARTÍNEZ MUÑOZ, JUAN ANTONIO, "El Derecho natural en Michel Villey", in *Revista de la Facultad de Derecho de la Universidad Complutense de Madrid*, 78, academic year 1990—1991, pp. 173—203.

—*El conocimiento jurídico*, Madrid, Servicio de Publicaciones de la Facultad de Derecho de la Universidad Complutense de Madrid, 1rst. ed. 2005, 2nd. ed. 2006.

—MARTÍNEZ SOSPEDRA, MANUEL (1947—), "El Tribunal Constitucional como órgano político", *Jornadas sobre el Tribunal Constitucional*, II, Madrid, Instituto de Estudios Fiscales, 1981, pp. 1.804 ff.

—MAURY, J., "Observations sur la jurisprudence en tant que source de Droit", in *Études ofertes à Georges Rippert, (« Le droit privé français au milieu du XX siécle »)*, I, Paris, 1950, pp. 28 ff.

—MEIJERS, E. M., "Le conflit entre l'équité et la loi chez les premiers glossateurs", in *Tijdschrift voor Rechtsgeschiedenis*, 17, 1941, pp. 117—135, also in his *Études d'Histoire du Droit, vol. IV, Le droit romain au Moyen Âge*, II, Leyden, Universitaire Leyden, 1996, pp. 142—156.

—MENCHEN HERREROS, P., "Jurisprudencia: unidad y evolución del Derecho", paper delivered in the *Jornadas sobre El Poder Judicial*, held by the Dirección General de lo Contencioso del Estado, III, Madrid, Instituto de Estudios Fiscales, 1983, pp. 1951—1981.

—MERRYMAN, JOHN HENRY, *The Civil Law Tradition*, Standford —California—, Stanford University Press, 1985.

—MIECHI, VINCENZO, *La forza obbligatoria della consuetudine considerate nelle sue basi sociologiche e giuridiche*, Perugia, Unione Tipografica e Cooperativa, 1899.

—MIEDZIANAGORA, J., "Juges, lacunes et idéologie", in *Le problème des lacunes en droit. Études publiées par Chaïm Perelman*, Bruxelles, Bruylant, 1968.

—MIGUEL ZARAGOZA, JUAN DE, "Sobre las funciones latentes del Tribunal Constitucional", in *Boletín de Información del Ministerio de Justicia*, 1238, 5 May 1981.

—MISCHKE, C., "The Inseparability of Powers: Judge—Made Law in the German Legal System", in *Publiekreg /Public Law*, 7, 1992, pp. 253—263.

—MONTERO AROCA, JUAN, *Independencia y responsabilidad del juez*, Cuadernos Civitas, Madrid, Civitas, 1990.

—MONTERO AROCA, JUAN – FLORS MATÍES, JOSÉ, *El recurso de casación civil. Casación e infracción procesal*, Valencia, Tirant lo Blanch, 2009.

—MONTESQUIEU, C.L. DE SECONDAT, *Del espíritu de las leyes*, Introduction by ENRIQUE TIERNO GALVÁN, translation into Spanish by MERCEDES

BLÁZQUEZ and PEDRO DE VEGA, Madrid, Tecnos, Colección "Clásicos del pensamiento", 1985.

—MONTROSE, JAMES LOUIS, *Precedent in English Law and Other Essays,* Harold Greville Hanbury (ed.), Shannon—Ireland, Irish University Press, 1968.

—MORAL SORIANO, LEONOR, "Los precedentes del Tribunal Supremo: el acercamiento de la jurisprudencia a la teoría de los precedentes", in *Revista del Poder Judicial,* 57, 2000, pp. 119—154.

—*El precedente judicial,* preface by ZENON BANKOWSKI and NEIL MACCORMICK, Madrid, Marcial Pons, Ediciones Jurídicas y Sociales, S. A., 2002.

—MORANGE, G., "Une categorie juridique ambigue: les principes généraux du droit", in *Revue de Droit Publique et de la Science Politique en France et à l'Étranger,* 1977, 4, pp. 761—778.

—MORENA Y DE LA MORENA, LUIS DE LA, "La jurisprudencia. ¿Fuente del Derecho?", in *Libro Homenaje al Profesor José Luis Villar Palasí,* 1rst. ed., Madrid, Civitas, 1989.

—MOSCHZISKER, ROBERT VON, "Stare Decisis in Courts of Last Resort", in *Harvard Law Review,* 37, 4, 1924, pp. 409—430.

—MOUTON Y OCAMPO, L., *Derecho consuetudinario español y europeo,* Madrid, 1911.

—Under "Costumbre" and "Derecho consuetudinario", in *Enciclopedia Jurídica Española,* Barcelona, Seix.

—MOZOS Y DE LOS MOZOS, JOSÉ LUIS DE LOS, "La equidad", in *Estudios de Derecho Internacional Público y Privado,* I, Oviedo, 1970.

—*Derecho civil español I. Parte General, vol. I, Introducción al Derecho civil,* Salamanca, Ed. Kadmos, 1977.

—"El sistema del 'common law' desde la perspectiva jurídica española", in *Revista de Derecho Privado,* LXVII, April 1983.

—MUNDAY, R. J. C., "New Dimensions of Precedent", in *Society of Public Teachers of Law,* 14, 3, 1978, pp. 201—217.

—MUÑOZ DELGADO, ADOLFO, *Algunas consideraciones acerca de la Jurisprudencia de la Suprema Corte de Justicia de la Nación y de los Tribunales Colegiados de Circuito,* Thesis, México, Facultad de Derecho, UNAM, 1976.

—MURILLO, GUILEBALDO, "La jurisprudencia obligatoria", in *Problemas jurídicos de México,* Sección de Derecho Constitucional, México, Editorial Ius, Asociación Nacional de Funcionarios Judiciales, 1953.

—NICOL, ANDREW G. L., "Prospective Overruling: A New Device for English Courts?", in *The Modern Law Review,* 39, 1976, pp. 542—560.

—NICOLÁS MUÑIZ, JAIME, "El Tribunal Constitucional y las fuentes del Derecho", in *Revista Vasca de Administración Pública,* 10, II, 1984, pp. 73—89.

—NIETO, ALEJANDRO, "El precedente judicial", in *Libro Homenaje al prof. Juan Roca,* Murcia, Universidad de Murcia, Secretariado de Publicaciones, 1989.

—"El precedente judicial en la doctrina del Tribunal Constitucional", in *Estudios Jurídicos en honor de D. José Gabaldón López,* Madrid, Trivium, 1990.

—*El arbitrio judicial,* Barcelona, Ariel, 2000.

—NINO, CARLOS SANTIAGO, *Introducción al análisis del Derecho*, Barcelona, 1983.

—NOCERA, GUGLIELMO, *Iurisprudentia. Per una storia del pensiero giuridico romano*, Roma, Bulzoni, 1973.

—NOVALVOS PÉREZ, MANUEL, "Arbitrio y actividad judicial", in *Revista de Derecho Privado*, June 1978.

—ODGERS, WALTER BLAKE, *The Common Law of England*, I, London, Sweet & Maxwell, 1911.

—OGAYAR Y AYLLÓN, TOMÁS, *Creación judicial del Derecho*, discurso del académico electo, leído en el acto de su recepción pública el día 3 de marzo de 1975, y contestación de Antonio Hernández Gil, Madrid, Real Academia de Jurisprudencia y Legislación, 1975.

— "Las fuentes del Derecho en el Novísimo Título Preliminar del Código Civil", in *Libro Homenaje a Ramón Mª Roca Sastre*, I, Madrid, Universidad Complutense de Madrid, 1976, pp. 607—656.

—OLIPHANT, HERMAN, "A Return to Stare Decisis", in *American Bar Association Journal*, 14, 2, 1928, pp. 71—77.

—OLLENNU, NII AMAA (1904—), *Judicial Precedent in Ghana*, Gahna, s. n., 1962.

—OLLERO TASSARA, ANDRÉS, *Igualdad en la aplicación de la ley y precedente judicial*, Madrid, Cuadernos y Debates, 19, Madrid, Centro de Estudios Constitucionales, 1989; 2nd. ed., 2005.

—ORTEGA CARCELEN, MARTIN C., "Análisis del valor de la jurisprudencia en el Derecho internacional", in *Revista Española de Derecho Internacional*, 2, July—August 1988.

—ORTÚZAR ANDÉCHAGA, LUIS, *Derecho y jurisprudencia en la Unión Europea*, Navarra, Aranzadi, 2003.

—ÖRÜCÜ, ESIN, "Equity in the Scottish Legal System", in A. MORDECHAI RABELLO (ed.), *Aequitas and Equity: Equity in Civil Law and Mixed Jurisdictions*, Jerusalem, The Harry and Michael Sacher Institute for Legislative Research and Comparative Law. The Hebrew University or Jerusalem, 1997. Second International Conference on Aequitas and Equity, 1993. (1rst. 1990: Equity and Contemporary Legal Developments, 1992), pp. 383—395.

—OST, FRANÇOIS, "Juge pacificateur, juge—arbitre, juge entraîneur", in *Fonction de juger et pouvoir judiciaire*, Bruxelles, Bruylant, 1983.

—"Quelle jurisprudence, pour quelle société ?", in *Archives de Philosophie du Droit*, 30, La jurisprudence, Paris, Sirey, 1985, pp. 9—35.

—"Júpiter, Hércules y Hermes: Tres modelos de juez", in *Doxa*, 14, 1993, pp. 169—194.

—PACCHINI, G., "I poteri creativi della giurisprudenza", in *Rivista di Diritto Comerciale*, X, I, Roma, 1912, pp. 40—44.

—PANIAGUA, JOSÉ, "La regla de oro de la jurisprudencia inglesa", in *Revista de los Tribunales*, Madrid, 1933.

—PATON, G. W. — SAWER, G., "Ratio Decidendi and Obiter Dictum", in *The Law Quarterly Review*, 63, 1947, pp. 461—485.

—PATTARO, ENRICO, "La completezza degli ordinamenti giuridici e i principi generali dell'ordinamento giuridico dello Stato", in *Materiali per una storia della cultura giuridica*, XVIII, 1988, pp. 145—161.

—PATTENDEN, ROSEMARY, "The Power of the Criminal Division of the Court of Appeal to Depart From its Own Precedents", in *The Criminal Law Review*, 1984, pp. 592—603.

—PATTERSON, EDWIN, *Jurisprudence. Men and Ideas of the Law*, Brooklyn, The Foundation Press Inc., 1953.

—PAVONE LA ROSA, Under "Consuetudine, f) Usi normativi e usi giudiziali", in *Enciclopedia del Diritto*, IX, 1961, pp. 513—31.

—PECES BARBA MARTÍNEZ, GREGORIO, "La creación judicial del Derecho desde la teoría del ordenamiento jurídico", in *Revista del Poder Judicial*, 6, March 1983.

—PECZENIK, ALEXANDER — ALEXY, ROBERT, *Grundlagen der juristischen Argumentation*, New York, Springer Verlag, 1983.

—"Sui Precedenti vincolanti", in *Ragion Pratica*, 6, 1996, pp. 35—43.

—PERA VERDAGUER, FRANCISCO, "Fuentes del Derecho, jurisprudencia y constitucionalidad", in *Jornadas de la Dirección General de lo Contencioso del Estado, sobre «La Constitución española y las fuentes del Derecho»*, III, Madrid, Instituto de Estudios Fiscales, 1981, pp. 1607—1628.

—"El T. S. y el nuevo ordenamiento constitucional", in *Jornadas de la Dirección General de lo Contencioso del Estado sobre el Poder Judicial*, III, Madrid, Instituto de Estudios Fiscales, 1983.

—PERELMAN, CHAÏM — OLBRECHTS—TYTECA, LUCIE, *Traité de l'argumentation. La nouvelle Réthorique*, Bruxelles, Université de Bruxelles, 1970.

—PÉREZ ÁLVAREZ, MIGUEL ÁNGEL, *Interpretación y jurisprudencia. Estudio del artículo 3.1 del Código Civil*, Pamplona, Aranzadi, 1994.

—PÉREZ GORDO, ALFONSO, *El Tribunal Superior de Justicia de las Comunidades Autónomas (Perspectivas procesales para el desarrollo de la previsión constitucional)*, Barcelona, Bosch, 1982.

—PÉREZ ROYO, JAVIER, *Las fuentes del Derecho*, Madrid, Tecnos, Colección Temas Clave de la Constitución española, 1984; there is a 3rd. ed.

—PÉREZ TREMPS, PABLO, *Tribunal Constitucional y Poder Judicial*, Madrid, Centro de Estudios Constitucionales, 1985.

—"Constitución, Ley Orgánica del Poder Judicial y jueces ordinarios", in *Documentación Jurídica*, 45—46, January—June, 1985, pp. 23—41.

—PETERS, ELLEN ASH, "Common Law Judging in a Statutory World: an Address", in *University of Pittsburg Law Review*, 43, 4, 1982, pp. 995—1011.

—PETEV, VALENTIN, "Structures rationnelles et implications sociologiques de la jurisprudence", in *Archives de Philosophie du Droit*, 30, La jurisprudence, Paris, Sirey, 1985, pp. 181—190.

—PIBERNAT DOMENECH, XAVIER, "La sentencia constitucional como fuente del Derecho", in *Revista de Derecho Político*, Universidad Nacional de Educación a Distancia, Madrid, Summer 1987, 24, pp. 57—85.

—PIERI, GEORGES, "Ius et prudentia", in *Archives de Philosophie du Droit*, XXX, *La jurisprudence*, Paris, Sirey, 1985, pp. 53—60.

—PILNY, H. L., *Präjudizienrecht im angloamerikanischen und deutschen Recht*, Baden—Baden, Nomos Verlag, 1993.

—PIOLA CASELLI, EDUARDO, "Giurisprudenza", in *Il Digesto Italiano*, XII, Torino, 1927, XII, pp. 831—853.

—POLLOCK, FREDERICK, *Jurisprudence*, London, MacMillan and Co., 1918.

—POLLOCK, FREDERICK — MAITLAND, FREDERIC WILLIAM, *History of English Law*, 2 vols. 1923.

—PORTOLÉS SERRANO, *El Derecho consuetudinario a través de la codificación civil castellana*, Thesis. Zaragoza. 1920.

—POSTNER, R. A., *The Problems of Jurisprudence*, Cambridge —Massachusetts—, Harvard University Press, 1990.

—POUND, ROSCOE, "Common Law and Legislation", in *Harvard Law Review*, 21, 6, 1908, pp. 383—407.

—"The Future of the Common Law", in *University of Cincinnati Law Review*, 7, 4, 1933, pp. 1—18.

—"The Development of American Law and Its Deviation from English Law", in *The Law Quarterly Review*, 67, January 1951.

—*El espíritu del "Common Law"*, Barcelona, Bosch, 1954.

—*Jurisprudence*, vols. I, II, III, St. Paul —Minn.—, West Publishing Co., 1959.

—PREDIERI, ALBERTO, "El sistema de fuentes del Derecho", in *La Constitución española de 1978, Estudio sistemático*, directed by professors PREDIERI and GARCÍA DE ENTERRÍA, Madrid, 1984, pp. 159—260.

—PRIETO CASTRO FÉRRANDIZ, LEONARDO, *Meditaciones sobre la jurisprudencia*, Madrid, 1966.

—PRIETO SANCHÍS, LUIS, *Ideología e interpretación jurídica*, Madrid, 1987.

—"Notas sobre la interpretación constitucional", in *Revista del Centro de Estudios Constitucionales*, 9, 1991, pp. 175—198.

—PRIEUR, JEAN, "Jurisprudence et principe de séparation des pouvoirs", in *Archives de Philosophie du Droit*, 30, *La jurisprudence*, Paris, Sirey, 1985, pp. 117—130.

—PUECH, MARC, "La jurisprudence pénale", in *Archives de Philosophie du Droit*, 30, *La jurisprudence*, Paris, Sirey, 1985, pp. 141—156.

—PUERTAS GÓMEZ, GERARDO FEDERICO JOSÉ, *El precedente judicial y la jurisprudencia en los sistemas norteamericano y mexicano*, Thesis, México, Universidad de Monterrey, March 1981.

—PUGLIATTI, SALVATORE, "La giurisprudenza comme scienza pratica", in *Rivista Italiana per le Scienze Giuridiche*, 87, 1950, pp. 49—86.

—PUGSLEY, DAVID F., "L'origine della regola stare decisis nella House of Lords e il Caso London Tramways (1898)", in VINCENTI, UMBERTO (a cura di), in cooperation with GIANNI SANTUCCI, Il *valore dei precedenti giudiziali nella tradizione europea*, Padova, CEDAM, 1998, pp. 235—252.

—PUIG BRUTAU, JOSÉ, *La jurisprudencia como fuente del Derecho (Interpretación creadora y arbitrio judicial)*, Barcelona, Bosch, 1979.

—PULIDO QUECEDO, MANUEL, *La Constitución española con la jurisprudencia del Tribunal Constitucional*, Pamplona, 1996.

—PUTNAM, J. P., *Digest of the Decisions in the Courts of Equity in the United States*, Boston, Little, 1851.

—QUINTANA REDONDO, CARMELO, "Las fuentes del Derecho en el Nuevo Título Preliminar del Código Civil", in *Libro Homenaje a Ramón Mª Roca Sastre*, I, Madrid, Universidad Complutense de Madrid, 1976, pp. 657—672.

—RABASA, OSCAR, *El Derecho angloamericano*, México, Porrúa, 2nd. ed., 1982.

—RADBRUCH, GUSTAV, "El espíritu del Derecho inglés", translation into Spanish by FERNANDO VELA, *Revista de Occidente*, 1958.

—RADCLIFFE—CROSS, *The English Legal System*, London, Butterworths, 6th ed., 1977.

—RAJAK, HARRY, "Equity v. Statute", in S. GOLDSTEIN (ed.), *Equity and Contemporary Legal Developments. Papers delivered in the First International Conference on Equity. The Faculty of Law. The Hebrew University of Jerusalem. June 1990*, The Harry and Michael Sacher Institute for Legislative Research and Comparative Law, The Hebrew University of Jerusalem, 1992, pp. 100—115.

—RAMIREZ DE LA TORRE, "Ley y costumbre en la bibliografia inglesa", in *Revista Crítica de Derecho Inmobiliario*, 1926.

—RAYNAUD, PHILIPPE, "La loi et la jurisprudence des Lumières à la Révolution française", in *Archives de Philosophie du Droit*, 30, *La jurisprudence*, Paris, Sirey, 1985, pp. 61—72.

—RAZ, JOSEPH, *La autoridad del Derecho. Ensayos sobre Derecho y Moral*, translation into Spanish by ROLANDO TAMAYO Y SALMORÁN, México, Universidad Nacional Autónoma de México, 1985.

—*The Morality of Freedom*, Oxford, Clarendon Press, 1986.

—"Authority and Justification", in JOSEPH RAZ, *Authority*, Oxford, Basil Blackwell, 1990.

—*Razón práctica y normas*, translation into Spanish by J. RUÍZ MANERO, Madrid, Centro de Estudios Constitucionales, 1991.

—RECASÉNS SICHES, LUIS, *Nueva Filosofía de la interpretación del Derecho*, México, Fondo de Cultura Económica, 1956; México, Porrúa, 1980

—"Equity and Logic of the Reasonable", in RALPH A. NEWMAN (ed.), *Equity in the World's Legal Systems, op. cit.*, pp. 411—425.

—*Tratado General de Filosofía del Derecho*, 8th. ed., México, Porrúa, 1983.

—REICHEL, HANS, *La ley y la sentencia (Orientación acerca de la doctrina actual sobre fuentes del Derecho y aplicación del último)*, translation into Spanish by EMILIO MIÑANA, Villagrasa, Madrid, Reus, 1921.

—REID, LORD, "The Judge as a Law Maker", in *Society of Public Teachers of Law*, 12, 1, 1972, pp. 22—29.

—REINHARDT, MICHAEL, *Consistente Jurisdiktion: Grundlegung einer verfassungrechtlichen Theorie der rechtsfestaltenden Rechtsprechung*, Tübingen, Mohr Siebeck, 1997.

—REQUEJO PAGES, JUAN LUIS, "Juridicidad, precedente y jurisprudencia", in *Revista Española de Derecho Constitucional*, 29, 1990, pp. 223—240.

—RHEINSTEIN, MAX, "Common Law and Civil Law. A Comparison", in *Pennsylvania Bar Association Quarterly*, 12, 1, 1940, pp. 7—19.

—RICCOBONO, SALVATORE, "Jurisprudentia", in *Nuovo Digesto Italiano*, VII, Torino, 1938, pp. 477—502.

—RICKETT, CHARLES E. F., "Precedent in the Court of Appeals", in *The Modern Law Review*, 43, 1980, pp. 136—158.

—ROBLES ÁLVAREZ DE SOTOMAYOR, ALFREDO, *El precedente judicial anglosajón y la jurisprudencia española*, Madrid, Instituto Editorial Reus, 1948. Also in *Revista General de Legislación y Jurisprudencia*, XV, 183, May 1948, pp. 508—561.

—ROBLES DE SOTOMAYOR, MARÍA ELODIA, "Los sistemas de interpretación de la ley", in *Revista de la Facultad de Derecho de México*, XXVIII, 110, México, UNAM, Dirección General de Publicaciones, May—August, 1978.

—ROCA—SASTRE MUNCUNILL, LUIS, *La jurisrprudencia*, Barcelona, Colection "Ciclo de conferencias sobre el nuevo Título Preliminar del Código Civil", held by the "Ilustres Colegios de Abogados y Notarial de Barcelona y la Academia de Jurisprudencia y Legislación de Cataluña", 1975.

—ROCA TRIAS, ENCARNA, "Jurisprudencia, precedentes y principio de igualdad", in *Revista Jurídica de Cataluña*, 4, 1986, pp. 7—40.

—RODRÍGUEZ DEL BARCO, JOSÉ, "La jurisprudencia como fuente jurídica en el nuevo Título Preliminar del C. C., aprobado por Decreto 1836/1974, de 31 de mayo", in *Revista de Derecho Privado*, LIX, 1975.

—RODRÍGUEZ MOURULLO, GONZALO, *Aplicación judicial del Derecho y lógica de la argumentación jurídica*, Madrid, Ed. Cuadernos Civitas, 1988.

—RODRÍGUEZ RAMOS, LUIS, "Hacia una teoría de las fuentes materiales del Derecho penal", in *Anuario de Derecho Penal y Ciencias Penales*, 1981, pp. 721—737.

—ROSS, ALF NIELS CHRISTIAN, *Towards a Realistic Jurisprudence*, Copenhagen, 1946.

—ROSSLER, JAMES BRIAN, "Prospective Application of Judicial Decisions", in *Alabama Law Review*, 33, 2, 1982, pp. 463—492.

—ROTA, A., "La concezione irneriana dell'aequitas", in *Rivista Internazionale di Filosofia del Diritto*, III, 26, 1949, pp. 241—257.

—RUBIO LLORENTE, FRANCISCO, "La Constitución española como fuente del Derecho", in *La Constitución española y las fuentes del Derecho*, I, Madrid, 1979, pp. 51—74.

—"Sobre la relación entre el Tribunal Constitucional y el Poder Judicial en el ejercicio de la jurisdicción constitucional", in *La forma del poder. Estudios sobre la Constitución*, Madrid, 1997, pp. 431—462; and in *Revista Española de Derecho Constitucional*, 4, Centro de Estudios Constitucionales, January—April 1982.

—"La jurisdicción constitucional como forma de creación del Derecho", in *La forma del poder. Estudios sobre la Constitución*, Madrid, 1997, pp. 463—504; and in *Revista Española de Derecho Constitucional*, 22—24, January—April 1988, pp. 9—51.

—RUBIO LLORENTE, FRANCISCO — ARAGÓN REYES, MANUEL, "Enunciados aparentemente vacíos en la regulación constitucional del control de constitucionalidad", in *Revista de Estudios Políticos*, 7, 1979.

—"La jurisdicción constitucional", in *La Constitución Española de 1978. Estudio sistemático,* directed by professors A. PREDIERI and EDUARDO GARCÍA DE ENTERRÍA, Madrid, 1984, pp. 831—886.

—RUIZ, GREGORIO, *Federalismo judicial (El modelo americano)*, Madrid, Civitas, 1994.

—RUIZ DE LA PEÑA, R., "El Tribunal Constitucional", in *Estudios sobre la Constitución española de 1978,* Zaragoza, Ed. M. Ramírez, Libros Pórtico, 1979.

—RUIZ MANERO, JUAN, *Jurisdicción y normas,* Madrid, 1990.

—RUIZ VADILLO, ENRIQUE, "El nuevo Título Preliminar del Código Civil (Comentarios a los capítulos I, II y III)", in *Libro Homenaje a Ramón Mª Roca Sastre,* I, Madrid, Universidad Complutense de Madrid, 1976, pp. 781—823.

—"Algunas ideas sobre el valor y significación de las fuentes del Derecho en el nuevo Título Preliminar del C. C.", in *Anuario de Derecho Civil,* XXX, I, 1977.

—RUMELIN, MAX, *Die Billigkeit im Recht,* Tübingen, Mohr, 1921.

— *Rechtsgefühl und Rechtsbewustein,* Tübingen, Mohr, 1925.

—SALINAS MARTÍNEZ, ARTURO, *La Suprema Corte de Jurisprudencia obligatoria,* Lecture delivered the 19 April 1975, in the "Suprema Corte de Justicia".

—SALMOND, JOHN W., "The Theory of Judicial Precedents", in *The Law Quarterly Review,* 16, 1900, pp. 376—391.

—*Jurisprudence,* London, Sweet & Maxwell, 9th ed., 1937.

—SALUDEN, MARIANNE, "La jurisprudence, phénomène sociologique", in *Archives de Philosophie du Droit,* 30, *La jurisprudence,* Paris, Sirey, 1985, pp. 191—206.

—SAMPER JUAN, JOAQUÍN (*et al.*), *La fuerza vinculante de la jurisprudencia,* Consejo General del Poder Judicial, 2002.

—SÁNCHEZ DE LA TORRE, ÁNGEL — HOYO SIERRA, ISABEL ARACELI (eds.), *Fundamentos de conocimiento jurídico. Teorías y aplicaciones sobre la noción de responsabilidad jurídica,* Madrid, Real Academia de Jurisprudencia y Legislación — Dykinson, 2009.

—SANTAMARÍA IBEAS, J. JAVIER, *Los valores superiores en la jurisprudencia del Tribunal Constitucional: libertad, justicia, igualdad y pluralismo político,* Madrid, Dykinson, 1997.

—SANTA PINTER, JOSÉ JULIO, *Sistema de Derecho anglosajón,* Buenos Aires, Depalma, 1956.

—SANTOS BRIZ, JAIME, "La aplicación de las normas jurídicas en el nuevo Título Preliminar del Código Civil", in *Libro Homenaje a Ramón Mª Roca Sastre,* I, Madrid, Universidad Complutense de Madrid, 1976, pp. 753—779.

—"El Tribunal Supremo como órgano jurisdiccional superior. Valor de la jurisprudencia", in *Revista de Derecho Público,* 84—85, July—December 1981.

—SANTOS VIJANDE, JESÚS MARÍA, *Doctrina y jurisprudencia del Tribunal Constitucional. Su eficacia respecto de los tribunales ordinarios,* Granada, 1995.

—SASSOFERRATO, BARTOLO DE, "In primam Codicem Iustinianeum partem, tit. De legibus et constitutionem principem", lex prima "Inter aequitatem", 7—10.

—SATTER, ROBERT, "Changing Roles of Courts and Legislatures", in *Connecticut Law Review,* 11, 2, 1979, pp. 230—246.

—SCHAUER, FREDERICK, "Precedent", in *Standford Law Review*, 39, 1987, pp. 571—605.

—SCHLÜCHTER, ELLEN, *Mittlefunktion der Präjudizien*, Berlin, Gruyter, 1986.

—SCHLÜTER, WILFRIED, *Das Obiter Dictum*, München, C. H. Beck, 1973.

—SCHMITTHOFF, CLIVE M., "Die Englische Equity", in *Festschrift für Ernst von Caemmerer zum 70 Geburstag*, Tübingen, pp. 1049—1066.

—SEASONGOOD, HAROLD J., "Jurisdiction", in ROBERT J. JANOSIK (ed.), *Encyclopedia of the American Judicial System*, II, New York, Charles Scribner's Sons, 1987, pp. 825—841.

—SENDLER, H., "Überlegungen zum Richterrecht und richterlicher Rechtsforbildung", in *Deutsches Verwaltungsblatt*, 103, 1988, pp. 828—839.

—SENN, FÉLIX, *Les origines de la notion de jurisprudence*, Paris, Recueil Sirey, 1926.

—SENTIS MELENDO, SANTIAGO, *El juez y el Derecho*, Buenos Aires, EJEA, 1957.

—SERENI, ANGELO PIERO, "L'equity negli Stati Uniti", in *Rivista Trimestrale di Diritto e Procedura Civile*, 2—3, 1952, pp. 311 ff. And in *Studi di Diritto Comparato*, I, Milano, 1956, pp. 68—147.

—SERVERIN, EVELYNE, *De la jurisprudence en droit privé (Théorie d'une pratique)*, Lyon, Presses Universitaires de Lyon, 1985.

—SILTALA, RAIMO, *A Theory of Precedent: From Analytical Positivism to a Postanalytical Philosophy of Law*, Hart Publishing, 2000.

—SILVA MELERO, VALENTÍN, "Jurisprudencia y evolución", in *Revista General de Legislación y Jurisprudencia*, LXIX, 237, October 1974.

—SMITH, ADAM (1723—1790), *Lecciones de jurisprudencia*, translation by ALFONSO RUIZ MIGUEL, Boletín Oficial del Estado, 1996.

—SMITH, T. B. (THOMAS BROWN, 1915—), *The Doctrine of Judicial Precedents in Scots Law*, Edinburgh, W. Green, 1952.

—"Legal Precedent", in *Dictionary of the History of Ideas. Studies of Selected Pivotal Ideas*, III, USA, Charles Scribner's Sons Publishers, 1973.

—SOHM, RUDOLPH, *Instituciones de Derecho privado romano. Historia y sistema*, 17rst ed., corrected by MITTEIS and WENGER, translation into Spanish by W. ROCES, Madrid, Ed. Revista de Derecho Privado, 1928.

—SOTO NIETO, FRANCISCO, *Cuestiones jurídicas (jurisprudencia creadora)*, I, Madrid, Ed. Montecorvo, 1976.

—SPOTA, ALBERTO G., *El juez, el abogado y la formación del Derecho a través de la jurisprudencia*, Buenos Aires, Ediciones Depalma, 1976.

—SPRECHER, ROBERT A., "The Development of the Doctrine of Stare Decisis and the Extent to which it Should Be Applied", in *American Bar Association Journal*, 31, 1945, pp. 501—509.

—SQUELLA, AGUSTÍN — GONZÁLEZ, ABEL, *Dos concepciones de la equidad*, Valparaíso, EDEVAL, 1981.

—STEVENS, JOHN PAUL, "The Life Span of a Judge—Made Rule", in *New York University Law Review*, 58, 1, 1983, pp. 1—21.

—STONE, JULIUS, "The Ratio of the Ratio Decidendi", in *The Modern Law Review*, 22, 6, 1959, pp. 597—620.

—"1966 and All That! Loasing the Chains of Precedents", in *Columbia Law Review*, 69, 7, 1969, pp.1162—1202.

—*Precedent and Law. Dynamics of Common Law Growth*, Sydney, Butterworths, 1985.

—STONE, ROY, "The Precedence of Precedents", in *The Cambridge Law Review*, 26, 1, 1968, pp. 35—38.

—SUÁREZ COLLÍA, JOSÉ MARÍA, *El principio de irretroactividad de las normas jurídicas*, Madrid, Actas, 1994.

—*La retroactividad. Normas jurídicas retroactivas e irretroactivas*, Madrid, Editorial Universitaria Ramón Areces, 1rst. ed. September 2005; 1ª reimpr. April 2006.

—SZANTON, PETER L., "Stare Decisis; A Dissenting View", in *The Hastings Law Journal*, 10, 4, 1959, pp. 394—403.

—TARDE, GABRIEL, *Les transformations du Droit*, Paris, 1893; there is a translation into Spanish, *Las transformaciones del Derecho*, with Preface and notes by ADOLFO POSADA, Madrid, La España Moderna, s. a.

—TARUFFO, MICHELLE, "Precedente ed exempio nella decisione giudiziaria", in *Rivista Trimestrale di Diritto e Procedura Civile*, XLVIII, 1994, pp. 19—36.

—"Dimensione del precedente giudiziario", in *Rivista Trimestrale di Diritto e Procedura Civile*, XLVIII, 1994, pp. 411—430.

—"Per un'analisi comparata del precedente giudiziario", in *Ragion Pratica*, 6, 1996, pp. 55—64.

—TOMAS Y VALIENTE, FRANCISCO, "Poder judicial y Tribunal Constitucional", in *Poder Judicial*, 11, 1989, pp. 13—41.

—*Escritos sobre y desde el Tribunal Constitucional*, Madrid, 1993.

—TORRES DEL MORAL, ANTONIO, *Principios de Derecho constitucional español*, 3rd ed., Madrid, 1992.

—TROPER, MICHEL, "Hans Kelsen et la jurisprudence", in *Archives de Philosophie du Droit*, 30, *La jurisprudence*, Paris, Sirey, 1985, pp. 83—94.

—TRUJILLO, G., "Juicio de legitimidad e interpretación constitucional: cuestiones problemáticas en el horizonte constitucional español", in *Revista de Estudios Políticos*, 7, 1979, pp. 145—158.

—TUNC, ANDRÉ, "Jurisprudence", in *Enciclopedia Universalis*, 9, 1968.

—"La Cour de cassation en crise", in *Archives de Philosophie du Droit*, 30, *La jurisprudence*, Paris, Sirey, 1985, pp. 157—170.

—"L'équité en droit anglais et en droit américain", in Various Authors, *Justice et équité. Número monográfico de Justices. Revue Générale de Droit Processuel*, January—March 1998. Dalloz.

—TUNC, ANDRÉ — TUNC, SUZANNE, *Le droit des Etats—Unis d'Amerique, Sources et Techniques*, Paris, Presses Universitaires de France, 1955.

—TWINING, WILLIAM — MIERS, DAVID, *How to Do Things with Rules*, London, Weidenfeld and Nicholson, 3rd. ed., 1991.

—UNIKEN VENEMA, C. AE., *Law en equity in het Anglo—Amerikaanse privaatrecht: rechtsvergelijkende beschouwingen bettreffende de belangrijkste structuren en begrippen in het Anglo—Amerikaanse privaatrecht*, Rjeenk Willink, Zwolle, 1990. London, Butterworth, 1924

—URÍAS MARTÍNEZ, JOAQUÍN PABLO, *La cuestión de inconstitucionalidad*, Madrid, 1996.

—VACCA, LETIZIA, "Sulla relevanza dei 'precedenti' nel diritto giurisprudenziale romano", in VINCENTI, UMBERTO (a cura di), in cooperation with GIANNI SANTUCCI, *Il valore dei precedenti giudiziali nella tradizione europea*, Padova, CEDAM, 1998, pp. 29—55.

—VALLARTA PLATA, JOSÉ GUILLERMO, "El poder judicial y el sistema de la Declaración de inconstitucionalidad en Latinoamérica", in *Función del Poder Judicial en los Sistemas Constitucionales Latinoamericanos*, México, Instituto de Investigaciones Jurídicas, UNAM, 1977.

—VALLET DE GOYTISOLO, JUAN BERCHMANS, "Algunas consideraciones acerca de la ley y la jurisprudencia de los Tribunales como fuente del Derecho", in *Estudios sobre el Título Preliminar del C. C. Parte General. Vol. I*, Academia Matritense del Notariado, Edersa, 1977.

—VANNI, ICILIO, *Della consuetudine nei suoi rapporti col Diritto e colla Legislazione.* Dissertazione di laurea, Perugia, Tipografia Santucci, 1877.

—VÁZQUEZ BOTE, EDUARDO, "El sistema de fuentes y la Ley Orgánica del Poder Judicial", in *Revista de Derecho Inmobiliario*, 575, July—August 1986.

—VIDAL ANDREU, GUILLERMO (dir.), *Poder judicial y estado compuesto: relaciones entre el Tribunal Supremo y los Tribunales Superiores de Justicia*, Madrid, Consejo General del Poder Judicial, 2005.

—VIDALES RODRÍGUEZ, CATY, *La eficacia retroactiva de los cambios jurisprudenciales*, Preface by JOSÉ LUIS GONZÁLEZ CUSSAC, Valencia, Tirant lo Blanch, 2001.

—VIEHWEG, THEODOR, *Tópica y jurisprudencia*, translation into Spanish by LUIS DIEZ—PICAZO, 1964.

—VIGO, RODOLFO, "La interpretación jurídica en Michel Villey", in *Anuario de Filosofía Jurídica y Social*, 9, 1989, pp. 171—194.

—VILAR BADÍA, R., "La sentencia judicial, proceso creador del Derecho", in *Revista de Derecho Procesal Iberoamericano*, 2 and 3, 1977.

—VILLAR PALASÍ, JOSE LUIS, *La interpretación y los apotegmas jurídico—lógicos*, Madrid, Tecnos, 1973.

—VILLEY, MICHEL, "Iusnaturalisme. Essay de definition", in *Revue Interdisciplinaire d'Etudes Juridiques*, 1986, pp. 25—32; also in *Revista de la Facultad de Derecho de la Universidad Complutense de Madrid*, 77, academic year 1990—1991, pp. 341—347, translation into Spanish by JOSÉ MIGUEL SERRANO RUIZ—CALDERÓN.

—VINCENTI, UMBERTO (a cura di), in cooperation with GIANNI SANTUCCI, *Il valore dei precedenti giudiziali nella tradizione europea*, Padova, CEDAM, 1998.

—"I precedente giudiziali: prospettive romanistiche", in VINCENTI, UMBERTO (a cura di), in cooperation with GIANNI SANTUCCI, *Il valore dei precedenti giudiziali nella tradizione europea*, Padova, CEDAM, 1998, pp. 1—29.

—VINOGRADOFF, PAUL, *Custom and Right*, Oslo, Aschehoug, Instituttet for Sammenlignende Kulturforskning. Serie A. Vol. III, 1925.

—VIVES ANTON, TOMÁS S., "Tribunales de Justicia y jurisprudencia constitucional", in *La libertad como pretexto*, Valencia, 1995, pp. 237—243, also in *Poder Judicial*, 2, June 1986, pp. 9—13.

—"Valoraciones ético—sociales y jurisprudencia constitucional", in *La libertad como pretexto*, Valencia, 1996, pp. 171—174.

—VULLIERME, JEAN—LOUIS, "La autorité politique de la jurisprudence", in *Archives de Philosophie du Droit*, 30, *La jurisprudence*, Paris, Sirey, 1985, pp. 95—104.

—Various Authors, *La Motivation des Decisions de Justice*, directed by CHAÏM PERELMAN and PAUL FORIERS, Bruxelles, Bruylant, 1978.

—*La jurisprudence*, vol. 30 of the *Archives de Philosphie du Droit*, 1985, Paris, Sirey, directed by FRANÇOIS TERRÉ.

—*La jurisdicción constitucional en España. La Ley Orgánica del Tribunal Constitucional: 1979—1994*, Madrid, 1995.

—WAGNER—DÖBLER, R. — PHILIPPS, L.; "Präjudizien in der Rechtsprechung: statische Untersuchungen anhad der Zitierpraxis deutscher Gerichte", in *Rechtstheorie*, 23, 1992, pp. 228—241.

—WALD, ABRAHAM, *Rapport brésilieu al T. XXXI, 1980 de les Travaux de l'Association H. Capitant (Les reationes de la doctrine à la création du droit par les juges), Journées italiennes de Florence*, Paris, Ed. Economica, 1982.

—WALINE, MARCEL, "Le pouvoir normatif de la jurisprudence. La technique et les principes du droit public", in *Melanges Scelle*, II, Paris, 1950.

—WALKER, DAVID M., "Equity in Scots law", in NEWMAN, R. A. (ed.), *Equity in the World's Legal Systems. A Comparative Study*. Congress held by the Hastings College of Law of the University of California in Bellagio, in August 1972. Dedicated to RENÉ CASSIN, Brussels, Établissements Émile Bruylant, 1973, pp. 187—205.

—WANBAUGH, EUGENE, *The Study of Cases*, Boston, 2nd ed, 1894.

—"How to Use Decisions and Statutes", in ARTHUR VANDERBILT (ed.), *Studying Law*, New York, Washington Square Publishing Comp., 1945, pp. 537—598.

—WANK, R., "Richterliche Rechtsforbildung und Verfassungsrecht", in *Zeitschrift für Unternehmens und Gesselschaft*, 3, 1988, pp. 314—380.

—WASSERSTROM, R., *The Judicial Decision. Towards a Theory of Legal Justification*, Stanford, Stanford University Press, 1977.

—WEBER, A., "La jurisdicción constitucional en Europa Occidental: una comparación", in *Revista Española de Derecho Constitucional*, 6, 1986, pp. 47—83.

—WEINBERGER, OTA, "Basic Puzzles of Discourse Philosophy", in *Ratio Juris*, 9, 1996, pp. 172—181.

—WHITNEY, EDWARD B., "The Doctrine of Stare Decisis", in *Michigan Law Review*, 3, 2, 1904, pp. 89—107.

—WINCKLER, ANTOINE, "Précédent: l'avenir du droit", in *Archives de Philosophie du Droit*, 30, *La jurisprudence*, Paris, Sirey, 1985, pp. 131—140.

—WISE, E. M., "The Doctrine of Stare Decisis", in *Wayne Law Review*, 21, 4, 1975, pp. 1043—1060.

—WOODARD, CALVIN, "Common Law and Common Law Legal Systems", in ROBERT J. JANOSIK (ed.), *Encyclopedia of American Judicial Systems*, II, New York, Charles Scribner's Sons, 1987, pp. 500—516.

—WRIGHT, LORD, "Precedents", in *The Cambridge Law Journal*, 8, 2, 1943, pp. 118—145.

—WRÓBLEWSKI, JERZY, "Legal Syllogism and Rationality of Judicial Decisions", in *Rechtstheorie*, 3, 1974, pp. 33—46.

—"La jurisprudence et la doctrine juridique en tant que source de droit", in *Rapports Polonais*, Varsovie, Ossolineum, 1974.

—"Evaluative Statements in Law. An Analytical Approach to Legal Axiology", in *Rivista Internazionale di Filosofia del Diritto*, 1981, 4.

—*"Sentido" y "hecho" en el Derecho*, translation into Spanish by FRANCISCO JAVIER EZQUIAGA GANUZAS, San Sebastián, Universidad del Pais Vasco, 1989.

—"The Judicial Application of Law", in Z. BANKOWSKI and N. MACCORMICK (eds.), Dordrecht, Kluwer, 1992.

—XIOL RÍOS, JUAN ANTONIO, "El precedente judicial en nuestro Derecho, una creación del Tribunal Constitucional", in *Revista Poder Judicial*, 3, September 1986, pp. 25—40.

—"El principio de igualdad en la aplicación de la ley", in *El principio de igualdad en la Constitución*, Madrid, 1991.

—*El precedente judicial y otros estudios sobre el proceso administrativo: técnicas de evitación del proceso contencioso—administrativo*, Madrid, Colegio Nacional de Registradores de la Propiedad y Mercantiles de España, 2005.

—ZACCARIA, GIUSEPPE, "L'obiettivitá del giudice tra esegesi normative e politica del diritto", in *Rivista di Diritto Civile*, XXV, 1979.

—ZAFRA VALVERDE, JOSÉ, "Sentencia constitutiva y sentencia dispositiva", in *La Constitución Jurídica Procesal*, Madrid, RIALP, 1962.

—ZAGREBELSKY, GUSTAVO, "La Corte constitucional y la interpretación de la Constitución", in Various Authors, LÓPEZ PINA (ed.): *División de poderes e interpretación (hacia una teoría de la praxis constitucional)*, Madrid, Tecnos, 1987.

—ZAGREBELSKI, VLADIMIRO, *Sulla consuetudine costituzionale nella teoria delle fonti del diritto*, Torino, Giappichelli, 1970.

—ZANDER, MICHAEL, *The Law—Making Process*, London, Weidenfeld and Nicholson, 3rd. ed., 1989.

—ZELLICK, GRAHAM, "Precedent in the Court of Appeal", in *The Criminal Law Review*, 1974, pp. 222—238.

—ZERTUCHE GARCÍA, HÉCTOR GERARDO, *La jurisprudencia en el sistema jurídico mexicano*, México, Porrúa, 1990.

— ZICCARDI, F., "L'integrazione del contratto", in *Rivista Trimestrale di Diritto e Procedura Civile*, 1969, pp. 108—90.

—ZULETA PUCEIRO, ENRIQUE, "Jurisprudencia y fuentes del Derecho", in *Estudios sobre el Título Preliminar del C. C., Parte General, vol. I*, Academia Matritense del Notariado, Edersa, 1977.

Index

aequitas 16, 26
Agreements adopted by the non-jurisdictional meetings of the Supreme Court 113-115
analogy 83, 97-98, 101-102, 108, 110, 124, 131-134, 165
Analytical Jurisprudence 151-152
Anglosaxon
  /Continental systems 45-55
  precedent 19-55, 122, 136, 138, 141, 145, 153, 158-159, 166
  system of sources 22-43
anima 86-88, 90-91, 123
animus 86-88, 90-91
anti-formalist revolt 143-157
aporetic perspective 154
Appeal to the Highest Instance (Appeal for Cassation) 60-63, 74-75, 81, 108, 118, 121
application of law 100-102, 115, 121, 123, 127, 132, 148
arbitration 50
argument
  ab exemplo 137-138
  a contrario 97-99, 102
  a fortiori 97-98, 102
  a maiori ad minus 98
  a minori ad maius 98-99
  authority 137-140
  literal 163
  pragmatic 141
  psychological 88
  systematic or *sedes materiae* 163
art 17-18
auctoritas / potestas 73, 114
audience 139-140
authority 15-16, 138-140, 145

capital punishment 158
casuistic method 51-52
causa legis 85, 87
Codification 48, 86
Codification Commission 112-113, 118
common law
  declarative and constitutive theories of the nature of 36-37
  in general 26, 36-37, 41-45, 48-49, 54, 96
Consejo de Castilla 60
Continental
  case law 52-55, 57-172
  legal systems 19, 22, 30-31
corpus 86-88, 91, 123
Corpus Iuris Civilis 86
County Courts 39
Court of Appeal 39
creation of law 103-104, 113, 115, 121-125, 132, 135, 163
crime of aggression 80
Crown Court 39
custom 91-96, 108-109, 118-120, 122, 126-127, 145, 152, 161-163, 169
Chancellor 26, 38, 43-44
change in case law 157-159

de facto assumption 83-85, 132
delegation 112
discretional / arbitrary power 129-131
dispersed / concentrated jurisdiction 53-54, 64-66
distinctions 33-34, 38

dossier 142-143
due process of law 42

edicts 15
egological conception 154
empiricism 49, 129
equity 25-27, 41-44, 101, 108, 122-131, 156
European
  Commission of Human Rights 77
  Court of Human Rights 59, 77-78
  Court of Justice 39
excellence 18
experimental logic 153

fact / legal act 87
Fazañas 60
force of law / binding value 171
Free School of Law 148-151
French
  legal anti-formalism 145-146
  Revolution 116
  Scientific School 145-146
  Sociological School 146

general principles of law 91-92, 102, 104, 108, 110, 118, 120, 122, 126-127, 161-163, 165, 169
General Department of Registers and Notaries Public 58, 81-82
German conceptual anti-formalism 147-151
glossators 14-15, 47-48, 86, 89, 124, 131
Goodhart test 34
Greek *logos* 85
grounds for judgements 168

hard cases 142
High Court of Justice 39
Higher Courts of Justice of the Autonomous Communities 58-59, 61, 74-76, 123
Historical School of Law 15, 94, 124, 132

House of Lords 38-39, 44
hypothetical
  judgment 83
  will 89

imputation / causality 83-85
Inquisition 158
institutions 147, 158
International Criminal Court 59, 79-81
interpretation
  criteria for 91
  literal 86, 100, 118, 149
  logical 86
  of law 100-101, 109, 112, 121, 123, 127, 132, 145, 147, 149-150, 154-155, 162
  sociological 91
  teleological 91
Iuriscientia 16
ius
  praetorium 15
  publicae respondendi 12-13

Judicature Acts 27
jurisconsult 10-13, 17
Jurisprudence
  of Concepts 147-149, 151
  of Interests 147-150
  superior / low 147
jurisprudential anti-formalism 151-153
Jurisprudenz 9-10

law
  British 21-22
  English 21-22, 30, 41, 43-48, 50, 52-53
  exceptional 111
  German 170-171
  in action / in the books 49
  individual 110-112, 117, 125
  integration of 102-103, 121, 123
  judge-made 24-27, 53
  natural 145-146, 150

objective 120
public / private 52
reporting system 39-40
Scottish 43-44
special 110-111
specific 112
statute 26-31, 54, 117-118, 161-163, 165, 169
legal
argumentation 97-99, 101-102, 139, 154
certainty 120-121, 129, 139
consequence 83-85, 98, 101-102, 132
doctrine 61-63, 165-166
system 19
legislation
community 28
delegated 28-29
domestic 28
primary 28
legislator
judge 172
's will 88-90
logoid elements 154
logos of the human or the reasonable 155-157

Magistrates' Courts 39
models of judge 141-143

ne bis in idem 119
non liquet 103, 116
North American
law 40-44, 53
Realism 152-153
Sociological Jurisprudence 151-152
nullum crimen sine lege 114

obiter dicta 34-36, 82-83, 97, 99
ocassio legis 87, 91
Oliphant thesis 34
open texture 107
opinio iuris 91, 95, 109
Organic Law regarding the Judiciary 169-170

Pandectists 47, 124, 132
papal bulls 158
paper / real rules 152
Philosophy of Law 45, 124, 148
Pontiffs 11-12
post-glossators 15, 47, 85-87, 89-90, 124, 131
Praetor 11-12, 15, 44
precedent
absolutely / conditionally obligatory 38
auto- 138
declarative / creative 37
horizontal 137-138
obligatory / persuasive 37-38
publication of 39-40, 44
vertical 137-138
preliminary ruling 76, 78
Preliminary Title of the Civil Code 160-165
prescriptive propositions 83
principle
of formal justice 140-141
of inertia 140-141
of legality 29, 167
of separation of powers 107, 115-117, 120, 169
principles 147, 161
privilege 111
progress 159
prudentia 10-11, 16-18, 155

question of unconstitutionality 73
ratio
decidendi 32, 34-36, 57, 82-99, 101, 103-104, 110, 120-121, 123, 131, 133-134, 171
eadem 98
historical / hypothetical 90
legis / legislatoris 87-89, 91
minor or contrary 99
major 98

rationality 95
reasonability 138-140
Reception 47-48, 112
recurso de amparo 69
re-sending 127-128
res judicata 119-120, 125
retrospective / prospective derogation 32-33
revolution 50
Roman
  classical law 7-9, 12
  iurisprudentia 7-18, 55, 124
  law 45, 47-48, 85-86
rule of law 114-115, 117, 167, 169
Rules of Civil Procedure 165-166

sapientia 10
Science of Law 9-11, 14, 16, 44-45
Secretariat for Disputes 58
source of law 15, 105-121, 133-136, 145, 150, 157, 159-170
sources-argument theory 136-141
Spanish
  Constitution of 1978 58, 64, 67-68, 70-72, 114, 116-117, 167-168
  Constitutional Court 53-54, 57-59, 64-73, 114, 122-123, 135
  legal system 57-170
  Supreme Court 38, 53, 57-59, 60-63, 69-70, 73-76, 82, 105-121, 157-159, 162, 164-165, 168
stare decisis 31-33, 37, 53
Stufenbau 107, 125, 142
subjective rights 120, 147, 168
subsumption 97-98, 101, 115-117
Swiss
  Civil Code 172
  legal system 112, 125

theory of the exclusive general rule 97-99
three-dimensionalism 83, 97
to complement / to complete 163-164
tradition 50, 141, 145, 158

use 95, 109, 118

voluntas legis / legislatoris 88-91

Wambaugh test 34
war crimes 80
Wirklichkeitsjurisprudenz 147

www.ingramcontent.com/pod-product-compliance
Lightning Source LLC
La Vergne TN
LVHW081515300926
849161LV00006B/1187
9789004204164